THE MAHATMA'S MANIFESTO

Rajesh Talwar has written forty-two books, which include novels, children's stories, plays, self-help and works of non-fiction covering issues regarding social justice, culture and law. His noted publications include *Courting Injustice: The Nirbhaya Case and Its Aftermath* (Hay House India, 2013), *How to Kill a Billionaire* (Juggernaut, 2016), *The Three Greens* (Orient Blackswan, 2005) and *How to Choose a Lawyer and Win Your Case* (Vision Books, 2017).

He has contributed to *The Economic Times*; *The Guardian* (UK); *The Pioneer*; *The Times of India*'s student edition, *NIE*; *The Patriot*; *Manushi*; *Sunday Mail*; *The Daily Guardian*; *CNN-News 18* and the *New Indian Express*. He is a sought-after speaker at literary festivals.

Rajesh has worked for the United Nations for over two decades, across three continents in numerous countries. Additionally, he has practised law, taught at Delhi University and Jamia Millia Islamia, and studied for shorter and longer durations at the universities of Harvard, Oxford, Cambridge, Nottingham and Delhi. In 2024, he was nominated for an Alumni Award by the University of Nottingham for service to the community and professional and academic excellence.

THE MAHATMA'S MANIFESTO

A CRITIQUE OF HIND SWARAJ

RAJESH TALWAR

Om Books International

First published in 2025 by

Om Books International

Corporate & Editorial Office
A-12, Sector 64, Noida 201 301
Uttar Pradesh, India
Phone: +91 120 477 4100
Email: editorial@ombooks.com
Website: www.ombooksinternational.com

Sales Office
107, Ansari Road, Darya Ganj,
New Delhi 110 002, India
Phone: +91 11 4000 9000
Email: sales@ombooks.com
Website: www.ombooks.com

ISBN: 978-93-6395-318-5

Printed in India

10 9 8 7 6 5 4 3 2 1

To

The Youth of India

Contents

PREFACE

It is said that when the French aviation pioneer Louis Bleriot first flew across the English Channel, Gandhi, who was in England at the time, was furious that massive crowds were acclaiming an event he considered to be inconsequential. Something similar happened to me when I started to read the Mahatma's manifesto, *Hind Swaraj*. As I worked my way through the slim volume, I got increasingly agitated—and determined to write something to express that anger. Even though I made allowance for the fact that Gandhi wrote his manifesto at a time when India was under colonial rule and therefore could reasonably have been expected to assume an angry tone, the manner in which he rails against things (machinery), language (the English language), institutions (the courts and Parliament) and even the idea of a well-rounded education appeared to me to be irrational, unwise and hypocritical.

To some extent, the word count of this book was set by the material it seeks to review. Gandhi's *Hind Swaraj* is itself a slender volume of hardly thirty thousand words. While this book seeks to analyse not only the contents of Gandhi's book but also Gandhi, the man, the 'saint' and the politician, it should not have greatly exceeded the word count of the original, given that the ancillary discussion is framed within the context of the review and critique of *Hind Swaraj*. As it happens, however, it is roughly twice its length. This is not so much because Gandhi is difficult to understand and explain but because his 'manifesto' is full of absurdities and contradictions that merit examination and discussion.

There is much that is wrong with Gandhi's manifesto, which forms the basis for the title of this book, but not *everything* is wrong or misguided. It is therefore not the case that in the book I simply criticise the Mahatma's views as expressed in *Hind Swaraj*. He is also praised whenever I feel praise is due. Unfortunately though, as far as the bulk of the text of the manifesto is concerned, I have found it to be lacking in both logic and substance. On one hand the Mahatma was a man with great practical intelligence, but at the same time some of his views, opinions and perceptions are irrational and even delusional. The problem is also that when the Mahatma makes his various criticisms, he doesn't offer any clear, alternative vision of how things ought to be. If he wishes to do without the present system of lawyers and courts, so be it; but what alternative vision of justice delivery does he promise? Alas, there is none. Gandhi believes that medical doctors are villains, and even worse than quacks. Even if, for the sake of argument, we grant that he was perfectly right in arriving at such a conclusion, what would he have proposed should have happened to the millions of Indians who contract malaria and tuberculosis every year?

I have quoted Gandhi extensively throughout this book. There are two reasons for this. First, many biographies (and history books, it may be said) become unreadable because they use too many secondary sources instead of referring to the primary source. When the primary source is at hand, as in the case with Gandhi's manifesto, why bother too much with secondary sources?

In a book such as the present one, which has the possibility of becoming controversial, an author needs to be careful not to put words into Gandhi's mouth. If I paraphrase Gandhi's views on electricity, women or Western civilisation, a reader predisposed to believe only good about the Mahatma may worry that I am distorting or even subverting his original meaning. If I am quoting him directly from the most authoritative source that exists (his own book), I immediately avoid this danger and take a huge step towards gaining the confidence of the reader. If Gandhi wished to carry out experiments with truth, I also wish to stay as close to the truth as possible.

Having said that, while I have quoted from the Mahatma's own writings extensively, I have also relied on his various biographers for additional information in relevant areas.[1] I have used endnotes judiciously, dispensing with references where facts are already well known and beyond dispute.

In reviewing the writings of Gandhi, contemporary readers, biographers and historians have tended to overestimate the quality and value of *Hind Swaraj*, owing to his subsequent greatness (and also because of the comparative lucidity of his other writings). All of us can be said to be influenced by a person's reputation and status when judging them. In the case of Indians, there is also the issue of a false sense of patriotism: how dare anyone criticise Gandhi?

Just as Gandhi wrote *Hind Swaraj* for the ordinary Indian, this book is also primarily intended for the lay reader and not for scholars. Is it relevant, someone may ask, to write a book on *Hind Swaraj* more than a century after it was first published? It is indeed relevant, for newer editions of Gandhi's book keep being published and released, and they sell very well. There are recent, enthusiastic reviews of new editions of *Hind Swaraj* on Amazon. The last time I checked, there were numerous five-star reviews, with one person calling it 'a must read', another suggesting that it was a book that 'everyone must read', and yet another going so far as to say how 'at sixty years, it was the best thing he had read'.[2] A young reviewer wrote that it was 'the best book' for 'real Indians'.[3] It is therefore apparent that Gandhi, as well as *Hind Swaraj*, continues to influence thousands of people, and the present book has been written to try to point out that while he remains relevant in some ways, many things said and written by him are actually not relevant anymore and should not be considered relevant, and their irrelevance—leaving aside the historical value because of his eminence—should be recognised and accepted.

This is not to deny that several observations made in *Hind Swaraj* ring true even today. Reading what Gandhi wrote on how British prime ministers were susceptible to subtle influences and could give awards for political consideration, one is reminded of the Cash for Honours scandal that erupted in the British Parliament in 2006, nearly a century after Gandhi wrote his critique.[4] Many similar scandals occur in democratic nations across the world from time to time.

Gandhi wrote voluminously. With his complete works running into a hundred volumes,[5] his writings were perhaps even more extensive than those of his sworn enemy Winston Churchill, and those of more traditional left-wing revolutionaries, such as Lenin and Stalin. *Hind Swaraj* remains one of the most significant pieces of writing Gandhi produced.

The three volumes of *Das Kapital* are among the most highly regarded writings of the great thinker Karl Marx, but they are also among his most abstruse and least readable works. It is the writing in the *Communist Manifesto* that stirred the blood of young student revolutionaries across the world. I would venture to suggest that, in Gandhi's case, *Hind Swaraj* represents his 'manifesto' more than anything else he wrote. Many will disagree and point to *My Experiments with Truth* as holding that position; there is no doubt that it is much more widely read across the world, but it is a reflective work, relatively speaking, and not a call to action in the way that *Hind Swaraj* is.

Hind Swaraj is presented like a manifesto, with various directions and 'commandments', and in this book I sometimes refer to it simply as 'the manifesto'. *My Experiments with Truth* has a straightforward and arresting title. The title of *Hind Swaraj*, on the other hand, would make little sense to a non-Indian, who would be mystified by the word '*Swaraj*', and only slightly less baffled by '*Hind*'.

Gandhi was only forty years old when he wrote *Hind Swaraj*. He would live for another forty years, and grow in stature, understanding and reputation. Is it fair for me to be critiquing a book he wrote when he was relatively young? Yes, it is, because Gandhi never repudiated anything that he wrote in that seminal manuscript. Even though the Mahatma was notoriously fickle, it is clear that he did not change his mind about *Hind Swaraj*. Just over two years before he was assassinated, in a letter to Jawaharlal Nehru dated 5 October 1945, he wrote: 'My experience has confirmed the truth of what I wrote in 1909. *If I were the only one left who believed in it, I would not be sorry.* For I can only testify to the truth as I see it.'[6]

As a thirty-nine-year-old Indian, Gandhi was well read, if not erudite, and had his own clear opinions and a vision of what was good for the country. When he included references to other great writers and thinkers of the period, he sought to kill two birds with one stone. First, he simply wanted to say: 'Listen, you people, my readers. I'm well read and conversant with all the great contemporary writing and thinking on all the important issues of the day.' Second, by including himself in the company of other globally acknowledged greats, he wanted to make sure that he could not be easily dismissed as an obscurantist, a medieval-minded ideologue, or a man who was against all kinds of progress.

Gandhi's own vision and world view were distinctive, in many ways highly original, but at the same time quite outlandish. He must have known this. There can be little doubt that none of the contemporary eminent thinkers and philosophers that he so admired would have agreed with him on the evils of the railway train or the vaccine.

Sections of the manifesto are written in the form of a dialogue, ostensibly for greater readability. The Mahatma wrote that 'the dialogue, as it has been given, actually took place between several friends, mostly readers of *Indian Opinion* and myself'.[7] His chosen format reminded me of Plato's *Dialogues*, but according to the historian Ramachandra Guha, Gandhi may have been thinking more along the lines of the Gita. A similar dialogue took place between the warrior Arjuna and Lord Krishna,[8] the former expressing his misgivings about entering a war where many lives would be lost, and thus seeking guidance in this regard. If this is indeed the case, which I am prepared to concede, it was certainly arrogant of Gandhi—and a measure of his ego, perhaps—to imagine that he was capable, like Lord Krishna, of dispensing pearls of timeless wisdom to someone who would come to him for guidance.

Given Gandhi's subsequent leadership of the Indian independence movement and of the Congress Party, and the important role he played in negotiations with the British government, any Indian writer who contemplated publishing a critique might have hesitated for fear of being branded as anti-national. However, intelligent criticisms of Gandhi came from Dr B.R. Ambedkar, who could not bear the Mahatma's sanctimonious attitude towards the Dalits and untouchability. We have to ignore the mindless criticism of Gandhi coming from right-wing fanatics both then and now.

Even with his status as a leader of the nation, Gandhi did come in for criticism for his sexual experimentation. A recent biographer writes on how much material known during his lifetime 'was distorted or supressed after his death during the process of elevating Gandhi into the "Father of the Nation"'.[9] Sometimes children tend to ignore the eccentricities of a 'father figure', although they may gossip about him behind his back and even make fun of him. Was Gandhi one such figure? It would certainly seem to be the case.

★ ★ ★

A word now about how I came to write this book. For some years, I have wished to write a biography. A writer always wants to stretch himself and to explore subjects and genres he has never attempted before. Having written some general non-fiction works on law, human rights, culture and politics, as well as works of fiction, including novels, plays and children's books, I wanted to try my hand at writing a biography, even a partial or incomplete one.

Much like an explorer, every writer wishes to go where no one has been before, and Gandhi had been thoroughly explored. There were already so many biographies about the great man (many of them in the nature of hagiographies), that were I to attempt another I would be treading a much-travelled road. And yet I thought it was important to try to explain to the reader that while Gandhi remains relevant, there is so much about him and his thoughts that is decidedly irrelevant and should be discarded. My research revealed that there wasn't much fair, contemporary analysis and examination of *Hind Swaraj* compared to that of the man himself. In other words, this pathway was not nearly as well trodden as were the attempts to write Gandhi's biography. So, I was determined that I would not write a biography as such, but instead an interpretation and criticism of *Hind Swaraj* that could perhaps double up as an incisive, though partial, biography of the Mahatma.

Hind Swaraj is an important book because, autobiographies apart, it was the only real book that Gandhi wrote. As the historian Ramachandra Guha comments: 'Although many thematic collections of his writings appeared in his lifetime, Gandhi published only three books *qua* books. Since the other two were works of autobiography, *Hind Swaraj* carries even more weight as representing, so to speak, his most important political statement.'[10] I would argue that *Hind Swaraj* went beyond being a 'political statement' and represented his deeply and sincerely held views on very many diverse subjects that might not come within the narrow compass of what we generally understand by that term.

The power and influence of the man are such that it is somewhat inevitable that 'products' on Gandhi will continue to appear regularly, for there are many researchers working within the field of what is known as 'Gandhian studies'. With the nationwide hype and propaganda about Gandhi, in a country where currency notes have his bespectacled smiling photo and where every town and city has at least one Mahatma Gandhi Road, square (*chowk*) or street, the real Gandhi has become lost somewhere. Millions of Indians actually believe Gandhi to be a completely different person from the man he really was. The reality of the man is far, far different from the image.

Just as Gandhi's voluminous writings have spawned an entire field of study, and thousands of people have spent a lifetime reading and researching his life and work, there are tens if not hundreds more who are now at the beginning of that process. As the Dalit leader B.R. Ambedkar wryly noted in a book published in 1945, 'quite recently a new "ism" has come on the Indian horizon. It is called Gandhism.' He added: 'It is true that very recently Mr Gandhi has denied that there is such a thing as Gandhism. This denial is nothing more than the usual modesty that Mr Gandhi wears so well. It does not disprove the existence of Gandhism.'[11] Gandhism is now more than a century old. In a letter to Subhas Chandra Bose dated 30 March 1939, the Mahatma himself used the expression 'Gandhiites', though—typical of his careful modesty—he added within parentheses 'to use that wrong expression'.[12]

* * *

There are many books on *Hind Swaraj* that are many times the length of the original—something that could be appropriate for interpreting a haiku, a poem, a sutra, or a work of dense philosophy, but does not sit so well with a book written so simply and directly.

Consider, for instance, *M.K. Gandhi's Hind Swaraj* by Suresh Sharma and Tridip Suhrud. This is a critical reading of *Hind Swaraj* authored by two social historians of repute and refers to the 'seminal and profound work' by the 'great soul' at a time of great historical importance (namely, the end of the First World War).[13] The irony of this particular work is that the Gandhian professors, while eulogising the Mahatma in every way, did not believe that his English was good enough for him to do justice to the translation of his own work into the language.

So they have done their own scholarly interpretation of *Hind Swaraj*, examining both the Gujarati and the English versions but hardly realising that their own English writing is far inferior to that of the Mahatma in terms of clarity. For whatever criticisms one might make of *Hind Swaraj*, one must concede that it is for the most part written in plain and simple English.

If the opinions expressed by Gandhi in *Hind Swaraj* are as evidently unreasonable as I claim, why has there been so little criticism of it? Indian and global media, as well as scholars in the world of academia, such as Sharma and Suhrud, are overindulgent towards Gandhi. It is not the case, these erudite professors argue, that Gandhi's arguments and explanations in *Hind Swaraj* are crude, primitive and simplistic in nature. Rather, Gandhi is centuries ahead of his time, and *Hind Swaraj* is a critique of modernity itself! This is what it says on the jacket: 'As a mode of exposition and argument *Hind Swaraj* stems from a cognitive universe that abides beyond the ambit of modernity.'[14] The praise for *Hind Swaraj* is couched in high-sounding academic prose. When the Mahatma critiques democracy and political parties, the authors nod their heads wisely and clarify that, unknown to the Mahatma, 'Machiavelli is perhaps the first to enunciate the idea of the party as the New Prince. It marks in the history of ideas and institutions a new and extraordinary kind of political artifact. Like all institutions it has a life beyond individuals.'[15] There also exist 'deconstructive' readings of *Hind Swaraj*, such as Prem Anand Mishra's *Hind Swaraj: A Deconstructive Reading*, and doubtless other more 'constructive' readings.

Hind Swaraj was expectedly critiqued by the British as well as by the Indians when it was first published, but as the decades have rolled on, with Gandhi gaining in stature in India and around the world, that criticism has died down. Even the historian Ramachandra Guha—who with two massive books on Gandhi has become a kind of global authority—chooses to treat *Hind Swaraj* with kid gloves. Somewhat disingenuously, he argues that Gandhi was provoked into writing *Hind Swaraj* because of an article by G.K. Chesterton that appeared around that time, in which the famous writer expressed contempt for emerging Indian nationalism on the grounds that it expressed no original ideas and was largely imitative. Chesterton wrote that he would have admired an Indian who stated that he preferred maharajas over civil servants, for at least that would be an authentic Indian, not a clone. Gandhi, Guha argues, took this criticism to heart—and therefore wrote *Hind Swaraj*! There are flaws with this line of reasoning. It treats Gandhi (and *Hind Swaraj*) as having been written while Gandhi was in reactive mode. This is clearly not the case. Gandhi genuinely believed in everything he wrote, and decades later, in 1947, he clearly confirmed in a letter to Nehru that he would continue with these expressed beliefs even if he were the last person on the planet who believed as he did. It appears rather that Guha, just like Suresh Sharma and company, admires Gandhi so much that he cannot help but downplay any criticism of him.

Furthermore, it is not fair to contend that we must read *Hind Swaraj* only in the historical context in which it was written, and not see it through the prism of current times. We are in this book examining the modern-day relevance of *Hind Swaraj* and therefore must perforce see it through a modern lens, and call out what we see as wrong, just as today we condemn Aristotle's approval of slavery. Gandhi's writings are far more recent than those of the Greek philosopher and must be judged for what they can mean for today's readership.

There exists in law a principle to be followed when it comes to interpreting legal text, and there is no good reason why the same principle should not be followed in general. It provides that when a text is clear enough on its own, we have to accord to it its plain meaning, referred to as the 'literal rule' or the 'plain meaning rule'.

Gandhi frequently contradicts himself in the manifesto—sometimes just a paragraph ahead and sometimes even in the very next line. This, however, is not reason enough to try to harmonise the two statements. Mostly, it is a case of Gandhi himself not being aware of the contradictions and paradoxes. In general, there is no reason to suppose that Gandhi did not understand what he was saying, or rather writing, or that he did not mean what he wrote. Sometimes scholars and interpreters try to say that the great man *could clearly not have meant* what he said and wrote. They cannot come to terms with what has been stated, for they admire Gandhi immensely; but when they interpret him against what is clearly the meaning of a text, they do him a great disservice.

A few words may be said about the writing style deployed in the present book. Often, a paragraph from the manifesto is quoted, and then one or two sentences from within that paragraph are repeated. This is to indicate to the reader that the arguments that immediately follow are linked to those particular lines. The repetition is there only to make it easier for the reader to focus on where I am targeting my criticism, and also to make it doubly clear that I am not quoting the lines out of context.

A few words now about the structure of this book. *Hind Swaraj* itself is divided into twenty chapters, with several running to barely a few pages in length. This book has only ten chapters, and they consolidate most of the themes that *Hind Swaraj* dwells upon.

Chapter 1 is titled 'Gandhi on the British Parliament'. In *Hind Swaraj*, Gandhi critiques democracy in general but maintains a special focus on the British Parliament. He presents a delightful, almost satirical account of Parliament, which he likens to a 'prostitute' with many owners. At the same time, he never, during the whole course of his life, really presented a viable alternative.

Chapter 2 is titled 'Gandhi on Civilisation'. When queried once about Western civilisation, Gandhi is famously supposed to have remarked: 'It is a good idea'—meaning thereby, somewhat ambiguously, either that it is only at the stage of an idea, or that it would be a good idea for the West to become civilised. Gandhi's manifesto itself has two chapters that are specifically on civilisation, though there is a critique of the West in several other chapters as well. Chapter VI of the manifesto is simply titled 'Civilisation', and Chapter XIII is titled 'What Is True Civilisation?' Gandhi critiques both ancient and modern Western civilisation, although he focuses on the latter. While he rubbishes Roman and Greek civilisation, he holds up ancient Indian civilisation as something that, despite British rule, continues to survive in the hearts and minds of the people, and that the rest of the world should look up to. Curiously, he sidesteps any discussion of the all-important issues of caste and untouchability that could be considered civilisational flaws in the Indian context. Chapter 2 also discusses Gandhi's rather controversial views on the railway, since he considered it to be an aspect of modern and industrial civilisation.

Chapter 3 of this book is titled 'Gandhi on Hindu–Muslim Relations'. As a Hindu, Gandhi knew that the Muslims would not trust him easily and therefore, on occasion, he went a little over the top in insisting that the Hindus should not object to any demands raised by the Muslims. Despite his being the 'Father of the Nation', some critics could call him the 'Father of Appeasement Politics' in independent India. Right-wing nationalists frequently argue that, with Pakistan, the Muslims have their own country. Had there been a need to appease the Muslims, it would have been in order to persuade them to remain in an undivided India; following the bloodiness of Partition, no such need remained.

Chapter 4 is titled 'Gandhi on Lawyers and Lawyering'. Gandhi worked as a lawyer for much of his life, but in his manifesto he reveals how much he loathed the profession. Nor did he think judges were much better. He condemned both lawyers and judges, along with the whole edifice of justice. And yet there is not one word of regret expressed for having himself been a practising lawyer for more than a decade. He does not argue for improvement or reform in the justice machinery but simply recommends that lawyers leave their profession and take up the handloom instead. This chapter is largely based on Chapter XI of *Hind Swaraj*, which is titled 'The Condition of India: Lawyers'.

The next chapter of the book, Chapter 5, is titled 'Gandhi on the Medical Profession'. If Gandhi gives short shrift to lawyers, he is the same, if not harsher, to doctors. While he steers clear of recommending touts over lawyers, there is a line in the manifesto where he actually suggests that 'quacks' might be doing a better job than doctors. He likens the medical profession to a parasitic, greedy scourge on society. It is in the utterly confounding Chapter XII of *Hind Swaraj*, titled 'The Condition of India: Doctors', that Gandhi expresses his view on the medical profession.

Chapter 6 of this book is titled 'Gandhi on Machinery'. There are two chapters in the manifesto that discuss this issue: the penultimate Chapter XIX of *Hind Swaraj*, simply titled 'Machinery', and an earlier chapter, Chapter IX, titled 'The Condition of India: Railways'. Railways are an aspect of machinery, and both are aspects or manifestations of science. It is interesting to note that Gandhi does not direct his anger at scientists and science to the extent that he does at machines, and that could be said to be a consequence or manifestation of science. Elsewhere in *Hind Swaraj*, he does not hesitate to accuse historians of arrogance and of pretending that they are the Godhead, but for some reason he spares scientists. Perhaps, he realised that it was all getting a bit much, with condemning politicians in the chapter on the British Parliament, and doctors and lawyers in dedicated chapters elsewhere. So there is no special chapter for scientists and scientific researchers.

Chapter 7 of this book is titled 'Gandhi on Education'. The Mahatma would have been horrified at the present state of Indian education, for at the time he wrote *Hind Swaraj* he was dead against Indians learning English. He went as far as saying: 'To give millions a knowledge of English is to enslave them.' This is ironic, given that he spoke and wrote so much in that foreign language. He translated the manifesto into English himself. His spoken and written English were both excellent. It was the link language for him, for example in his communications with Tolstoy; for Gandhi could neither speak nor write Russian, and of course Tolstoy would not have understood a single word of Gujarati or Hindi.

Should we be surprised at the contradictoriness of Gandhi? Probably not. It would be an understatement to say that consistency was never his strong suit. He was a lawyer for many years and yet he rails against lawyers. He worked as a male nurse assisting doctors for many years but ended up despising the medical profession. So why would he not talk and write in English himself while discouraging other Indians from learning the alien tongue? This is just what Gandhi does. Had India chosen to follow Gandhi's advice and tried to discourage its population from learning English, we would not have had the success as a global service provider in the outsourcing and software industries that we have had. It is another matter that Gandhi might not have thought much of that success.

Chapter 8 of this book is titled 'Gandhi on Ahimsa'. The Mahatma is best known the world over for non-violent political protest, and therefore it is absolutely necessary to have a chapter on ahimsa, the Sanskrit word for non-violence. Gandhi deals with the subject of non-violence in two separate chapters in the manifesto, namely Chapter XVI titled 'Brute Violence' and Chapter XVII titled 'Passive Resistance'. Both these chapters contain certain wonderful and seminal ideas that display a wisdom that sometimes seems bewildering when contrasted with Gandhi's views on the importance of conserving semen or getting rid of all the machinery in the world. In reviewing the manifesto, or indeed Gandhi's legacy itself, there is always a danger of allowing the wisdom displayed in certain areas to cloud one's assessment of the bizarre thoughts revealed in others; and of course, there is the other danger, which critics often fall victim to, of assessing Gandhi's contributions to the theory and practice of non-violence as marginal or trivial given his seeming absurdity in other areas. If I have been critical of Gandhi's views as expressed in most of *Hind Swaraj*, I found his views on non-violence brilliantly expressed.

Chapter 9 of this book is titled 'The Saint's Commandments'. It analyses and discusses the various directives and/or instructions given by the Mahatma at the end of *Hind Swaraj*.

Chapter 10, the final chapter of the book, is titled 'In Conclusion' and seeks to wrap up the preceding discussion. It also draws some conclusions about the man himself and about the relevance of his thoughts to the modern world—and to the conflicts that rage all across it.

Are there important thoughts of the Mahatma that are *not* discussed in this book? Yes, indeed. The Mahatma was so prolific that this was more or less inevitable. However, I should highlight two important themes that are omitted. I have spoken about Gandhi's attitude towards women and sex whenever it is relevant to do so, but never in much detail. Regarding the troublesome issue of caste, which Gandhi did not discuss in his manifesto, I have alluded briefly to his changing—or should I say 'evolving'—attitude in the last chapter of this book. Both women and caste are important themes on which the Mahatma had definite views and a certain practice, and they deserve a separate book in their own right.

* * *

The anarchist Pierre-Joseph Proudhon wrote a famous book, *The Philosophy of Poverty*. In response to this, Karl Marx wrote a classic rebuttal, a book that was deliberately and ironically titled *The Poverty of Philosophy*. We do not know where the Mahatma stood in that philosophical debate. What is clear, however, is that he profoundly understood the 'power of poverty', or rather of 'dressing down' to the extreme in a poor country, such as India. The costume he adopted was a masterpiece in terms of its impact on his 'target audience', which was of course the poor and the very poor of India, and was something that neither Versace nor Yves Saint Laurent nor any of the other great French or Italian designers could ever have hit upon. He did not have the physique to look impressive in the finest Western attire; ironically enough, it was a rough cloth wrapped around his body that focused the world media's attention on to him. The 'naked fakir', who 'nauseated' Churchill,[16] had worn very different clothes as a young man in London. In Piccadilly, he was seen dressed in a pin-striped morning suit, stiff Gladstone collar, a silk top hat, spats over his patent leather shoes and even 'a flashy tie', as a fellow Indian student recalled.[17]

The new costume that the Mahatma adopted was a far cry from his top-hat days and not at all glamorous, but therein lay its strength. Some would argue that despite this, and despite his frequent lectures on the importance of the handloom and simplicity, he was not himself impervious to glamour—witness his choice of Nehru, the rose-buttonholed and always elegantly dressed disciple, as successor[18] and prime minister (PM) of independent India, instead of the much older, staid-looking Patel.

Of course, the very poor who dressed in the selfsame dhoti would not be able to maintain the high standards of cleanliness that the Mahatma maintained. He was notoriously fastidious in this regard: when a drop of mango juice fell on his loin cloth, he scratched at it intermittently for an hour.[19]

As someone who believed that machinery was evil, Gandhi was opposed to mills that manufactured cloth. He believed in the virtue of the khadi he wore. This does not mean that he was ignorant about how striking his costume would be and how it would create, among many people who saw him so dressed, faith in his own higher virtue.

Gandhi was not fond of travelling. As a matter of fact, in *Hind Swaraj* he speaks of how, if God had wanted man to travel so much, he would have equipped him with something more than hands and feet. (One could equally argue—and it has indeed been argued thus—that God created the world so that we might explore and see it from corner to corner.) The trademark dress Gandhi adopted—of plain dhoti, showing his bare chest—made travel more complicated for him, and once this dress of his had attained the stature of a national, even international, symbol, he became a victim of that symbolism.

So it was that when he travelled to address mill workers in the north of England, he could not, despite the freezing temperatures, abandon the costume. Instead he used woollen socks and other clothing aids to keep him warm. 'I don't think that's such an important person at all,' a little girl in the audience, who had been told they were going to see someone important, said to her mother. Years later, when she interviewed with the BBC as an elderly woman, she commented: 'He looked like a muppet to me.'

Gandhi remained until his death a man who largely stood by the ideas stated in *Hind Swaraj*. On the question of Western civilisation, he wrote in *Young India* in January 1921, more than a decade after *Hind Swaraj* was published, about the book being 'a severe condemnation of "modern civilisation"'. *Hind Swaraj* was written in 1909, and thirteen years later Gandhi stated: 'My conviction is deeper today than ever. I feel that, if India would discard Modern Civilisation, she can only gain by doing so.'[20]

I found it difficult to read *Hind Swaraj*, not because it was difficult to understand but because of the nature and quality of the arguments presented. I'm sure that Gandhi opted to write large sections of it in the form of a dialogue between two imaginary characters because he thought, accurately, that he could explain his position on self-rule, or Swaraj, in simple terms.

He also thought, somewhat naively and inaccurately, that he could pre-empt all criticism by putting it into the mouths of the Reader (one of the two participants in this imaginary dialogue) and deal with it by using devastating and impeccable logic through the responses of the Editor, the other character in the dialogue. In fact, he exposed himself at several junctures as a man with a fairly inflated ego who displays a false sense of modesty.

I don't doubt the Mahatma's motives at all, or that he was anything but well intentioned towards the nations' best interests. However, as evidenced by my reading of this single book, he was a curious combination of sincerity and falsehood, or rather self-deception.

Since the present book is not intended to be hagiographic in character but rather an unbiased assessment, let me point to an example of both sincerity and false modesty that surfaces at almost the very outset. As an example of his sincere expression, Gandhi wrote as follows: 'Whilst opinions were being invited as to the advisability of publishing this work, news was received that the original was seized in India. This information hastened the decision to publish the translation without a moment's delay.'[21]

Gandhi's paranoia as an author was sincere and legitimate. Any author understands the panic he must have experienced, especially since we are talking of times in which there was no word processing or saving of text on a computer. However, he then adds the following statement: 'But, without the financial assistance of the many Indians who promised to buy copies for themselves and for distribution, it might never have seen the light of day.'[22]

This is an example of false modesty. Clearly, Gandhi was pretending to be poorer than he is. His personal wealth aside, even in 1910, when the preface to the English translation was written (and from which both of the above extracts are taken), Gandhi was a hugely important figure on the Indian landscape, and he could not have been unaware of this. Indeed, his awareness is evident in what he writes towards the end of the same preface: 'But, occupying the position that I do, it would have been cowardice on my part to postpone publication under the circumstances just referred to.'[23] He means here the seizure of the original.

The conversational style that Gandhi adopts suffers from the fact that his characters are completely wooden and lack all personality. No serious attempt was made to make the Q & A sound natural. It is too obviously fabricated for it to be an engaging read. When Gandhi, as the Editor, states that it is his duty to try to remove the questioner's prejudice, the natural thing for the questioner would have been annoyance at the presumptuousness of this remark.

'How dare you call me prejudiced!' such a person would have responded; and an Englishman would probably have added: 'You pompous ass! You …'

Instead, we have the plastic and completely unreal character of the Reader saying: 'I like that last statement.'

I *like* that last statement? Would a man engaged in a contentious debate respond in such a fashion?

According to Guha, while the Editor was clearly Gandhi himself, the Reader was 'almost certainly modelled on Pranjivan Mehta'.[24] I don't know much about Mr Mehta except that he was a physician and a friend of Gandhi, but I find that difficult to believe because the Reader is so bereft of any real personality that he is scarcely human.

Let me give another example. In the manifesto, Gandhi argues (Chapter VII) that India was not taken by the British, but rather was *given* to them. It is a bald statement, and hardly any arguments are advanced for the conclusion that 'they [the British] are not there because of their strength but because we keep them'. In any natural conversation, we would expect the questioner to strenuously object to such bland assertions on Gandhi's part. Not only does the fictional questioner (i.e., the Reader) not object, but on the point at issue he caves in unceremoniously: 'You are right. Now I think you will not have to argue much with me to drive your conclusions home.

I am impatient to know your further views. We are now on a most interesting topic. I shall therefore endeavour to follow your thoughts and stop you when I am in doubt.'[25]

The Reader is rather too humble and sounds a bit like a caricature of Gandhi himself. Since Gandhi is himself responsible for the address, being the author of the dialogue and the man who pulls at the strings of his two puppets, it is as if the Reader has become the Editor's *chamcha*, or acolyte.

It is clear that despite his greatness in the political sphere, and his love for religious and moralistic tales, Gandhi himself hadn't exactly mastered the storytelling format.

The Mahatma was a past master at using modesty as a weapon. No one of such eminence has used humility and modesty (sometimes genuine, often fake) quite as cleverly as Gandhi. See, for instance, the following paragraph from the very beginning of *Hind Swaraj*: 'Whilst the views expressed in *Hind Swaraj* are held by me, I have but endeavoured humbly to follow Tolstoy, Ruskin, Thoreau, Emerson and other writers ...

And then in order to ensure that he does not appear too Western-oriented, he adds the words: '... besides the masters of Indian philosophy'.

When Gandhi lumps 'Tolstoy, Ruskin, Thoreau, Emerson' all together, he glosses over their individual differences. One is at a loss to understand how he endeavoured, and that so humbly too, to follow all these highly individual thinkers at the same time.

★★★

Although this is, to my mind, a critical but fair work, it is not the case that I am completely out of sync with the Mahatma's feelings. Thirty years ago, when I made my first trip overseas and travelled to London and New York, I too felt extremely alienated and deeply uncomfortable. I missed India with all its chaos, its crowds, its smells and indeed its filth, and I felt overwhelmed, even unnerved, by the fast trains, the Metro and the avalanche of technology that surrounded me on all sides. I have always been a technophobe, and in some ways it is extremely ironical that I should have written this book. Perhaps I would have accepted a case for reasonable curbs on the advancement of technology, but what the Mahatma and I consider to be 'reasonable' are worlds apart.

Many Gandhi lovers may hate the book and accuse me of having been overly critical of the Mahatma. Even those who do not love him might feel that this venture is somewhat unpatriotic. I would like to believe, however, that I have only expressed an honest opinion on the merits of the manifesto, and on a few of Gandhi's eccentricities. After all, he himself would have liked to be judged by the highest standards of moral integrity and rational thinking—and indeed of gender sensitivity.

Throughout the book, I quote directly from *Hind Swaraj* and Gandhi's other writings extensively, to exclude the possibility of any misinterpretation. I have, however, emphasised part of a quote in italics in order to make my own commentary more intelligible to the reader. This usage of italics is the only modification that I have made to the Mahatma's original words. In any event, the original manuscript of *Hind Swaraj* follows my critique, and the reader may refer to it should they wish to do so.

New Delhi, 2025   Rajesh Talwar

CHRONOLOGY

It is beyond the scope of this book to give an exhaustive list of historical dates relevant to Gandhi's life. The dates mentioned here are all relevant to the writing of *Hind Swaraj* and to the present book.

- 1869. Gandhi was born on 2 October at Porbandar, Gujarat. He was the third son of a prominent bania family. Although he hailed from a business/trading community, his father was a high-ranking official of the regional government.[1]

- 1883. Gandhi got married at the age of thirteen to Kasturba, who was fourteen—an age that would not be considered early by the standards of Gujarat at that time.[2]

- 1885. Two years later, Gandhi left the bedside of his dying father to engage in conjugal relations with his wife. By the time he returned, his father had passed away. Gandhi thereafter considered 'lustful love' for his absence around the time of his father's death.[3]

- 1888. Three years after the death of his father, against the wishes of a family elder and caste leader, Gandhi sailed for England to study law. The family jewellery was pawned to support this venture.

- 1891. Three years later, Gandhi received his official licence to practise law in court and became a barrister. Weary of life in England, he soon returned to India.

- 1893. Gandhi struggled for two years in India trying to make it as a lawyer. He was not successful and therefore accepted an offer to work as a legal consultant for an Indian trading and shipping company in South Africa.[4]

- 1894. Gandhi created the Natal Indian Congress with the help of other Indian rights activists, with the idea of giving Indians a voice in South African politics.[5]

- 1899. At the start of the Second Boer War, Gandhi organised an Indian Ambulance Corps. He was sympathetic to the cause of the Boers but decided that he owed allegiance to the British and needed to demonstrate his loyalty to the Empire.[6]

- 1906. Gandhi commanded a corps of Indian volunteers to work with the British forces to suppress the Zulu rebellion.[7]

- 1906. At the age of thirty-nine, Gandhi took a vow of *brahmacharya* (celibacy).

- 1906. Gandhi organised the first satyagraha campaign to protest against the Transvaal Asiatic Law Amendment Act—a law that required the fingerprinting and registration of all Indians living in the Transvaal. He continued his protests against the 'Black Act' (as this law came to be known) until 1911, when it was finally repealed.[8]

- 1907. Within a year of his vow, convinced that he had taken a great step forward, he recommended in his newspaper, *Indian Opinion*: 'It is the duty of every thoughtful Indian not to marry. In case he is helpless in regard to marriage, he should abstain from sexual intercourse with his wife.'[9]

- 1908. Gandhi was incarcerated in a British prison in South Africa, where he reportedly disparaged his fellow inmates, the so-called kafirs, as being filthy and living like animals.

- 1909. Gandhi authored and published *Hind Swaraj*. It was written on board a steamer, the *Kildonan Castle*, between 13 and 22 November. It was first published under the title *Hind Swarajya*, in two instalments, in the Gujarati columns of *Indian Opinion*. The first twelve chapters were published on 11 December and the remaining eight on 18 December.[10]
- 1910. The work was published in English with the title *Hind Swarjaya* by the International Printing Press, Phoenix, Natal, South Africa. The text was translated by Gandhi himself, and published with his Foreword. In March, less than three months after its publication, copies were intercepted in Bombay (now Mumbai). On 24 March, copies were proscribed by the Government of Bombay.
- 1914. Gandhi decided to return to India.
- 1919. The first Indian edition of *Hind Swaraj* was published.
- 1924. The first American edition of the book, edited by Haridas T. Mazumdar and with an introduction by John Haynes Holmes, was published under the title *Sermon on the Sea* by the Universal Publishing Co., Chicago.[11]

Chapter 1

GANDHI ON THE BRITISH PARLIAMENT

*That which you consider to be the Mother of Parliaments is like a
sterile woman and a prostitute.*

*It [the British Parliament] is like a prostitute because it is under
the control of ministers who change from time to time.*

— Mahatma Gandhi

There is much that is great about Gandhi, but it is also true that
Indians have not evaluated the man, his writings and his legacy
critically enough. Gandhi himself might have disapproved of
this criticism, but if we are to take him at his words, he was a
believer in honest disagreement. He wrote: 'If the readers of
Indian Opinion and others who may see the following chapters
will pass their criticism on to me, I shall feel obliged to them.'[1]

Gandhi reassures his readers that he is not vain enough
to think that he could not make errors in his writing. He
acknowledges in his preface to the English translation: 'I am
aware of the many imperfections in the original. The English

rendering, besides sharing these, must naturally exaggerate them, owing to my inability to convey the exact meaning of the original.'[2]

In an early chapter in the manifesto titled 'The Condition of England' (Chapter V), Gandhi provides a simple, homespun and yet at the same time powerfully worded critique of the British parliamentary system. While making his attack, Gandhi is not sophisticated enough to realise that he is making fairly rough and crude comparisons. This, for instance, is what he says about the British Parliament in response to a question:

> That which you consider to be the Mother of Parliaments is like a sterile woman and a prostitute. Both these are harsh terms but exactly fit the case. The Parliament has not yet of its own accord done a single good thing; hence I have compared it to a sterile woman. The natural condition of that Parliament is such that without outside pressure it can do nothing. It is like a prostitute because it is under the control of ministers who change from time to time. Today it is under Mr. Asquith, tomorrow it may be under Mr. Balfour.[3]

'The Parliament has not yet of its own accord done a single good thing. Hence, I have compared it to a sterile woman.'

If Gandhi was meaning to shock his readers by using such language, he certainly succeeds, but not necessarily in the way he intended. Isn't this a terrible and unfair thing to say about sterile women? Are sterile women incapable of 'a single good thing'? Is producing children the only 'good thing' that women are capable of? Possibly the Mahatma did not mean to abuse or disrespect the sterile women, but as a person who believed that real India lived 'in its villages', he could not but have been aware of the stigma faced by barren or sterile women in rural environments for failing to produce offspring. The Hindi word *baanj* is uttered almost as a term of abuse.

A modern man or woman, including in India, would be outraged by the comparisons that Gandhi makes. Is a prostitute any less of a human being, or does she deserve less respect than any other woman? The Mahatma has slighted all women when he makes such a comparison. Was there no other appropriate metaphor that the Mahatma, with his fertile brain and imagination, could have devised?

Gandhi dwells on the sheer wastage of time in the British Parliament. According to him: 'If the money and the time wasted by the Parliament were entrusted to a few good men, the English nation would be occupying today a much higher platform. The Parliament is simply a costly toy of the nation.'[4]

How are these 'few good men' to be selected and placed in charge? This important question does not concern the Mahatma, and he does not offer any suggestion as to how it might be accomplished.

As for 'the English nation would be occupying today a much higher platform', what is his own platform, and that of his people, that he should worry about the English? And what 'higher platform' is the Mahatma talking about? The English were already ruling much of the world. But the Mahatma makes this assertion and does not elaborate, and he follows the same pattern elsewhere in the book too. After all, this is a manifesto.

Expanding the meaning of his metaphor in comparing the Parliament to a prostitute, he writes on how 'Parliament is without a real master. Under the prime minister its movement is not steady, but it is buffeted about like a prostitute.'

In India, it is a matter of record that as things stand today, a high percentage of members of the Indian Parliament have a criminal record, and the percentage is still higher in the state assemblies. One shudders to think how Gandhi would have reacted to this situation. Despite his immense sacrifices in terms of proposing and trying to work out a concrete alternative to the British parliamentary model that India adopted, he certainly did not appear to do anything to prevent it from happening. In his manifesto, this is what he says about the British parliamentarians: 'One of the members of that Parliament recently said that a true Christian could not become a member of it. Another said that it was a baby. And if it has remained a baby after an existence of seven hundred years, when will it outgrow its babyhood?'[5]

The English feel proud and boast about the long history of their Parliament, but Gandhi cleverly runs it down, saying that they have not managed to improve it in all those centuries.

Author Sunil Khilnani, an admirer of Gandhi, suggests that the latter possibly envisaged something beyond the nation state. This is possible, of course, but the point is that Gandhi himself does not say anything of the kind.

If the ordinary British parliamentarian is subjected to harsh criticism (as above), the PM is not dealt with in any kinder fashion. Gandhi wrote: 'The Prime Minister is more concerned about his power than about the welfare of the Parliament. His energy is concentrated upon securing the success of his party. His care is not always that Parliament shall do right. Prime ministers are known to have made Parliament do things merely for party advantage.'[6]

This is a valid perspective and argument, but one that would have been immeasurably strengthened had Gandhi proposed an alternative. A little later, his tone turns shriller:

I can have nothing against Prime Ministers, but what
I have seen leads me to think that they cannot be

considered really patriotic. If they are to be considered patriotic because they do not take what is generally known as bribes, let them be so considered, but they are open to subtler influences. In order to gain their ends, they certainly bribe people with honours. I do not hesitate to say that they have neither real honesty nor a living conscience.[7]

Hind Swaraj clearly enunciates Gandhi's strong and valid conviction that India should not be imitative of British political institutions; the problem, though, is that he does not posit a clear and viable alternative. It is all very well to point to inadequacies in a political system, but you have to suggest concrete alternatives. Gandhi mulled over the situation for many years—decades even—but nearly thirty-eight years later, as India's independence approached, for a man with his prolific written output he had said or written precious little in terms of an alternative agenda beyond vague and general talk about empowering village panchayats and councils.

It is also remarkable that while Gandhi critiques the functioning of the British Parliament, he does not raise the issue anywhere in his manifesto of the hypocrisy of so-called democratic nations that practise democracy at home and autocracy overseas. It would have been logical for him to have pointed out that while the English enjoyed their rights and freedoms at home, in territories colonised by the English across the world, people were enslaved. But he does not make that argument (with which no one could have taken issue), arguing instead that the British were not in India because of their strength but because 'we keep them'.

★ ★ ★

If Gandhi did not believe in the parliamentary system, which embodies democratic values in the political sphere, can it therefore be inferred that he did not believe in democracy itself? It is certainly possible that this was the case. Not only was Gandhi not a democrat, he did not feel in the least ashamed about this.

The adage that 'power tends to corrupt' is certainly true—even if it is somewhat doubtful that absolute power corrupts absolutely, for who in the world has absolute power, and what is really meant by 'absolute power' or for that matter 'absolute corruption'? It could be rather said that while power tends to corrupt, greater power tends to corrupt even more. Gandhi certainly enjoyed power and the trappings of power in his own way. His dictatorial tendency is evident both in the political sphere and in his personal life, where he indulged his sexual peccadilloes. In the political sphere, possibly the most shocking exhibition of the dictator hiding within the saint came to light when he overruled by Gandhian diktat the democratic election of Subhas Chandra Bose as Congress party president. The dictator within Gandhi was also on full display when he chose to sit on a fast unto death unless the Dalit leader B.R. Ambedkar withdrew his demand for separate electorates for the scheduled castes.

Khilnani wrote about how Gandhi actually subverted the democratic idea on very many occasions. 'For the duration of Gandhi's dominance, from 1920 until the early 1940s', he wrote:

Gandhi preferred not to be a formal member of the Working Committee yet he used it repeatedly to push through decisions that contradicted the wishes of party members. Most conspicuous was his removal of Subhas

Chandra Bose from the elected office of Party President in 1939. Gandhi did establish a culture of dialogue and publicity with Congress but his fierce disciplinary regimes – fasts, silences, penances – gave him a grip on the party that relied at once on coercion and seduction. *These were the immensely effective techniques of an eccentric parent, but they were not designed to nourish commitment to democratic institutions.*[8]

As regards Bose's election, Gandhi had in fact nominated someone else to be the candidate for party president that year and suggested that he be elected unopposed. Bose had not fallen in line with the Mahatma's wish and decided to contest the election, which he won hands down. On 29 January 1939, Bose was elected Congress party president. Despite this victory, he could not properly savour its taste. Gandhi was extremely unhappy and declared: 'Sitaramayya's defeat is my defeat.'[9] When Gandhi thus expressed his unhappiness, Bose was compelled to leave the party. Was this not hypocrisy on the part of the Mahatma? If he didn't want anyone else but the person he nominated, why suggest the charade of an election?

It could be argued that Bose had a different world view from Gandhi's proclaimed non-violent approach, and so despite his popularity they could not have coexisted in the same institution. At the same time, it is saddening that Bose's contributions have been neglected. Even if one were to completely dismiss unsubstantiated rumours that Nehru allowed Bose to die in a Soviet prison pending release of still unclassified documents,[10] there is no doubt that part of the reason why Bose has become a shadowy figure, rather than being treated fairly as in the mainstream of the Indian independence movement, is that Gandhi's protégé Nehru was appointed as PM of the new India.[11]

Bose supported the Germans and the Japanese in the Second World War because from his perspective the British were the Nazis of India.

While Khilnani acknowledges Gandhi's eccentric and dictatorial ways, in a misguided attempt to temper that criticism he also refers to 'Gandhi's powerful vision of direct self-rule, with the majority in possession of political power unmediated by a state'.[12] The truth is that while Gandhi mocked Western-style democracy beautifully, he never offered any powerful alternative vision. Even the communist ideology speaks of how the state might 'ultimately' wither away. Gandhi had grander notions of doing away with the state right away—but never concretely suggested how this might be made possible. There was enough time—nearly four decades—after *Hind Swaraj* was first published to have made those concrete suggestions (had there been any) but none was ever made.

When Gandhi criticises the British parliamentary model in *Hind Swaraj*, it is somehow implicit that he considers his critique to be equally valid and relevant for other variants, such as the American and French ones. In other words, he is criticising all Western models of democracy!

Had Gandhi passed away a few years later after writing all his criticisms of parliamentary democracy, he would have kept the world guessing whether he actually had some real ideas up his sleeve. Perhaps his followers might argue that the Mahatma had many bright ideas about how to implement 'true' democracy, but simply did not have the time to properly enunciate or articulate them. Such is the man's reputation that Gandhians all over the world continue to detect and interpret hidden meanings in those expressed views, though he had enough time to spell out what he truly meant, if he meant anything at all. In point of fact, he never attained clarity in his views on federalism, as is evidenced by his conversation with his biographer Louis Fischer in 1942. Fischer wrote:

> Gandhi asserted that a federal administration would be unnecessary in an independent India. I pointed out the difficulties that would arise in the absence of a federal administration. He was not convinced. I was baffled. Finally, he said, 'I know that despite my personal views there will be a central government.' This was a characteristic Gandhi cycle: he enunciated a principle, defended it, then admitted with a laugh that it was unworkable.[13]

The point is also that if Gandhi really believed in 'true' democracy, or 'grassroots' democracy, he should have nurtured whatever democracy was possible. Certainly, he was not edging India closer to grassroots democracy by behaving like a dictator. Did it not smack of hypocrisy when, despite his simple attire and famed modesty and politeness, he behaved like a feudal lord insofar as decision-making within the Congress was concerned?

The decision to appoint Jawaharlal Nehru as the PM of India was Gandhi's alone, not of the Congress party. Gandhi was the kingmaker; he knew it, and he never thought for a moment that he should step aside and allow the Congress party to take its first, tentative steps towards democracy. True democracy, or grassroots democracy, whatever Gandhi might have meant by it, was still a long way off.

In the years preceding full independence, it became clear that whoever assumed the post of president of the Indian National Congress would automatically be invited by the British to be the first PM of India.

The author M. Brecher refers to the Mahatma as a 'super-President' and speaks of how 'contests were rare, the most noteworthy being the bitter campaign of 1939 when Bose defeated Sitaramayya'.[14]

It was the Mahatma who, as the 'super-president', decided who would be the next president of the Congress—and future PM of the country. This is what he wrote to Maulana Azad, who had been president of the Congress for the previous six years.

> Please go through the enclosed cuttings ... I have not spoken to anyone of my opinion. When one or two Working Committee members asked me, I said it would not be right for the same President to continue ... If you are of the same opinion it may be proper for you to issue a statement about the cuttings [the news item Gandhi had sent him] and say that you have no intention to become the President again ... In today's circumstances, I would, if asked, prefer Jawaharlal. I have many reasons for this. Why go into them?[15]

Certain details about how the selection of the first Indian prime minister took place have only recently surfaced. Maulana Azad, who was the Congress president at the time, was asked by Gandhi to step aside and make way for Nehru. According to the Maulana's will, a certain part of his biography, published posthumously in 1959, was to be withheld for thirty years after his death. Two of these previously undisclosed paragraphs stated the following:

> I acted according to my best judgement but the way things have shaped up since then has made me realise that this was perhaps the greatest blunder of my political life ...
> The second mistake was that when I decided not to stand myself, I did not support Sardar Patel.[16]

Despite the Mahatma's clear support for Nehru, had there been a contest there is little doubt that Sardar Patel (who subsequently became home minister) would have been elected president and would have been the first PM of India. Out of fifteen Pradesh Congress Committees, the only bodies with the power to nominate and elect the president of the party, twelve nominated Sardar Patel.[17] Not a single Congress committee nominated Nehru, but at the end of the day that did not matter. He was the Mahatma's blue-eyed boy. Gandhi acted like the feudal lord he pretended he wasn't and 'advised' Patel to withdraw his candidature. He asked Acharya Kripalani to find a proposer and seconder for Nehru's candidacy.

As the historian Rajmohan Gandhi recorded, 'as soon as Nehru had been formally proposed', Kripalani handed Patel a fresh piece of paper with the latter's withdrawal written out on it. Vallabhbhai was pulling out, Kripalani's draft said, 'so that Nehru could be elected unopposed'.[18]

Clearly, the Mahatma had contempt for the views of the Congress committees, considered his own opinion to be vastly superior, and did not hesitate to veto the views of the majority. Would a genuinely modest man so easily and readily overrule the views of twelve Pradesh Congress Committees? Did this action on Gandhi's part augur well for the future of the world's largest democracy—to have its PM chosen in such a feudal manner? Given the Mahatma's actions, should educated Indians even take seriously his views on how some fictitious 'grassroots' democracy was infinitely superior to parliamentary democracy? Was democracy only to be practised in the superior system that resided in the Mahatma's imagination alone, and not in the system India was actually hurtling towards?

Politics apart, despite his so-called modesty (another reason to argue that it was fake is the fact that genuinely modest people do also tend to be democratic) there are innumerable examples of Gandhi tending to act as a dictator in his personal life. The press and even scholars have tended to focus on his dealings with Kasturba, his wife, but there are other equally serious examples. These are discussed briefly in the last chapter of this book.

Gandhi's critique of the parliamentary system and so-called democracy in the West may have been scathing, but he was saying nothing new or particularly original. Winston Churchill famously said: 'No one pretends that democracy is perfect or all-wise. Indeed it has been said that democracy is the worst form of government except for all the other forms that have been tried from time to time.'[19]

* * *

On the hypnotic role of the media in beguiling the masses, Gandhi sounds startlingly similar to Noam Chomsky, the dissident American intellectual and professor. In a way, he was more qualified than Chomsky to comment on the issue, for he himself was something of an expert in manipulating public opinion. Certainly, he used his fasting to great effect both in terms of affecting public opinion and in terms of achieving what he desired even if it went against common consensus. Anyhow, if Chomsky has written about the manipulation of public opinion in the context of the various American wars, this is what Gandhi says about the gullible English people and their mental manipulation by a partisan media:

> To the English voters their newspaper is their Bible. They take their cue from their newspapers which are often dishonest. The same fact is differently interpreted by different newspapers, according to the party in whose interests they are edited. One newspaper would

consider a great Englishman to be a paragon of honesty, another would consider him dishonest.[20]

Biased and politicised as the media might be, Gandhi does not stop to consider that sometimes reading opposing viewpoints can actually help people make up their own minds.

A lover of the common man and a believer in humanity, the Mahatma nonetheless demonstrates that he holds the opinions of the masses, including those of the English people, in utter contempt. For this he blames the media, but not it alone. He wrote: 'What must be the condition of the people whose newspapers [described above] are of this type?'[21]

A little later in *Hind Swaraj*, he elaborated on that condition: 'These people change their views frequently. *It is said they change them every seven years.*'[22]

It's interesting that Gandhi speaks of seven years. This means two election cycles really, assuming a five-year term. If we think of the American system in contemporary times, it would give the president of the USA two terms. And so Bill Clinton had two terms, George W. Bush had two terms, Barack Obama had two terms. Food for thought admittedly, but this is not the place to carry out an analysis of the veracity or truth in Gandhi's observations on this seven-year cycle of public opinion. At any rate, it is not his original contribution to political thought; he is only regurgitating views expressed by Western critics themselves.

Elaborating on the fickleness of public opinion and of the English, Gandhi concluded: 'These views [those of the English] swing like the pendulum of a clock and are never steadfast. The people would follow a powerful orator or a man who gives them parties, receptions, etc. As are the people, so is their Parliament.'[23]

'The people would follow a powerful orator ... As are the people, so is their Parliament.'

Can we interpret this to mean that other people, for instance Indians, are *more* steadfast? Is Gandhi implying that the Indians are more discerning than the English since they are not swayed by mere oratorical skills? Gandhi was certainly well aware of his own extreme limitations as a public speaker, and he seems to suggest that on this account Indians are more discerning. Certainly, the Indians were steadfast in their admiration and love for the Mahatma, which persists till this day. Reading between the lines, there seem to be two hidden compliments here: one for the Indian people, and one for their leader—Gandhi himself.

Admirers of the Mahatma believe that it was Gandhi's travel to England and time spent in South Africa that made him see India dispassionately and with a critical eye. This is undoubtedly true. Gandhi thought of himself as authentically Indian, not a westernised Indian. But this is not entirely true.

One of the ways in which Gandhi is Indian is that he too has the Indian way of perceiving great Indians with a completely uncritical eye. The Irish poet W.B. Yeats writes of this Indian tendency in his famous introduction to Rabindranath Tagore's *Gitanjali*: 'Other Indians came to see me and their reverence for this man [Tagore] sounded strange in our world where we hide great and little things under the same veil of obvious comedy and half-serious deprecation.'[24]

While Yeats admired this Indian tendency, he was in the Irish–British way being too polite. For, as he acknowledges in that very same introduction, how will society come to an awareness of what is better without criticism?

Most Indians too will not tolerate anything said against Gandhi. Gandhi is like a god to them. Apart from Gandhi, if something is even said against a contemporary politician or actor there can be riots. This is also true of some South Indian actors, such as Raj Kumar in the past and Rajinikanth in present times. We are not only an idol-worshipping people, but we really idolise our people. *Indian Idol* should have started before *American Idol* and not the other way around.

Let me give an example of how Gandhi too can be seemingly uncritical. In response to a critical question with respect to Mr Gokhale, Gandhi conceded that criticism can be made, but in the very next breath he added: 'Our chief purpose is not to cry down his work, but to believe that he is *infinitely greater* than we, and to feel assured that compared with his work for India, ours is *infinitesimal*.'[25]

Chapter 2

GANDHI ON CIVILISATION

Indian civilisation is the best, and ...
European is a nine days' wonder.

— Mahatma Gandhi

The chapter in *Hind Swaraj* titled 'Civilisation' does not contain the famous phrase attributed to Gandhi.[1] When asked for his view of Western civilisation, Gandhi is reported to have said: 'It is a good idea.' This was no vitriolic attack but a gentle admonition or reproach to indicate that Western civilisation was only at the stage of an idea, and not a historical development that had actually taken place!

The Mahatma's views on civilisation do not take us entirely by surprise, for Gandhi has prepared the reader somewhat in his earlier comments on the British Parliament. Indeed, he gives us a broad hint of what is to follow in his preface to the English translation via his following remark: 'But, I must frankly confess that I am not so much concerned about the stability of the Empire as I am about that of the ancient civilisation of India, which, *in my opinion, represents the best that the world has ever seen.*'[2]

Gandhi is well known for his politeness, but he pulls no punches while attacking Western civilisation describing it as evil, with few, if any, redeeming features. As he writes: 'The British Government in India constitutes a struggle between the Modern Civilisation which is the Kingdom of Satan (no less) and the Ancient Civilisation, which is the Kingdom of God.'[3]

If there had been a real questioner in *Hind Swaraj*, and not Gandhi's puppet, such a questioner might have been tempted to ask, in sarcastic humour or jest: 'And where exactly does the medieval world fit in between these two kingdoms, Mahatma?'

Satan is invoked several times in *Hind Swaraj*, even though in polytheistic Hindu India, just as is the case with gods, goddesses and goodness, evil has, in general, taken a decentralised shape with a variety of *rakshasas* (demons). Has Gandhi made the satanic references deliberately with a view to shaming some of the Western Christians who might read *Hind Swaraj*? It could be a plausible explanation; however, the references are more likely due to the influence that Christianity itself had on Gandhi. In Chapter XVI, invoking the Devil twice, he wrote: 'I am not likely to obtain the result flowing from the worship of God by laying myself prostrate before Satan. If therefore anyone were to say: "I want to worship God, it does not matter that I do so by means of Satan" it would be set down as ignorant folly.'[4]

These are words that more properly belong in the mouth of a Christian priest, albeit a misguided one, not a polytheistic Hindu for whom morality is not seen in such black and white terms. In Hinduism, while there are all manners of rakshashas, there exists no central satanic entity; it is a 'democracy', with many gods and demons, and not a single God and Devil. (It is true that Islam and Judaism too invoke the Devil, but they are less likely referents here—Gandhi never came across anything in the Old Testament or the Holy Quran that he found as moving as the Sermon on the Mount.)

This is not to say that he does not invoke Islam as well in condemning Western civilisation. Gandhi observes that '[a]ccording to the teachings of Mohammed, this would be considered to be a Satanic civilisation'. It is unfortunate that Gandhi does not further elaborate on the connection that he draws between the teachings of the Prophet and Western civilisation. Gandhi had studied Islam; at one point in his life, he even had Muslim friends who were trying to persuade a confounded Gandhi to convert to Islam. He was not therefore just talking off the top of his head. He must have had things in mind, which he did not, however, spell out. Modern-day jihadis, including those from the Islamic State, would undoubtedly agree with the Mahatma's assessment of the West and its civilisation, although they are unlikely to be quoting Gandhi in support of such an assertion. In any event, should such a jihadi happen to come across *Hind Swaraj* and read through it, for all his disagreements with Gandhi's pacifism and non-violence he would probably both agree with and take comfort from Gandhi's observation that Western civilisation will eventually self-destruct. Gandhi wrote: 'This civilisation is such that one has only to be patient and it will be self-destroyed.'[5]

Gandhi's criticism of Western civilisation is part of a broader critique of modernity, and is an impressive and lucidly stated one, even if it frequently tends to go over the top. For instance, he wrote: 'Formerly, the fewest men wrote books that were most valuable. Now, anybody writes and prints anything he likes and poisons people's minds.'[6]

And who, if the Mahatma could be asked, is to be the judge of what is poisonous? Judging by the seizure of *Hind Swaraj*—

an unexpected development that sent him into a panic and thereafter led him to not 'lose a moment' in its publication—there are clearly people who judged his work as poisonous. One man's poison is another's nectar, and vice versa.

'Now, anybody writes and prints anything he likes …' The Mahatma's stance is rather elitist here when he speaks of 'anybody' in his remark that 'anybody writes and prints anything he likes'. And what should anybody write and print if not something that he (anybody) likes—and believes in?

Although Gandhi made full use of the postal service in communicating with eminent personalities across the world, it was not spared from the sharp edge of his pen. He wrote: 'Formerly, special messengers were required and much expense was incurred in order to send letters; today, anyone can abuse his fellow by means of a letter for one penny.'[7]

Realisation dawns that the point is exaggerated and over the top. Pre-empting accusations of hypocrisy, he hastily concedes in the very next sentence: 'True, at the same time one can send one's thanks also.'[8]

One wonders what Gandhi would have thought of the Internet and email.

★ ★ ★

In his book *The Idea of India*, Khilnani suggests that Gandhi's 'costume' was carefully designed. Possibly so, but upon reading Gandhi's views on civilisation we find that his simple folksy attire not only reflected his identification with the poor of India but completely fell in line with his critique of industry and modern civilisation.

In the previous chapter, we spoke of how Gandhi's views on women were indirectly revealed when he compared the British Parliament to a barren woman. In his views on civilisation, he goes a step further in suggesting that the true role of a women lies within the confined space of a family or home. Dismayed at what he perceives to be the 'plight' of Western women, he observes that '[w]omen who should be the queens of households, wander in the streets or they slave away in factories'.[9]

So are these the only three alternatives that are truly available to the Western woman: to be a 'queen of the household', or to 'wander in the streets', or to 'slave away in factories'?

Although there is, prima facie, nothing wrong in a woman being a 'queen of the household', a modern woman could take umbrage and point out that the so-called queen is all too often under the thumb of the master or king of the household! They would consider this comment evidence that the Mahatma's mind was cast in an overbearing, patriarchal mode, which would appear to be in line with some of his other behaviour, such as in asking young girls to sleep next to him in the bed[10] (with their consent, as would be argued by Gandhi apologists, or at least with the consent of their husbands, the masters and kings of the household). Was Gandhi's wife, Kasturba, a 'queen of the household'? Or was she a queen only in name, and completely subservient to the wishes of the king of the household, Gandhi himself?

Once, when Kasturba refused to do Gandhi's bidding with a smile on her lips while cleaning the toilets of lower castes, he almost threw her out of the house.

He wrote in his autobiography:

Even today I can recall the picture of her chiding me,
      her eyes red with anger, and pearl drops streaming

down her cheeks, as she descended the ladder pot in hand ...

I was far from being satisfied by her merely carrying the pot. I would have her do it cheerfully. So, I said, raising my voice: 'I will not stand this nonsense in my house ...'

I caught her by the hand, dragged the helpless woman to the gate, which was just opposite the ladder and proceeded to open it with the intention of pushing her out ...[11]

She had not even refused to do his bidding; it was merely the absence of a 'smile' that so infuriated our saintly dictator. As Gandhi himself conceded until at least 1898—barely ten years before he wrote *Hind Swaraj*—he was of the view that 'the wife was the object of her husband's lust, born to work at her husband's behest, rather than as a helpmate, a comrade and a partner in the husband's joys and sorrows'.[12]

But was it ever really a true partnership? We see that Gandhi did not even bother to discuss his views with Kasturba, or see whether they met with her approval. He concluded that such an exercise was futile: 'Kasturba perhaps does not even know whether she has any ideals independently of me. *It is likely that many of my doings have not her approval even today. We never discuss them. I see no good in discussing them.*'[13]

To return to the text of *Hind Swaraj*, what exactly did Gandhi mean by women who 'wander in the street'? As a revolutionary leader, he should not have been against the wandering spirit, unless by 'wander in the street' he meant women who were forced to offer their bodies for sale (those women who are so very like that awful British Parliament we spoke about a little earlier).

To be fair, Gandhi does have the support of some modern men—and women. As the contemporary and controversial historian Hanne Nabintu Herland wrote, 'In a country that is increasingly characterised by a deterioration of traditional values, the woman sits drunk and alone in bars at night in mini-skirts—and thinks she is free.'[14] (She has also expressed the view that feminism has created many harsh Norwegian women and that she understands why men prefer Thai and Russian brides.[15])

Doubtless, household work is easier and healthier than working under unhygienic conditions for long hours, but Gandhi's real intent appears to have been against women working outside the home itself; otherwise he would have spoken of better working conditions for all workers, and especially for women. His remarks can be construed as having such a meaning: 'For the sake of a pittance half a million women in England alone are labouring under trying circumstances in factories or similar institutions.'[16]

He did want women to properly cover up their bodies. One doubts that he would have been against the 'scarf', the Muslim headgear that has created so much controversy in France, although he was against covering the face and against purdah. Once he reprimanded his niece Manu for not covering her head. This is how she recollected the incident:

When I got to Bapu I was wearing a sari. As usual I kept my head covered, but as I bowed down to greet him, the sari slipped off my head and I was not aware of it. As I put my head in his lap, he affectionately pulled my ear and said, 'So you have come?' The same night at Shrirampur he told me, *Gujarati saris are for rich women who have nothing else to do but to loll in sofas or drive about*

in cars. Moreover, a Gujarati sari with head uncovered
looks so immodest that one cannot bear to see it.'[17]

Gandhi and the Artefacts of Modern Civilisation: The Railways

In the very opening pages of *Hind Swaraj*, Gandhi hails Dadabhai Naoroji as the 'grand old man of India'. He wrote on how Dadabhai 'dedicated his life to the service of India', and how 'we have learned what we know from him'.[18]

The famous 'drain theory' with which Dadabhai is credited argued that there were six different ways in which the British were draining or siphoning away the wealth from India. He felt some tribute could be paid to the British, as rulers, for introducing railways in the country, but only within reason; the British were, on the other hand, like vampires draining the lifeblood from the Indian economy.[19]

The Mahatma paid lip service to Dadabhai. But while the venerable gentleman felt that the payment of a tribute to thank the British for introducing railways might be in order, Gandhi turned such logic upon its head.

In an Chapter IX of his manifesto titled 'The Condition of India Railways',[20] he grandly announced to the questioner: 'When I give you my views as to the poverty of India, you will perhaps begin to dislike me because what you and I have hitherto considered beneficial for India no longer appears to me to be so.'[21]

And then he drops an intellectual bombshell (he probably hoped it would create an intellectual earthquake among the classes if not the masses): 'Railways, lawyers and doctors have impoverished the country so much so that if we do not wake up in time, we shall be ruined.'[22]

Even at a first quick appraisal, the argument seems to self-destruct, for railways existed in England long before they came to India. If they had not impoverished the conqueror, why would they impoverish India? It is, after all, the trains themselves that are evil, according to Gandhi, not the use to which they are being put.

The world's first train journey took place more than a century before Gandhi wrote *Hind Swaraj*. It was way back in 1804 that the first steam engine train chugged along in South Wales, in the UK.[23] At the time when *Hind Swaraj* was published, more than half a century had elapsed since the first train ran in India. The first passenger train service had been inaugurated from Bori Bunder in Bombay (today Mumbai) to Thane in 1853.[24] So, before the arrival of the devilish machine in 1853, had the Indian condition been that much better? Gandhi did not bother to elucidate further.

An important argument that could have been made against the railways was that they were used by the colonial power in many instances to export foodgrain outside the country, particularly during the Second World War. Here too, though it was not the railways—that is to say the machines and the technology—that were to blame, but the *use* the railways were being put to. The Mahatma did not, however, make this argument or indeed refer to the export of foodgrain as a cruel and harmful policy.

What then are Gandhi's arguments against the railways? (Doctors and lawyers are dealt with in later chapters.)

Diseases spread faster. Point taken. Could the coronavirus have spread across the world so easily if we didn't have railways and aircraft? But is that reason enough for mankind to dispense with railways and aeroplanes altogether?

Yes, Gandhi did resort to such specious and—dare one suggest?—crude reasoning. This is what he said: 'The railways, too, have spread the bubonic plague. Without them, masses could not move from place to place. *They are the carriers of plague germs.*'[25]

Modern-day global charities, such as the Melinda and Bill Gates Foundation, Oxfam, and United Nations agencies such as the Office for the Coordination of Humanitarian Affairs, use all available means of transport to reach areas where food relief is urgently required. Unlike Gandhi, these charities do not see railways as the primary cause of the famines. This is Gandhinomics at its most incredible! Industrialist G.D. Birla is said to have remarked in the context of Gandhi's economic ideas that the Mahatma was positively 'hallucinating'.

In Gandhi's view of the matter, there are two ways in which the railways cause famine. First, he wrote: 'Railways have also increased the frequency of famines because owing to facility of means of locomotion people sell out their grain and it is sent to the dearest markets.'[26]

The Mahatma did not see that there was an opportunity for the farmer to get a better price for his produce. He would rather that the poor farmer remain in the grip of the moneylender, and the sale of his agricultural products be confined to where bullock carts and horses could easily carry them.

He hands out what he believes are homespun truths in *Hind Swaraj*, with little argument or discussion. It is as if he is making pronouncements from a pulpit. Ours is not to reason why …

Look at the second reason he advances in support of his argument that trains have caused famine. He writes: '[p]eople become careless and so the pressure of famine increases'.[27]

It is a casual comment, almost a careless one, and yet it is made on an issue that could not be more serious—that of famine.

People become *careless* and so the pressure of famine increases! And why exactly is it that people become careless? It is because they feel secure that grain will reach them because there are trains. Gandhi would have us believe that it would be better for people to live on the brink of famine and remain alert, rather than feel a sense of reassurance that even if the crop fails, there are trains that can bring in grain. It almost seems that he is scouting for arguments, and that he is prepared to advance even the flimsiest one in defence of his case.

What would the Mahatma have said when the charities wished to transport food and grain to a famine-struck region by means of goods trains? Would the train then not have been an instrument of good? A man of his intelligence would surely have pre-empted such questioning even while writing and subsequently publishing *Hind Swaraj*.

The Mahatma could not but concede this, but he does so grudgingly. Well, he seems to say that had the trains not been there in the first place, there *would* have been no famine.

Am I putting words in the Mahatma's mouth? Not at all. He clearly said so when he wrote: 'An opium eater may argue the advantage of opium eating from the fact that he began to understand the evil of the opium habit after having eaten it. I would ask you to consider well what I had said on the railways.'[28]

★ ★ ★

Surely it would have crossed the Mahatma's mind that even the Indian National Congress, the leading political organisation in the country over which he exercised enormous influence, would not, after a read-through of the text of *Hind Swaraj*, proceed to pass a resolution raising a political demand for the stoppage of all trains, and indeed the disbandment of the railway itself, as being the major cause of famines.

Eventually, Gandhi does concede this much: Railways as the cause of famine might be a debatable proposition, but it is beyond doubt that they promote evil and corrupt the very nature of man.

'Railways,' the Mahatma wrote, '*accentuate* the evil nature of man.'[29] They cause an increase in criminality, to be sure, for '[b]ad men fulfil their evil designs with greater rapidity'.[30]

Even 'the holy places of India have become unholy'.[31] Why and how has this happened? The Mahatma observed: 'Formerly, people went to these places with very great difficulty. Generally, therefore, only the real devotees visited such places. Nowadays rogues visit them in order to practise their roguery.'[32]

Gandhi's views on the railways are so fearful of the advent of a new kind of technology that they are reminiscent of how, in Gabriel Marquez's famous novel *One Hundred Years of Solitude*, residents of the imaginary village of Macando react to the first arrival of a train as if it were a devil incarnate. 'It's coming,' she cries. 'Something frightful like a kitchen dragging a village behind it.'[33]

Could a man such as Gandhi, who took on the might of the British Empire, have been frightened? Many would dismiss such a suggestion, but the bravest among us still have our—sometimes completely unfounded—fears. There are analysts and writers who argue, for instance, that the hippie movement and 'flower children' of the 1960s represented an extraordinary anti-technological movement that grew out of fear.[34]

Despite his misgivings, Gandhi himself travelled by train frequently, taking care to travel third class. Did travelling third class lessen the evil? It is not clear whether he thought this was the case, but it was potent symbolism, despite its absurdity.

As an aside, we may mention here how the poet Sarojini Naidu revealed the truth about Gandhi's train journeys in a conversation with Lord Mountbatten. 'Ah,' she laughed, 'you [Mountbatten] and Gandhi may imagine that when he walks down that Calcutta station platform looking for a suitably crowded third class carriage, that he's alone, he is unprotected. What he does not know is that there are a dozen of our people dressed as Untouchables, walking behind him crowding into that carriage.'[35]

Gandhi denounced the railways but used them nonetheless for his political work. He was also against modern devices such as the radio but agreed to do an interview on All India Radio. He was against modern contraptions but used a watch and could fly into a rage if he was delayed on account of someone else. (His niece Manu vividly recalled how he once scolded her severely for delaying him by five minutes.) He read and wrote extensively in English, although he discouraged others from doing so.

Even with all these contradictions and deviations from his own views, Gandhi was able to sway and influence millions of Indians. This would not have been possible had it not been for his hugely impressive simplicity and abandonment of modern conveniences.

Louis Fischer expressed it rather well, 'There he sat, four-fifths naked, on the earth, in a mud hut in a tiny Indian village without electricity, radio, running water or telephone.'[36]

Sarojini Naidu quipped famously on how 'it costs a great deal of money to keep Gandhiji living in poverty'.[37]

* * *

If it were up to him, Gandhi would have limited human mobility and movement across the globe. Although he himself, during the course of his life, travelled widely, he would rather that most people stayed put exactly where they were. Privy, like Prophet Muhammad, to God's most secret thoughts, he believed that God too would have wished as much and therefore set natural limits on man's powers. He wrote: 'God set a limit to a man's locomotive ambition in the construction of his body. Man immediately proceeded to discover means of overriding the limit.'[38]

At this point in the argument, Gandhi's view of God appears to be anthropomorphic; and not so very differently from the priest in a religion, he goes on to prey on the sense of guilt, which many worshippers suffer from, when he says: 'God gifted man with intellect that he might know his Maker. Man abused it, so that he might forget his Maker.'[39]

In philosophical terms, it would seem that Gandhi believed that God is clearly not All Powerful, or All Knowing. Evil Man fiddled about with God's creation, and thereby created all kinds of technology and 'maddening conveniences'[40]—all really more akin to the Devil's handiwork.

The Mahatma wasn't only against the railways but against all modern forms of transportation.[41] He wrote:

I should however like to add that man is so made by nature as to require him to restrict his movements as far as his hands and feet will take him. If we did not rush about from place to place by means of railways and other such *maddening conveniences*, much of the *confusion* that arises would be obviated.[42]

Gandhi travelled the world, from his very first journey to England, to South Africa and other parts of the African continent. Yet he does not appear to have particularly enjoyed his voyages. Rather, his travels disturbed, confused and confounded him. From his remarks noted just above, we get a sense of the massive cultural shock he must have suffered on his first voyage to England. While other Indians, notably Nehru, took to English culture and its material trappings like ducks to water, they came from more elite westernised backgrounds than Gandhi, who felt bewildered and confused.

Gandhi wrote in Chapter X of *Hind Swaraj*: 'I am so constructed that I can only serve my immediate neighbours, but in my conceit, I pretend to have discovered that I must with my body serve every individual in the Universe. In thus attempting the impossible, *man comes into contact with different natures, different religions and is utterly confounded.*'[43]

Before he managed to read books on vegetarianism and defended it before the rest of the world almost as an article of his faith, he was overcome by the arguments made by a friend in England soon after his arrival in the country that he should now forget vows made to an illiterate mother back home and take up meat eating. He wrote in his autobiography:

> One day the friend began to read to me Bentham's Theory of Utility. I was at my wits' end. The language was too difficult for me to understand. He began to expound it. I said, 'Pray excuse me. These abstruse things are beyond me. *I admit it is necessary to eat meat.* But I cannot break my vow. I cannot argue about it. *I am sure I cannot meet you in argument.* But please give me up as foolish and obstinate.'[44]

Subsequently during his time in England, Gandhi went on to read books on vegetarianism, which emboldened him, and with his new-found confidence he was able to not only defend his take on vegetarianism but also convince others to follow suit. In his autobiography, Gandhi recounts with apparent glee an episode where an English mother pleads with him to leave her son alone, for she worries that under the Mahatma's influence the young man might give up eating meat. Though Gandhi grew and matured in his thoughts and ideas as a result of his travels and wider reading, it appears that he did not wish others to experience personal growth and preferred that they remain stuck and stunted.

Gandhi's Love for Ancient India

Ancient India is the paradise, the veritable Garden of Eden from which Indians were cast out. There are fundamentalist Muslims who believe that the world was perfect at the time of Muhammad (despite all the wars during that period), and such people long to go back to those days—if only it were possible. There are right-wing Hindus (and others) who also hark back to a 'golden age'. And so, too, does Gandhi—but his vision of ancient India is considerably different.

What of the violence in India prior to the arrival of the train (and indeed of the English)?

Despite all his professed ahimsa, the non-violence for which he is known and beloved the world over, it turns out that the Mahatma can be accommodating of violence when it takes place in a more traditional and primitive context. Thus, he defends the violence of the Pindaris, the Bhils and the Thugs with great gusto. And what arguments does he use to defend their acts of violence? What arguments *can* there be to defend violence that is not for self-defence or a just cause?

Even in the cause of the freedom of India, Gandhi would not countenance any violence. The antics of the right-wing nationalists dismayed him. He was no admirer of Subhas Chandra Bose, the militant Indian nationalist. A small act of violence— the throwing of stones, for instance—would be anathema to the Mahatma, and indeed he would possibly go into a fast unless those responsible eschewed all violence. But we see him defending the violence of certain Indian tribes and communities: 'If you will give the matter some thought, you will see that the terror [by the Bhils, Pindaris and Thugs] was by no means such a mighty thing. If it had been a very substantial thing the other people would have died away before the English advent.'[45]

By 'other people' here one can only assume that Gandhi meant all Indians other than the Bhils, Pindaris and Thugs.

So the terror was not such a 'mighty thing' because the rest of the Indians were not exterminated. The Bhils, Pindaris and Thugs did not carry out large-scale mass slaughter or genocide after the American and Australian fashion—in the United States of the Native Indians, and in Australia of the Indigenous People. Since there were no large-scale massacres, no genocide, it doesn't deserve to be condemned outright, so the argument conceivably runs.

And what would you do, Gandhi ji, the questioner could possibly bait him, if you yourself were to be so attacked?

Although not framed in the form of a question, Gandhi pre-empts such a query, and his response is startling and unequivocal: 'I should prefer to be killed by the arrow of a Bhil,' he wrote with much bravado, 'than to seek unmanly protection.'[46]

Perhaps Gandhi wishes to highlight the greater savagery of modern warfare, having himself participated in British wars in Africa, and that could surely make for an important and interesting argument. But I do not wish to put words into the Mahatma's mouth.

Gandhi and the City

The modern city too is a product of industrial civilisation, and it is therefore only logical that Gandhi hated the city, terming it a 'snare'. It was for him a symbol both of evil and of Western civilisation. As compared with villages and small towns, cities have evidently more machinery such as buses, trains, etc., and for this reason he concluded that cities were intimately connected with 'machinery', something that he considered evil. He wrote, 'Where there is machinery, there are large cities; and where there are large cities, there are tram cars and railways; and there only does one see electric light.'[47]

Were Gandhi alive today, the big Indian cities such as Mumbai, Delhi and Kolkata would seem to him to be brimming with evil energy and force. He would not have thought of traffic jams as mere nuisance or health hazards, as does the modern metropolitan Indian. Cities would have seemed positively ghastly because of all the evil machines running over the roads. It is not clear, at least from a reading of *Hind Swaraj*, how the Mahatma felt about towns. We may fairly conclude that he would have been opposed to the bigger towns that approached the status of cities.

What about small towns? My guess is that he would have tolerated those that were just above village status but would have hated any further urbanisation.

There is undoubtedly much that is great about Indian civilisation—respect for the elderly and the greater importance of family values, for instance. What is true of India is also true of several other Asian countries. The West has much to learn from India and Asia. India can and should, however, learn from other cultures too, including those in the West. The problem with Gandhi's critique of Western civilisation is that it is a mixture of truth, half-truth and untruth.

★ ★ ★

When reading *Hind Swaraj*, it sometimes felt to this reader as if Gandhi were using ahimsa almost as a pretext to mask his real and virulent hatred for modern civilisation and industrialisation. This explains why, earlier in the narrative, he justifies the violence of tribal communities such as the Bhils as necessary for the development of courage and manliness in the land. Even though at the time of writing *Hind Swaraj* the English ruled India, it is according to Gandhi not really India but England that was in a pitiable state. As far as India is concerned, he feels that there are many places where civilisation has not penetrated, and therefore glorious India in its ancient splendour still exists! 'And where this cursed modern civilisation has not reached,' he concluded, '*India remains as it was before.*'[48] When Gandhi talks of the glory of India, he does not mean its riches; he means the simplicity of the countryside. 'The inhabitants of that part of India,' he continued, 'will very properly laugh at your new-fangled notions. The English do not rule over them, nor will you ever rule over them.'[49]

'I believe,' he wrote, 'that the civilisation India has evolved is not to be beaten in the world. Nothing can equal the seeds sown by our ancestors.'[50]

Chapter 3

GANDHI ON HINDU–MUSLIM RELATIONS

A man is just as useful as a cow no matter whether he be a Mohammedan or a Hindu.

— Mahatma Gandhi

Professor John J. Mearsheimer has written an interesting book on why political leaders tell lies in international politics. The professor draws a distinction between two kinds of lies: the selfish lie, which is intended only for the leader's own political benefit; and the strategic lie, which takes into account the national interest, or what is best for the people.[1] There is much in Gandhi's manifesto that cannot be taken at face value; we may consider that the Mahatma may in many instances have been telling strategic lies, keeping the national interest uppermost in his mind.[2] Of course, the strategic lie may often also have personal political benefits.

There is a fair amount of creative untruth-telling in the manifesto when Gandhi writes on the relations between the

Hindus and the Mohammedans (Chapter X). Several of the Mahatma's assertions are historically inaccurate, even if they are well intentioned. Gandhi always pretended to himself and to others that the Muslims had never tried to forcibly convert Hindus, impose special taxes on them or commit various atrocities. The Sikhs suffered greatly defending the Hindu faith. There are those who even argue, not without reason, that had it not been for the valour and sacrifices of the Sikh community, who stood up as a bulwark against the forcible conversion of Hindus, India today would have been a completely Muslim-dominated country, just like Malaysia or Indonesia. It is one thing to say that the past should be forgotten and that it is no longer relevant or useful to talk about any atrocities or injustices that may have occurred—an idea that I completely support—and another thing entirely to say that there *were* no atrocities.

Papering over the troublesome past, Gandhi wrote instead: 'Pray remember that we did not cease to fight only after British occupation. The Hindus flourished under Moslem sovereigns and Moslems under the Hindu.'[3]

This is Gandhi doublespeak at its cleverest. Someone who had no knowledge of Indian history could assume from this statement that sometimes the Hindus were on top and sometimes the Muslims were on top, but that they both 'flourished' under each other's sovereigns.

And then in the very next sentence, Gandhi follows up with a historical falsehood that would hide all the sacrifices made by the Sikh gurus, and the oppression by Mughal emperors such as Aurangzeb: 'Each party recognised that mutual fighting was suicidal, and that neither party would abandon its religion by force of arms.'[4]

Although the Mahatma's intentions cannot be doubted here, one can see why there were Hindus who were angered by such observations. This is another example of doublespeak, but the falsehood peeps out: 'Each party recognised that mutual fighting was suicidal …'

Not true at all. Gandhi's words could have been an accurate, albeit simplistic, explanation of the Cold War that ensued between the US and the former Soviet Union, but it was a distortion of historical truth as far as Indian history was concerned. Gandhi transposes what he wished had happened into what had actually happened. 'Each party recognised that mutual fighting was suicidal' somehow suggests that, generally speaking, there was a balance of power. This was, however, clearly not the case: '… and that *neither* party would abandon its religion by force of arms.'

The sentence seems to suggest that both Hindus and Muslims were trying to get the others to convert, and that is completely and utterly wrong. The Hindus did not even believe in converting others to their faith, so how could the question arise of converting Muslims to Hinduism by 'force of arms'? As a matter of fact, till the middle of the nineteenth century and the arrival of the Arya Samaj movement, a Hindu who had converted to Islam under duress was not even permitted to return to the fold!

Gandhi in *Hind Swaraj* is behaving like a parent who is trying to bring two quarrelling boys together. He adopts a technique commonly adopted by both parents and teachers. Instead of apportioning blame, he pretends that both boys are equally guilty, and should therefore now make up and be friends. Gandhi might be well intentioned, as any parent would be, but he does not necessarily exhibit an example of 'good parenting'. His aim may be that one of the boys (the Hindu) would realise that the parent is correct and that he has been behaving just as terribly as the other youngster, or that he would agree to let bygones be bygones and shake hands in friendliness. This kind of parenting might work in some scenarios but not in others. For instance, where one boy has been distinctly unfair and has been beating up the other, it would be an example of bad parenting, not good parenting, for the father to insist that both have been 'bad boys' and should now 'kiss, hug and make up'. The boy who was being beaten up would feel he had been treated unfairly, and the boy who was doing the beating up could feel emboldened that he could get away with beating up the other boy. Greater subtlety and nuance are called for in handling such a situation in order to ensure an enduring reconciliation.

Let's examine the issue more closely. From a parenting perspective, can it ever be justified that a parent treats one child with more favour than the other? Possibly yes. For instance, take a situation where one child is weaker than the other in an important respect, such as mental capacity or physical strength. Someone could make out a valid argument that equals deserve to be treated equally: if two parties are unequal, equal treatment would actually be unfair.

Were the Muslims unequal in any respect, compared to the Hindus? Perhaps yes. In an undivided India, they would have constituted a large minority, undoubtedly, but a minority nevertheless. They would have wondered if they would be able to trust the Hindu majority to treat them fairly. Many would be conscious of the fact that there had been Muslim invaders over the years, and Mughal rulers such as Aurangzeb had meted out harsh treatment to the Hindus. They might have asked themselves whether the Hindus would not seek revenge. In fact, there might have been a Hindu fanatic who would have wished to exact revenge for past wrongs, both real and imagined. There would be others who would not so much seek revenge as simply feel bitterness over the past.

On the other hand, there could be Muslims who felt nostalgic and recalled past 'glorious' centuries in which the minority Muslims had ruled over the majority Hindus. Alas, those times were now left behind forever. A few Muslim fanatics (for there are always bound to be some of those around) would also rack their brains and try to think and imagine ways in which the former glory of the Mughal dynasty could be somehow restored and the Muslims could rule India once again!

So, Gandhi, it can be argued, in order to assuage all these various feelings and misgivings, behaved with greater kindness towards Muslims than he did towards his own Hindu brethren.

There is a second important reason for the Mahatma's somewhat uneven, if not skewed, behaviour. He himself was a Hindu, and understood that his complete neutrality and impartiality could still be regarded as somewhat suspect by the Muslims—after all, he was not one of them. To counteract such an impression, and to take the metaphor of an Indian mother doling out halwa to her two children, he would throw an extra spoonful into the Muslim boy's plate, for he would be watching carefully, and could suspect the parent of unfairness even if the portions were distributed equally.

These are both important reasons that can provide a plausible and reasonable explanation for Gandhi's behaviour, and there is possibly a third, often less acknowledged, reason too. The Muslims were not only in the minority, but were in general less educated than the Hindus. This added to their fear of the Hindus, and there were Muslim preachers and leaders who did not hesitate to prey upon this fear. Consider, for instance, what a Bengali preacher said in Sylhet, implicitly referring to the greater education of the Hindus.

In Sylhet (now Bangladesh), Maulana Azad Sobhani made a speech on 27 January 1939, some translated paragraphs of which are worth quoting in full.[5] He appears to have been really paranoid about an imagined threat from the Hindus.

I want that there should be no fight with the English on behalf of the Muslim League. Our big fight is with the 22 crores of our Hindu enemies, who constitute the majority. Only 4½ crores of Englishmen have practically swallowed the whole world by becoming powerful. *And if these 22 crores of Hindus who are equally advanced in learning, intelligence and wealth as in numbers, if they become powerful, then these Hindus will swallow Muslim India and gradually even Egypt, Turkey, Kabul, Mecca, Medina and other Muslim principalities, like Yajuj-Majuj (it is so mentioned in Koran that before the destruction of the world, they will appear on the earth and destroy whatever they will find).*

The English are gradually becoming weak … they will go away from India in the near future. *So if we do not fight the greatest enemies of Islam, the Hindus, from now on and make them weak, then they will not only establish Ramrajya in India but also gradually spread all over the world.* It depends on the 9 crores of Indian Muslims either to strengthen or weaken them (the Hindus). So it is the essential duty of every devout Muslim to fight on by joining the Muslim League so that the Hindus may not be established here and a Muslim rule may be established in India as soon as the English depart.

Though the English are the enemies of the Muslims yet for the present our fight is not with the English. At first we have to come to some understanding with the Hindus through the Muslim League. Then we shall be easily able to drive out the English and establish Muslim rule in India.

Be careful! Don't fall into the trap of Congress Maulvis, because the Muslim world is never safe in the hands of 22 crores of Hindu enemies. [emphasis mine]

According to the summary of the speech given by the correspondent for the *Anandabazar Patrika*, the Maulana went on to describe various imaginary incidents of oppression of Muslims in Congress provinces. The correspondent wrote about the Maulana as follows:[6]

He was again thinking that before India became independent some sort of understanding had to be arrived at with the Hindus either by force or in a friendly way. *Otherwise, the Hindus, who had been the slaves of the Muslims for 700 years, would enslave the Muslims.*[7] [emphasis mine]

This may have been the additional reason why the Mahatma showed greater acceptance of Muslim demands. As the Bengali preacher hectored, 'these twenty-two crore Hindus ... are equally advanced in learning', comparing the Hindus to the English. While that issue might be debatable, it was certainly true that the Hindus were in general more advanced in learning than the Muslims.[8]

It isn't necessarily the case that the Mahatma was being patronising with respect to the Muslims; it might be that he experienced not only sympathy for but empathy with the average Muslim's lack of learning and education, relative to that of the Hindu. As *Hind Swaraj* goes on to show in a subsequent chapter titled 'Education', Gandhi was opposed to Western learning in general. On a plain reading of this part of the manifesto, it is clear that Gandhi was in favour of students *not* learning the sciences. This was a part of Gandhi that strongly believed in 'backwardness', from which it can be concluded that he had not only sympathy but also actual and genuine admiration for the relative backwardness of the Muslims. The Hindus were more educated, which also meant that they were more westernised. There was a part of Gandhi that loved the backward mind (an attitude we would today classify as non-progressive).

There is a fifth, highly uncharitable explanation for Gandhi's slight bias in favour of Muslims that deserves mention. His assassin, Nathuram Godse, argued that it was naked political ambition that led Gandhi to favour the minority community. According to Godse, the Mahatma 'lived in the hope of becoming the common leader both of the Hindus and the Muslims'. According to the assassin, the more setbacks Gandhi encountered as far as donning the mantle of Muslim leadership was concerned 'the more he indulged in encouraging the Muslims by extravagant methods'.[9]

To continue with the parenting simile, it would have been naive for Gandhi to imagine that the extra portion he tossed into the Muslim boy's bowl would go unnoticed by the Hindu boy. He may have thought that the Hindus would understand that, as someone with the same religious faith, Gandhi would never do anything against Hindu interests. While this may indeed have been how the majority of Hindus felt, there were always bound to be someone who would see hidden motives and even duplicity in Gandhi's conciliatory approach to the Muslims.

★ ★ ★

Gandhi may have realised that there would be some among the better-read Hindus who would accuse him not merely of simplifying but of using doublespeak to cleverly distort history because he very well knew that he was doing exactly that. Gandhi announces in *Hind Swaraj* and elsewhere how it is his deep conviction that the ends do not justify the means. However, in the context of dealing with the Indian past, he clearly believed that the ends *do* justify the means. He believed that adducing false arguments or half-truths (his simplifications of Indian history) is justified because in his view it furthered a moral cause, which is to bring two communities together. Gandhi clearly believed in the 'good lie', namely a lie that is told to benefit others.

Gandhi was prepared to counter those who accused him of distorting history, and he did so in a clever, manipulative way.

These thoughts are put into our minds by selfish and false religious leaders. The English put the finishing touch. They have the habit of writing history; they pretend to study the manners and customs of all peoples. God has given us a limited mental capacity, but they usurp the functions of the Godhead and indulge in novel experiments. They write about their own researches in most laudatory terms and hypnotise us into believing them. We in our ignorance then fall at their feet.[10]

The English, Gandhi wrote, 'pretend to study' the manners and customs of all peoples. He could have said 'aspire to', but by using the term 'pretend to' instead he intends to impute an agenda to English sociology and history writing. And then he cleverly adapts one of his own earlier arguments in the context of the evil trains. Just as we should not try to travel faster than God meant us to since he only gave us hands and feet, we should accept our mental limitations and not try to rise above our station. God has his 'functions', and we humans have ours. We should not try to 'usurp' the functions of the Godhead. Henry Ford famously said, 'History is more or less bunk'; the humble Mahatma goes one step further and suggests that not only history but sociology too (which would include the study of manners and customs that Gandhi alludes to) is mostly bunk, all being purely God's business, not ours.

Social historian Khilnani said this about Gandhi vis-à-vis history:

> Gandhi rejected the idea that past history was a source for defining future possibilities or orienting present action. The British fascination with historical dissertations was expressive of their desire to dominate: history was used to justify colonial rule and to show that past dissensions prohibited the possibility of future unity for India. It was only by kicking the British 'habit of writing history' that Indians could release themselves from the cultural harassments of their rulers. 'I look upon Gibbon and Motley as inferior editions of the *Mahabharata*.'[11]

Khilnani observed that, in contrast to nationalists who sought to construct a reliable future out of a selected past, Gandhi expressed profound distrust for the historical genre, turning instead to legends and stories from India's popular religious traditions. Clearly the Mahatma preferred their lessons to those of history. The fact that so many on the subcontinent found these fables accessible, and recognised in them their predicaments and symbols, itself testified to a shared civilisational bond.[12]

'I believe,' Gandhi is quoted by Khilnani as saying, 'that a nation is happy that has no history.'[13] He clearly thought that the study of history could not do any good for the strength and unity of India, especially if the country were undivided as he hoped it would be. In holding such views, he was by no means alone.

The great French philosopher Ernest Renan, for instance, emphasised the importance of forgetfulness as a factor in forging national unity.

> Forgetfulness, and I shall even say historical error, form an essential factor in the creation of a nation; and thus it is that the progress of historical studies may often be dangerous to the nationality. Historical research, in fact, brings to light the deeds of violence that have taken place at the commencement of all political formations, even of those the consequences of which have been most beneficial. Union is ever achieved by brutality. The union of Northern and Southern France was the result of an extermination, and of a reign of terror that lasted for nearly a hundred years. The king of France, who was, if I may say so, the ideal type of a secular crystallizer, the king of France who made the most perfect national unity in existence, lost his prestige when seen at too close a distance. The nation that he had formed cursed him; and today the knowledge of what he was worth, and what he did, belongs only to the cultured.[14]

He went on to observe: ' … the essence of the nation is that all its individual members should have things in common; and also that all of them should hold many things in oblivion.'[15]

And so Gandhi, for these reasons perhaps, wished to forget about the history of India and focus instead on the common moral truth in the two religions.

Gandhi's apparent favouring of the Muslims understandably riled a certain section of the Hindus. As regards the Muslim demands for greater concessions from Lord Morley, this is what he had to say in *Hind Swaraj*:

> There is mutual distrust between the two communities. The Mohammedans therefore ask for certain concessions from Lord Morley. Why should the Hindus oppose this? If the Hindus desisted, the English would notice it, the Mohammedans would gradually begin to trust the Hindus, and brotherliness would be the outcome. We should be ashamed to take our quarrels to the English. Everyone can find out for himself that the Hindus can lose nothing by desisting. That man who has inspired confidence in another has never lost anything in this world.[16]

Gandhi is resorting to a confidence-building measure, and is only well intentioned, but it is easy to understand how a section of the Hindus could perceive this as him favouring the Muslims over them.

In several places in *Hind Swaraj*, Gandhi states that there were invaders who came to India and became part and parcel of the nation, and thus the English too are welcome if they become Indian. When Gandhi wrote that the Muslim invaders became Indianised, he was speaking a truth but also counterposing and contrasting Mughal rule with British rule. It is no doubt absolutely true that from an economic point of view the British bled India far more than the Mughals ever did (or even Muslim invaders such as Ghori and Ghazni, who robbed and looted). However, as the old adage goes, 'man does not live by bread alone'. The Hindu psyche suffered greatly as a result of the Muslim minority's governance over a Hindu majority community. No minority can rule over a majority in any part of the world without the use of force and without deploying a certain level of cruelty. It is partly for this reason that scholars such as Nirad C. Chaudhuri welcomed British rule: he regarded their replacement of the Mughals as a period when the subject Hindu population could regain their composure.[17]

Gandhi does not spell it out in *Hind Swaraj*, but we have to grant that his bias in favour of the Muslims was due to his understanding that in the new India they would be a minority, and that too a minority with memories of a glorious Mughal past when they had ruled the Hindus in vast swathes of territory, so to speak. What of the Hindus? History beckoned once more. This was their moment. Was it reasonable for Gandhi to ask the Hindus to bend over backwards and get them to accept his suggestion that Muslim League leader Jinnah be made PM in order to prevent the partition of the country?

Gandhi Hoped for the Best, but Did Not Prepare for the Worst

Though an Indian, Dalit leader B.R. Ambedkar brought the special perspective of the impartial outsider to Hindu–Muslim relations. Coming from the untouchable caste, he despised the caste hierarchy in Hinduism, and eventually converted to Buddhism. It is also true that he was not blind to the flaws in Islam. Quoting approvingly from a pamphlet, Ambedkar found it to sum up the differences between Hindus and Muslims in their divergent approaches to history:

> In history the Hindus revere the memory of Prithviraj Partap, Shivaji and Beragi Bir, who fought for the honour and freedom of this land (against the Muslims), while the Mohammedans look upon the invaders of India, like Mohammad Bin Qasim and rulers like Aurangzeb as their national heroes.[18]

History apart, as Ambedkar goes on to point out, 'In the religious field, the Hindus draw their inspiration from *Ramayana*, *Mahabharata*, and *Geeta*', whereas the 'Musalmans, on the other hand, derive their inspiration from the Quran and the *Hadis*'.[19]

Ambedkar himself is of the view that 'the pity of it is that the two communities can never forget or obliterate their past. Their past is imbedded in their religion and for each to give up its past is to give up its religion. To hope for this is to hope in vain.'[20]

Ambedkar brought great practical intelligence to bear on the problem of Partition long before it actually transpired. Gandhi, on the other hand, could be said to have been far too unrealistic and optimistic.

Gandhi wished with all his heart for Hindus and Muslims to live together in peace, but he allowed this idealistic and deep desire to cloud a dispassionate assessment of Partition and its benefits. Yes, the two communities may have lived in peace, but when Gandhi says we should focus on the peace that ensued between the two communities instead of the conflict that erupted from time to time, he is, to some extent, being disingenuous. After all, the mere fact that there was no *continuous* civil war between Hindus and Muslims could not be said to be evidence of great communal amity without any cracks within.

Be that as it may, working for the undivided India of the future might have been a wonderful idea, except for the fact that Gandhi never envisaged a Plan B. A stubborn, idealistic streak would not allow him to properly consider such a possibility and to think how Partition might best be managed, were it to happen—until the time when it became a reality. It is perhaps true that no one could have anticipated the sheer scale of communal carnage that was unleashed following Partition— but that there would be killings and disturbances should have been reasonably predictable. The great irony is that India's road to freedom was relatively free of bloodshed vis-à-vis the British, the colonial power; but there was enormous bloodletting, carnage and suffering as a result of Hindu–Muslim violence on that very same road to freedom.

Can we exempt Gandhi and the Congress party completely for having failed to anticipate the ensuing large-scale violence between the two communities and take preventive measures? There were, after all, increasing incidents of communal violence as the date for Independence approached.

What *could* have been done to prevent the carnage that happened? Is it fair to blame Gandhi alone? Surely the British, who always argued that the Hindus and Muslims could not live together peacefully, could have anticipated this and thought up preventive measures? What about other leaders?

The only person who could see the writing on the wall was the bipartisan Dalit leader B.R. Ambedkar. As far back as 1940, seven years before Partition took place, Bhim Rao Ambedkar made concrete suggestions with regard to Partition in his book on the subject titled *Pakistan, or the Partition of India*— suggestions that were, alas, ignored. It is worthwhile discussing his suggestions at some length.

After carefully examining 'the distribution of the population in the areas affected' by a possible partition of the country, he comes to the conclusion that, taking Punjab for instance, 'there are certain districts in which the Musalmans predominate', and likewise 'there are certain districts in which the Hindus predominate'.[21] Furthermore, 'there are very few [districts] in which the two are, more or less, evenly distributed', and moreover 'the districts in which the Muslims predominate and the districts in which the Hindus dominate are not interspersed'.[22]

With regard to the formation of East Pakistan, he observes that 'one has to take into consideration the distribution in both the Provinces of Assam and Bengal'. Here too, a scrutiny of the population figures reveals that 'in Bengal there are some districts in which the Muslims predominate' and 'in others the Hindus predominate', and this is also true of Assam. Furthermore, 'Districts in which the Muslims predominate and those in which the Hindus predominate are not interspersed' and they 'form separate areas'. Additionally, 'the districts of Bengal and Assam in which the Muslims predominate are contiguous'.[23]

Given these facts, Ambedkar concludes that 'it is perfectly possible to create homogeneous Muslim states out of the Punjab, Bengal and Assam by drawing their boundaries in such a way that the areas which are predominantly Hindu shall be excluded'.

It's not all so completely simple, Ambedkar concedes, and goes on to observe:

In the North West Frontier Province and Sind, the situation is rather hard ... As may be seen from the Appendices there are no districts in which the Hindus in the North West Frontier Province and Sind are concentrated. They are scattered and are to be found in almost every district of the two provinces in small, insignificant numbers. These appendices show quite unmistakably that the Hindus in Sind and the North West Frontier Province are mostly congregated in urban areas of the districts. In Sind, the Hindus outnumber the Muslims in most of the towns, while the Muslims outnumber the Hindus in villages. In the North West Frontier Province, the Muslims outnumber the Hindus in towns as well as in villages.[24]

What could be done? Ambedkar put forward what appears at first to be an extreme and radical proposal but, on closer examination, is the only logical and sensible solution.

'In the North West Frontier Province and Sind,' he wrote, 'owing to the scattered state of the Hindu population, alteration of boundaries cannot suffice for creating a homogeneous state. There is only one remedy, and that is to shift the population.'

One can imagine the outcry that would greet such a recommendation, especially since at the time of making this proposal, Partition, which would happen only seven years later, was far from being a 'done deal'. Gandhi and the Congress would have reacted with predictable outrage had Ambedkar's proposal reached the level of mainstream debate. 'We are brothers, the Hindus and the Muslims,' Gandhi and the Congress would have claimed with over-righteous anger.

The erudite Dalit was fully prepared for such sneering:

Some scoff at the idea of the shifting and exchange of population. But those who scoff can hardly be aware of the complications which a minority problem gives rise to, and the failures attendant upon almost all the efforts made to protect them. The constitutions of the post-war states, as well as of the older states in Europe which had a minority problem, proceeded on the assumption that constitutional safeguards for minorities should suffice for their protection and so the constitutions of most of the new states with majorities and minorities were studded with long lists of fundamental rights and safeguards to see that they were not violated by the majorities. What was the experience? Experience showed that safeguards did not save the minorities. Experience showed that even a ruthless war on the minorities did not solve the problem. The states then agreed that the best way to solve it was for each to exchange its alien minorities within its border, for its own which was without its border, with a view to bring about homogeneous States. This is what happened in Turkey, Greece and Bulgaria. Those who scoff at the idea of transfer of population will do well to study the history of the minority problem, as it arose between Turkey, Greece and Bulgaria. If they do, they will find that these countries found that the only effective way of solving the minorities' problem lay in exchange of population. The task undertaken by the three countries was by no means a minor operation. It involved the transfer of some 20 million people from one habitat to another. But undaunted, the three shouldered the task and carried it to a successful end because they felt that the considerations of communal peace must outweigh every other consideration.

That the transfer of minorities is the only lasting remedy for communal peace is beyond doubt. If that is so there is no reason why the Hindus and the Muslims should keep on trading its safeguards which have proved so unsafe. If small countries, with limited resources like Greece, Turkey and Bulgaria, were capable of such an undertaking, there is no reason to suppose that what they did cannot be accomplished by Indians. After all, the population involved is inconsiderable and because some obstacles require to be removed, it would be the height of folly to give up so sure a way to communal peace.[25]

According to Ambedkar's plan, it would have been possible to have a largely homogeneous population of Muslims in West

Pakistan by shifting the Hindus to India (and the Muslims to Pakistan). It was also possible to have a largely homogeneous population of Muslims in East Pakistan (now Bangladesh) in the same manner. What would be rather more difficult to achieve would be to have a homogeneous Hindu India. Ambedkar wrote:

> It must be admitted that by the creation of Pakistan, Hindustan is not freed of the communal question. While Pakistan can be made a homogeneous state by redrawing its boundaries, Hindustan must remain a composite state. The Musalmans are scattered all over Hindustan—though they are mostly congregated in towns—and no ingenuity in the matter of redrawing of boundaries can make it homogeneous. The only way to make Hindustan homogeneous is to arrange for exchange of population. Until this is done, it must be admitted that even with the creation of Pakistan, the problem of majority vs minority will remain in Hindustan and will continue to produce disharmony in the body politic of Hindustan.[26]

Although admittedly it would have been rather more difficult to achieve a largely homogeneous Hindu India following Partition under this scheme, by creating a homogeneous Pakistan (including present-day Bangladesh), the minority problem in those countries would have been solved. Hindus would have been saved from persecution in those countries.

Ambedkar views such a situation as not being without benefits to the Hindus. He wrote:

> This distribution of the Muslim population, in terms of the communal problem, means that while without

Pakistan the communal problem in India involves 6½ crores of Muslims, with the creation of Pakistan it will involve only 2 crores of Muslims. *Is this to be no consideration for Hindus, who want communal peace? To me, it seems that if Pakistan (viz. the creation of) does not solve the communal problem within Hindustan, it substantially reduces its proportion and makes it of minor significance and much easier of peaceful solution.*[27]

But, it will be argued that even after the announcement was made that there would be a partition, there was no bar to Hindus moving to India. So why blame Gandhi and the rest? Such an argument does not carry merit. The question of political leadership comes into play. Great leaders provide greater options for people to choose from. Partition itself was rushed through. There was no organised process facilitating population exchange. Gandhi and the Congress party were still living out a fantasy that ignored the communal question. Gandhi stated famously and proudly that following Partition he would not use a passport to visit Pakistan. What fantasy! Had a process been started by the political classes providing suitable incentives and assurances that the new countries would welcome anyone who wished to be part of the new nation, and had people been properly guided that given the worsening Hindu–Muslim relations that had been clearly evidenced between the 1920s and 1940s it made practical sense for the Hindus of Pakistan to move to India, much of the terrible carnage that followed could have been prevented. But such sagacious and honest leadership did not exist—neither in Gandhi nor in the Congress party that he largely controlled.

Chapter 4

GANDHI ON LAWYERS AND LAWYERING

The first thing we do, let's kill all the lawyers.

— Dick the Butcher

In his writings in *Hind Swaraj*, Gandhi appears to be mentally on the same page as Dick the Butcher, a character in Shakespeare's *Henry VI: Part 2*, who brightly suggests to a revolutionary friend that they should 'kill all the lawyers'.[1] Incidentally, Shakespeare himself appears to have been appreciative of lawyers and attorneys as upholding justice in society.[2]

Gandhi says to the Reader: 'I have no desire to convince you that they have never done a *single* good thing.'[3]

How terrible is that!

What about Gandhi himself? Did he do a single good thing in all the years that he spent practising as a lawyer? Clearly, Gandhi did not think of himself as a lawyer anymore; or even if he did, he regarded himself to be an exception to the rule. This would seem to be the case, based on what he told his niece Manu, who quotes him in her book: 'You had better use the word *upadhi* for a degree. A degree is really a burden. *I regret having become a barrister, and, if you believe me, I am not even conscious of being one.* Because of my experience, I would rather save others from that burden.'[4]

What about all the other lawyers and ex-lawyers in the Congress fraternity—Jinnah, his favourite Nehru, Vallabhbhai Patel and C. Rajagopalachari, to name only a few? Were they all to be similarly regarded as 'exceptions to the rule'? And if that is the case, with so many 'exceptions to the rule', what would become of the rule itself? Would it even remain a 'rule'?

While he grudgingly concedes that it is 'believable' that the Congress owes something to lawyers,[5] Gandhi says this is because some goodness may survive despite their being lawyers. The only exception he actually makes, in response to a question, is a concession that the late Manmohan Ghose 'helped the poor'.[6] In general, though, Gandhi's 'firm opinion' is that 'the lawyers have enslaved India, have accentuated Hindu–Mohammedan dissensions and have confirmed English authority'.[7]

Gandhi writes as if it were the English who invented the institution of courts and lawyers. If we go back in history, even to the ancient India of Gandhi's imaginings, we find that it too had courts and lawyers. The issue of the existence of judges and courthouses in ancient times in India is beyond doubt.[8] A clear case of a lawyer appearing for a fee appears in Asahaya's commentary on *Narada Smriti*.[9] Does Gandhi then exempt those lawyers and judges of antiquity from his criticism of the community?

No one will deny that lawyers can be a greedy, grasping lot. In general, the Mahatma may even to an extent be right when he argues that 'men take up that profession, not in order to help others out of their miseries, but to enrich themselves'.[10] But the same can be said of many a vocation, business or profession. People take them up in order to 'make a living' and, if possible, to 'enrich themselves'. No one but a self-righteous 'waffly idealist' would expect anything else, or blame individuals who do so. Not everyone can be a social worker. It is probably not even desirable that everyone *should* be a social worker, and it can be argued that even social workers suffer from 'greed', albeit of a somewhat different variety.

'Men take up that profession, not in order to help others out of their miseries, but to enrich themselves ...'[11]

Not true. Many people became lawyers in India during Gandhi's time (and even now) *because they had no other option.* Until two decades ago, law school was the easiest to get into.[12] Most lawyers in Gandhi's time (just as is the case in India today) simply managed to eke out a living, on the whole neither constituting a wealthy class at the time when Gandhi was writing nor today. A few among them—some but not all of the London-trained barristers, who were the super elite within the lawyer community—were enormously wealthy, it is true, but you could not, as Gandhi attempted to do in these pages, paint them all with the same brush.

At the time when Gandhi was writing his manifesto, there were very different kinds of lawyers in India broadly classified into vakils, pleaders, advocates, barristers, and so on. It was only post-Independence, with the passage of the Advocates Act 1961, that a single class of legal practitioner, the advocate, was created—a legal functionary who would be entitled to practise in any court in the country. In Gandhi's time there were, for instance, many lawyers who could not appear before the higher courts. So exactly which kind of lawyer is Gandhi talking about when he writes that 'it is one of the avenues for becoming wealthy'? He does not make this clear, but appears to lump them all together, in a simplistic analysis, with blanket condemnation.

Gandhi, being a lawyer himself, could certainly not have been unaware of all the different kinds of lawyers that existed. Although he was right when he wrote that 'petty pleaders actually manufacture them [disputes]' and 'their touts like so many leeches suck the blood of the poor people' This is often typical of the situation in poorer nations with underdeveloped legal systems. The solution is greater investment into the judicial system, not doing away with lawyers themselves, which in effect would mean getting rid of the institution of justice without having anything with which to replace it.

Gandhi does not set out the full picture, for if truth be told these 'petty lawyers' and their 'touts' lead a hand-to-mouth existence. Neither category has fantasies about becoming enormously wealthy, nor is it likely that they ever will. Within the lawyer community, Gandhi has chosen the easiest target to hit!

The other thing is that lawyers do not in any way constitute a separate species, as the Mahatma seems to suggest. They mirror society as a whole. As regards their alleged ruthlessness and grasping nature, members of the legal fraternity often argue, not without truth, that it is their clients who teach them to behave as they do.

Gandhi's arguments would have been more authoritative had he argued that the justice institutions and lawyers indirectly legitimised British rule in the country. He does make the point that British rule would 'disappear in a day' if lawyers stopped working, but he does not develop that side of his argument.

Yes, lawyers may be a parasitical class in a sense, but this does not mean that we should go so far as to classify the institutions of justice and lawyers as essentially evil. The solution is not to 'do away with them' but to introduce reform to ensure that the courts provide fair and speedy verdicts and that lawyers follow the code of conduct they have sworn to uphold. This is why professional codes of conduct for lawyers exist in the first place.

After all, disputes will never entirely disappear from the face of the earth; they existed even in ancient India which, for Gandhi, was equivalent to the golden age. The courts and institutions of justice (which include lawyers) constitute a peaceful method of resolving disputes and an alternative, it might be said, to the jungle law that says 'might is right'.

The Mahatma is unwilling to concede this. He wrote, 'If people were to settle their own quarrels, a third party would not be able to exercise any authority over them.'[13]

'If people were to settle their own quarrels' … But people are *not able to* settle their own quarrels peacefully, and that's precisely why a third party is needed.

Gandhi's arguments run counter to modern jurisprudential ideas, which attribute value to a neutral arbitration whenever two sides quarrel. He seems to have little faith in the notion of a peacekeeper or peacemaker.

Indeed, the lines following those previously quoted confirm this impression, for the Mahatma now reveals that he considers the idea of neutral arbitration positively emasculating: 'Truly, men were *less unmanly*, when they settled their disputes either by fighting *or by asking their relatives to decide for them.*'[14]

In the context of inter-caste disputes within a village—that quintessential Indian village where Gandhi was convinced that 'true India lives'—it is not clear whether he would advocate for each caste's relatives to pick up sticks and once and for all decide the matter in a 'manly' fashion.

It is clear, though, that according to the Mahatma men became more unmanly and cowardly when they resorted to what we consider in modern times the 'rule of law'. Was he advocating a return to the times of the 'noble savage'?

'It was certainly a sign of savagery,' Gandhi concedes, 'when they settled their disputes by fighting.' However, he soon questions if it is *any the less so if I ask a third party to decide between you and me*.

What is so savage about asking a third party to mediate in a dispute?

I could not wait to read what fresh and amazing arguments the Mahatma would advance in support of his proposition that asking for third-party mediation (whether through the institution of a court, through arbitration, even through a village panchayat or otherwise) was akin to 'savagery'. It appears, though, that the Mahatma intended it to be a merely rhetorical question, since he simply leaves it hanging in the air. You may read that bit of the text twice to make sure you haven't inadvertently missed an explanation, but none is provided.

Gandhi goes on to invert the rules of logic by pointing out how '[s]urely the decision of a third party is not always right'.[15] Yes, judges have been known to make mistakes. But no one had asserted the contrary proposition, that is to say that judges *never* make mistakes. It should be enough for any supporter of rule-of-law institutions such as the courts, and to sustain the common man's faith in the courts, if judges and other such neutral umpires are right 'most of the time'. But no, Gandhi maintains or rather insists that 'the parties *alone* know who is right'.[16]

Quite often in disputes the parties do know who is right, but it cannot be claimed that this is always the case. The Mahatma appears to completely do away with the idea of a 'subjective' viewpoint and in so doing provides the reader with an insight into his own character. This might explain, for instance, his stubbornness, his uncompromising nature and his insistence that he is right on so many occasions. He genuinely doesn't seem to realise that all too often there are two or more sides to a dispute, and 'the parties' do *not* know who is right because *each* party thinks, believes and is absolutely convinced that he or she is right and that the other party is totally wrong.

But at this point in the writing Gandhi does not seem to envisage such a possibility. He asserts that 'we in our simplicity and ignorance imagine that a stranger *by taking our money* gives us justice'.[17]

In the last paragraph of the chapter on lawyers, he suggests that if only 'pleaders were to abandon their profession and consider it just as degrading as prostitution, English rule would *break up in a day*'.[18] In the opening part of the manifesto, the Mahatma had stated that the British Parliament was like a prostitute because it was *'under the control of ministers who change from time to time'*. Now it appears that the legal profession is also like a prostitute! Gandhi has, it seems, run out of disparaging similes.

★ ★ ★

There are more jokes against lawyers than there are against judges, but Gandhi considers judges and lawyers to be birds of a feather, and doesn't exempt judges from his general criticism of judicial institutions and their major players. Although he is against the entire system of justice that existed in India, he does not classify it as 'bourgeois' or argue against it from a communist perspective. He maintains: 'What I have said with reference to the pleaders necessarily applies to the judges, they are first cousins, and the one gives strength to the other.'[19]

It almost seems as if it occurred to Gandhi, sometime after he finished writing this chapter, that in the India of yore too there surely must have been lawyers. After all, the lawyer, like the cockroach, is an ancient species, and is said to exist in Hell as well as in Heaven! Rather than edit the chapter to make it more reasoned and reasonable, he saves the caveat for a later chapter, where he explains: 'This nation [that is to say, Ancient India] had courts, lawyers and doctors, but they were all *within bounds*.'[20]

* * *

Gandhi was never a successful lawyer. He was a thinker, a brilliant organiser, a great political negotiator and many other things, but he could not become a truly successful lawyer. There were reasons for this. Unlike Nehru, he did not have a prominent lawyer for a father; second-generation lawyers are always at an advantage. His facial features (with the exception of his eyes) were ugly, according to one of his biographers.[21] The American writer Pearl S. Buck described him as a 'plain, little man'.[22] By all accounts he did not have a physically impressive personality, which can be useful in a court of law. Many lawyers, however, overcome such physical hurdles. The main reason that the Mahatma could never have become a truly successful lawyer was that he was a complete failure when it came to public speaking. His drafting skills were never in doubt, and he could certainly have drafted agreements very well. His negotiating skills were also excellent. This helped him to settle deals, agreements and compromises between opposing sides. All this is part of bread-and-butter law practice, but to be a real star a barrister has to be able to speak extempore, and with passion and eloquence, before judges. This, alas, Gandhi could not manage to do.

We find evidence of his chronic shyness at many places in his autobiography. He wrote: 'This shyness I retained throughout my stay in England. Even when I paid a social call, the presence of half a dozen or more people would strike me dumb.'[23]

At a meeting for the promotion of vegetarianism, Gandhi was called upon to speak. He describes what happened:

I had ascertained that it was not considered incorrect to read one's speech. I knew that many did so to express themselves coherently and briefly. To speak extempore would have been out of the question for me. I had therefore written down my speech. I stood up to read it, but could not. My vision became blurred and I trembled, though the speech hardly covered a sheet of foolscap. Sergt. Mazmudar had to read it for me. His own speech was of course excellent and was received with applause. I was ashamed of myself and sad at heart for my incapacity.[24]

He tried again and again to overcome this public shyness, but his incapacity continued till the day before he was due to depart from England, when he invited his vegetarian friends for dinner at the Holborn Restaurant.

My last effort to make a public speech in England was on the eve of my departure for home. But this time too I only succeeded in making myself ridiculous ...

I had read of [Joseph] Addison that he began his maiden speech in the House of Commons repeating

'I conceive' three times, and when he could proceed no further a wag stood up and said, 'The gentleman conceived thrice, but brought forth nothing.' I had thought of making a humorous speech taking this anecdote as the test. I therefore began with it and stuck there. My memory entirely failed me and in attempting a humorous speech, I had made myself ridiculous. 'I thank you, gentlemen, for having kindly responded to my invitation,' I said abruptly and sat down.[25]

The public speaking improved somewhat when he went to South Africa but not sufficiently for him to make his mark.

It was only in South Africa that I got over this shyness, though I never completely overcame it. It was impossible for me to speak impromptu. I hesitated whenever I had to face strange audiences, and avoided making a speech whenever I could. Even today I do not think I could or would even be inclined to keep a meeting of friends engaged in idle talk.[26]

One of Gandhi's biographers includes in the life history of the great man an article titled 'Briefless Barrister',[27] which talks about how Gandhi could not get legal work. The biography by Louis Fischer also speaks of how 'Gandhi's speeches were delivered in a weak, unimpressive, conversational tone'.[28]

When Gandhi returned with his fine qualifications, there was an expectation in his family that he would quickly start to earn pots of money. He had, however, no knowledge of Indian law, or any idea of how the courts in India conducted business. In Mumbai, 'the timid barrister was further discouraged by stories of barristers "vegetating" for many years'. Those were the days of legal luminaries such as Badruddin Tyabji and Sir

Pherozeshah Mehta. 'The stories of stalwarts such as these would unnerve me,' the Mahatma wrote. After some time, he got a case to argue before the Small Causes Court. When called upon to cross-examine a witness, he could not perform adequately. 'My head was reeling, and I felt that the whole court was doing likewise,' Gandhi wrote. 'I could think of no question to ask. The judge must have laughed, and the lawyers no doubt enjoyed the spectacle.' He returned the fees of ₹30 to his client and never dared to enter another courtroom in India for the rest of his stay there.[29]

Had Gandhi succeeded as a lawyer in India, he would probably never have left for South Africa.[30] He could not overcome his shyness even there. A reporter who covered some of his appearances wrote about how he 'prefaced his speeches and comments by repeated sibilants, for instance: "Ess-ess-ess your worship, ess-ess-ess this poor woman was attending an invalid sister and was on her way home after the curfew bell had gone when she was arrested. I ask ess-ess-ess that she should not be sent to gaol, but cautioned ess-ess-ess."'[31]

It is true that Gandhi eventually gained a kind of success as a lawyer in South Africa, but that was not on account of his eloquence. Rather it was because he had a captive clientele, being the lawyer for all Natal Indians, irrespective of class, caste, creed or religion.[32] Even while he succeeded, his speaking deficiencies would have made him the butt of jokes at the Bar.

★ ★ ★

Could Gandhi's hatred for lawyers have something to do with his own, rather unsuccessful lawyering past? Lawyers often try to curry favour with judges and are known to be notoriously competitive with one another. The camaraderie that one finds in the armed forces is often missing in the profession as a whole. Successful lawyers often mingle only with other successful lawyers, and the less successful trial court lawyers often try to get close to their more successful brethren in the high courts in order to have work referred to them. Successful lawyers are also known to be arrogant, and to treat less successful lawyers as their inferiors. Lawyers can undoubtedly be a greedy, competitive bunch, and Gandhi well understood the milieu he had spent so much of his life within, but with all these failings and limitations, there is no denying that the institutions of justice, together with lawyers and judges, serve an important purpose in society.

The celebrated journalist Khushwant Singh was an unsuccessful lawyer for many years, and wrote on how he came to hate the courts and the legal profession. Could it be that in Gandhi's case too his lack of success in the profession, the snubs he may have received at the hands of judges, and the dismissive manner in which he may have been regarded by more successful lawyer colleagues succeeded over the years in creating so much hatred in him that he determined that there was actually no need for rule-of-law institutions? In other words, he decided to throw the baby out with the bathwater.

His sharp and pungent diatribe in *Hind Swaraj* on justice and lawyers may have been motivated in part by a desire to seek revenge on the functionaries of the institution that had directly or indirectly caused him suffering and humiliation. It may also have been the case that as a relatively new entrant into the Congress party—he attended his first meeting in Calcutta (now Kolkata) in 1901—he wished for the very many lawyers in the party to know what he, Gandhi, thought of their fine qualifications, and to show them their place.

Chapter 5

GANDHI ON THE MEDICAL PROFESSION

He [the doctor] will understand that if by not taking drugs, perchance the patient dies, the world will not come to grief, and that he will have been really merciful to him.

It is better that bodies remain diseased, rather than that they are cured through the instrumentality of the diabolical vivisection that is practised in European schools of medicine.

— Mahatma Gandhi

After gaining legal qualifications, Gandhi practised law for very many years. He therefore had a ringside view of the courts, lawyers and judges. His views may be considered to be over the top, but he was nonetheless talking, with a degree of authority, about a familiar territory. Did he have any such close encounter with the medical profession that might similarly entitle him to judge doctors and their profession? As a matter of fact, he did work on healthcare issues alongside the practice of law. One of his biographers said that Gandhi in his thirties worked as 'a volunteer in the ambulance corps, assisting the British Empire in its wars in Southern Africa'.[1] It was 'on long marches in sparsely populated land in the Boer War and the Zulu uprisings [that] Gandhi considered how he could best "give service" to humanity'.[2]

Gandhi loved nursing. The practice of law in South Africa did not sufficiently satisfy his humanitarian instincts. The dull nature of his legal work and the fact that, at the time, he was appearing largely before lower courts in non-controversial matters made him feel dissatisfied.

He recounted in his autobiography:

I longed for some humanitarian work of a permanent nature. Dr Booth was the head of St Aidan's Missions. He was a kindhearted man and treated his patients free. Thanks to Parsi Rustomjee's charities it was possible to open a small charitable hospital under Dr Booth's charge. *I felt strongly inclined to serve as a nurse in this hospital.* The work of dispensing medicines took from one to two hours daily, and I made up my mind to find that time from my office work, so as to be able to fill the place of a compounder in the dispensary attached to the hospital. Most of my professional work was chamber work, conveyancing and arbitration. I of course used to have a few cases in the magistrate's court but most of them were of a non-controversial character and Mr Khan, who had followed me to South Africa and was then living with me, undertook to take them if I was absent. So I found time to serve in that small hospital. This meant two hours every morning, including the time taken in going to and from the hospital. This work brought me some peace. *It consisted of ascertaining the patient's complaints, laying the facts before the doctor and dispensing the prescriptions ...*

The experience stood me in good stead, when during the Boer War I offered my services for nursing the sick and wounded soldiers.[3]

Clearly, then, Gandhi was not speaking off the top of his head, having worked in close contact with the medical profession as a nurse and formed ideas about it. He studied obstetrics at length and himself helped deliver his fourth son, Devdas, on 22 May 1900. He claimed to have not been nervous at all; after the birth, he also took care of the infant himself.[4] In other words, he was qualified to express an opinion on the medical profession even if his conclusions bordered on the absurd and the ridiculous.

★ ★ ★

There are animal rights activists who are strongly against vivisection, that is to say the carrying out of surgery on live animals with a view to ultimately benefiting humans from a medical point of view. They raise valid ethical arguments, such as subjecting the animals to pain and experiments. Gandhi was of the same view, and felt deeply and passionately about the subject. He wrote: 'I abhor vivisection with my whole soul. I detest the unpardonable slaughter of innocent life and humanity, so-called, and all the scientific discoveries stained with innocent blood, I count as of no consequence.'[5] No one can quarrel with such a position; however, few will go to the extent of despising the medical profession as a consequence.

In despising vivisection prescribed under the 'European school of medicine', Gandhi did not stray very far from the thinking prevalent in his own family. This was not a new evil he had discovered, but part of the very reason why he did not take up the medical profession, for Gandhi's first career preference had been to become a doctor, not a barrister. He penned down in his autobiography:

> So I jumped at the proposal and said the sooner I was sent the better. It was no easy business to pass examinations quickly. Could I not be sent to qualify for the medical profession?
>
> My brother interrupted me: 'Father never liked it. He had you in mind when he said that we Vaishnavas should have nothing to do with dissection of dead bodies. Father intended you for the Bar.'[6]

It is reasonable to assume that if the family were opposed to the dissection of dead bodies, which forms part of the training to become a doctor, they would have been equally, if not more, opposed to vivisection which involves experimentation with live bodies.

At that youthful stage in his life, when Gandhi thought of becoming a doctor, he did not see anything terribly wrong with vivisection but rather was persuaded against the profession by his brother. And that was not the only reason why he didn't pursue that option; a family friend had urged that law was a much better career path than medicine.

It was only many years later that he came around to his father's view, and then extended it to consider not only the dissection of dead bodies but also the vivisection of live bodies reprehensible. Now he began to see many aspects of the medical profession as an evil, not only for members of his own caste but for the world at large. Indeed, it is fair to assume that during the Boer War, in his capacity as a nurse, he would have assisted many doctors performing those terrible 'vivisections' on injured soldiers. Eventually, he would allow doctors to perform surgery on his own body to remove his appendix.

In Chapter XII of *Hind Swaraj*,[7] he tells the reader: 'I was at one time a great lover of the medical profession. It was my intention to become a doctor for the sake of the country. I no longer hold that opinion. *I now understand why the medicine men (the vaids) among us have not occupied a very honorable status.*'[8]

It would initially appear that if Gandhi despises the medical profession as practised by European doctors, he also does not consider the Indian *vaids* and 'medicine men', who practised the indigenous system of medicine, to be accomplishing anything very honourable. It may be true that the vaids did not occupy an honourable status even in 1910, but that is not because of any intrinsic demerit. Rather, it is because Western-style medicine had already entered the country, and crushed the domestic and indigenous system of medicine to an extent. Even today, Western-style doctors hold a higher status in India among the common people, who often out of respect do not even dare to question their procedures. For an ordinary person, doctors tutored in Western-style medicine are almost godlike. Just as the indigenous handicraft industry was suppressed, so too were all other indigenous systems. In short, Indians lost confidence in their own culture and indigenous systems that had served them well in the past.

In the same chapter, Gandhi writes on how 'sometimes I think that quacks are better than highly qualified doctors'. Was his comment a symptom of latent jealousy? Immediately following this statement, he analyses the entire system of medicine, illnesses and treatment in a few sentences, in a manner that indeed a quack might have been proud of (but not a social or physical scientist): 'Their business [that of doctors] is really to rid the body of diseases that may afflict it. How do these diseases arise? *Surely, by our negligence or indulgence.* I overeat. I have indigestion ...[9]

It is nonsensical to say that all (or even most) diseases arise by 'our negligence or indulgence'. There are so many diseases that arise without our apparently doing anything to contribute to them. Measles, chickenpox, smallpox, cataracts—the list where patients might not have done anything to contribute to the disease afflicting them is endless. Such diseases were simply not considered by Gandhi.

Once he has formed the assumption in *Hind Swaraj* that diseases are only caused 'by our negligence or indulgence', the rest of the argument is easily enough made.

> I overeat. I have indigestion. I go to a doctor, he gives me medicine. I am cured. I overeat again. I take his pills again. Had I not taken the pills in the first instance, *I would have suffered the punishment deserved by me* and I would not have overeaten again. The doctor intervened and helped me to indulge myself. My body thereby certainly felt more at ease, but my mind became weakened. A continuance of a course of medicine must therefore result in loss of control over the mind.[10]

Had Gandhi simply said that people should not rush to the doctor for every small ailment, but should instead let nature do its work, few could have taken issue with the proposition. He himself clearly suffered from stomach ailments—including constipation, with which he was plagued and for which he tried many remedies including dietary changes, use of hip bath, and earth treatments.[11] However, on the whole he remained healthy. From his own bodily condition, he seems to have concluded that the rest of the world was pretty much the same, and illnesses were caused by indulgence. And what were these indulgences that he was referring to? Sex, food and drink. Remove these and, according to the Mahatma, all ailments will automatically disappear.

Here again is Gandhi's analysis of how doctors create unhappiness in society: 'I have indulged in vice. I contract a disease, a doctor cures me, the odds are that I shall repeat the vice. Had the doctor not intervened, nature would have done its work, and I would have acquired mastery over myself, would have been freed from vice and would have become happy.'[12]

The logic is almost simplistic. There are scenarios where it would indeed work but these are limited. If a child overeats and suffers a stomach ache as a consequence, it may be best in some cases not to give him a pill for the stomach ache, so that he remembers what happened when he overate and doesn't repeat the mistake.

So far, so good. But Gandhi's truths apply to a very limited set of ailments. A child gets smallpox, chickenpox, malaria … none of these is caused by vice. And medical help is needed. Gandhi is clearly, in the context of medicine (as he was with legal institutions), throwing out the baby with the bathwater.

What is interesting is that Gandhi does not allude to his own experiences as a nurse in the Boer War. As part of the Ambulance Corps, he attended on the sick and wounded. It could not have failed to occur to him what a vicious cycle this business of war was—getting wounded, getting treated, going back to war. It would have been a poignant example to give the context of the arguments he makes in this chapter, but he does not speak at all of that experience.

Possibly he is somewhere guilty and regretful for having served in the British army but is unwilling to concede that his participation in the Boer War, against Boers, was an act of misguided recklessness. Yes, Gandhi cared for the wounded, but the British treatment of their prisoners was terrible. A 'scorched earth' policy was followed by the British commanders, with farms being razed to the ground. In numerous concentration camps, hundreds of prisoners perished without even a record. The great irony is that there were many sections within British society and the British Parliament itself that held grave misgivings about the Boer War, but the Mahatma was at the time troubled by no such uncertainties.[13]

Another major nursing opportunity presented itself in 1906, although Gandhi would himself have preferred to fight. Of this engagement, the author Gary Beene wrote:

> Perhaps even more surprising is Gandhi's position on the appropriate role of Indians in the South African Zulu War of 1906. After the British introduced a new poll tax, Zulus in South Africa killed two British soldiers. In response the British declared a war against the Zulus. It was not a war at all, but rather the legalized sport hunting of unarmed humans of Zulu descent. Gandhi actively encouraged the British to recruit Indians to aid the British army in this slaughter. He argued that Indians should support the war effort in order to legitimize their claims to full citizenship. The British however refused to commission Indians as army officers. Nonetheless they accepted Gandhi's offer to let a detachment of Indians volunteer as a stretcher bearer corps to protect wounded British soldiers. This corps was commanded by Gandhi himself.[14]

Gandhi wished for himself and other Indians to be involved in actual combat, but this was denied to him. 'If the Government only realised what reserve force is being wasted,' he wrote, 'they would make use of it and give Indians the opportunity of a thorough training for actual warfare.'[15]

One cannot help but wonder whether, as a nurse, Gandhi suffered at the hands of arrogant doctors, who may sometimes treat nurses, whether male or female, with less than the respect they deserve. It is conceivable that Gandhi was on several occasions upbraided and even reprimanded by doctors on his performance as a nurse, despite his utmost sincerity in this regard, and that he was never able to forgive the medical profession. Perhaps he thought to himself when slighted by a young medical professional: 'You arrogant fool! I could have become a doctor myself—and I would have been a better one than any of you!'

Clearly, Gandhi did not enjoy the legal profession very much but nursing, which he loved, did not have the *status* that he desired. However, the time spent as a nurse did not go waste. In his ashram, he could bring his passion for nursing to full fruition. This passion was such that he even got the rest of the family involved.

During this stay in Bombay I called on my brother-in-law who was staying there and lying ill. He was not a man of means and my sister (his wife) was not equal to nursing him. The illness was serious and I offered to take him to Rajkot. He agreed, and so I returned home with my sister and her husband. The illness was much more prolonged than I had expected. I had put my brother-in-law in my room and remained with him night and day. I was obliged to keep awake part of the night and had to get through some of my South African work whilst I was nursing him. Ultimately however the patient died but it was a great consolation to me that I had an opportunity to nurse him during his last days.

My aptitude for nursing gradually developed into a passion, so much so that it often led me to neglect my work, and on occasions I engaged not only my wife, but the whole household in such service.[16]

Is it possible that his diatribe against the medical profession was partly a case of revenge for past insults that were never completely forgotten or forgiven, despite his new stature as a great Indian leader—and partly a case of sour grapes? One cannot help but wonder.

* * *

Gandhi wrote on how preparations by the doctors that were 'intrinsically worth a few pence, cost shillings'. This would appear to be a misguided attack on the medical profession. It would have made far more sense if the Mahatma had targeted profit-seeking pharmaceutical companies.

More than a hundred years after the publication of the manifesto, it would still be perfectly reasonable to argue that the profits made by Big Pharma are often at the cost of the lives of many poor people who cannot afford to pay for the medicines. But Gandhi would not want you to buy those medicines anyhow—cheap or expensive.

As a writer from *The Harvard Crimson* observes:

When Gandhi's wife was stricken with pneumonia, British doctors told her husband that a shot of penicillin would heal her; nevertheless, Gandhi refused to have alien medicine injected into her body, and she died. Soon after, Gandhi caught malaria and, relenting from the standard applied to his wife, allowed doctors to save his life with quinine. He also allowed British doctors to perform an appendectomy on him, an alien operation if ever there was one.[17]

Penicillin was not something so new on the world stage that Gandhi could have entertained concerns about any side effects. It was discovered by Alexander Fleming in 1928, and had already been used globally to great effect.[18] There was no need to suspect any adverse reactions. Their son Devdas actually sent for penicillin for his mother, but Gandhi disallowed it. 'You cannot cure your mother now, no matter what wonder drugs you may muster,' said Gandhi. 'She is in God's hands now.'[19]

In Afghanistan (where I worked for the UN for many years), there are traditional tribesmen who would not allow their wives to be treated by a male physician even if she were dying. In the context of Kasturba's illness, how differently did the Mahatma behave? Instead of objecting to a male physician attending to Kasturba, he objected to the injection of penicillin. Who could say which is more backward and superstitious? His justification at the time was on the lines of: 'I tell you in all sincerity that if I were in the same situation, in which Kasturba is now placed, I would have reacted no differently.'[20]

The irony is that Gandhi, a self-proclaimed Hindu, exhibited greater flexibility with regard to the consumption of beef than to a shot of penicillin. In South Africa once, Kasturba was so ill that the doctor suggested beef broth for her to regain strength and fully recover. Knowing this to be a 'painful duty', he posed the question to her, stating that she was 'not bound to follow' him.[21] She refused to partake of the soup and eventually recovered. Interestingly enough, Gandhi did not offer her the option of chicken soup, which could have been equally effective, but against which there was no prohibition in Hinduism. As a Hindu woman, Kasturba understood that beef was taboo—but was hers a case of 'informed consent' with regard to penicillin? Definitely not.

Manu, Gandhi's niece, provides a description of the manner in which Kasturba breathed her last.

> On the 22 February, 1944, God took away this darling mother of mine from me. That whole day, with tears trickling down my eyes, I stood almost transfixed and gazed at Ba as she lay with her head on Bapu's lap, bidding adieu to this world for ever amidst the holy sounds of Ramadhun and the recitation of the Gita. Before she died, she begged pardon of us all. She said to me, 'My child, you have served me a lot. May God bless you,' and to Bapu, 'Now I am going.' Even Bapu could not help shedding two drops of tears.[22]

What was the point of the Ramadhun, when it was a timely shot of penicillin that was needed?

That Gandhi was not being completely insincere or dishonest is clear from an instance referred to by his niece when he too refused to take medicine prescribed by a doctor, and instead preferred to chant the name of Lord Ram.

> At that time Bapu was suffering from a severe cough, cold and fever. The cough at times was so violent that a bystander could hardly bear to look on … The doctors therefore requested him to take a penicillin injection so that he may have some relief during that period. There was a tussle between the doctors and Bapu about this.
>
> He said: 'And what about my Ramayana? If Ramayana saturates my heart, I am sure my cough

will vanish tomorrow; and if it continues for your three weeks period, I am prepared to proclaim to the world that I was found wanting in the matter of Ramayana.'

A doctor argued, 'Maybe, but how can you dismiss summarily all these laborious researches in science? Bring me your most perfect devotee of Ramayana and I will infect him with cholera.'

Bapu said, 'That is only a presumptuous claim of science. Science has yet a long way to go to get at truth. But I am sure that one who chants the Lord's name with real faith can never fall ill.'[23]

A penicillin injection? It would have been difficult for a man with Gandhi's conscience to allow the doctors to administer it to him even three years after Kasturba's death, given that it was the very same injection that he had forbidden the doctors to administer to her. And his was only a case of chronic cough, while she had been on her deathbed. So he did display some sincerity here.

That the Mahatma was not being *completely* honest is clear from the fact that when he caught malaria a mere six weeks after Kasturba's death and the *only* cure available was through modern medicine, he took huge doses of quinine.[24] He did not give in immediately though, and started with a diet of fruit juice and fasting. When that did not work, he allowed himself to be persuaded by the doctors to try out the sovereign remedy against malaria.[25] Where was his moral integrity then? Where was the man who said that had he been in Kasturba's situation (medically speaking) he would not have taken penicillin himself?

Kasturba was not the only one who had to pay the price for Gandhi's views. We can never know if she would have survived had penicillin been administered, but certainly his son Manilal might not have contracted smallpox had he been duly vaccinated. Gandhi was dead set against all manner of vaccines, whether for smallpox or chickenpox, and thought dying would be preferable. As a result of his harsh views on modern medicine, it is likely that none of the children were vaccinated. Gandhi's granddaughter, who also became her father Manilal's biographer, wrote about it.

> We know next to nothing for example of his encounter with smallpox and how this was treated. Yet his face bore the marks of the disease and it also affected his eyesight. Gandhi the chronicler was absent when this disease took root and it does not feature in the autobiography.[26]

Both then and now, campaigns are run to carry out mass vaccinations in order to save the lives of hundreds of thousands of children across the globe. Innumerable charities and foundations are engaged in these activities, and many selfless people devote their lives to such work. The Mahatma's powerful voice resonated across the country, and when he spoke against modern medicine it could potentially have negatively impacted many such planned ventures.

Poor, sick and suffering India was crying out for many of the things that Gandhi—who claimed to be the voice of the poor—would, ironically enough, deny. Fischer, one of Gandhi's biographers, describes the India that he encountered in 1942.

> One did not have to be in India for more than a few days to realize how abysmally poor the people were. American and many European farmers would consider it bad for business to keep their livestock in

accommodation as unhealthy as the tenements I visited with Dr Ambedkar in Bombay; hundreds of thousands lived in them. *Gandhi was fully dressed compared to the nakedness of peasants one saw in villages.* The vast majority of Indians are always, literally always, hungry.

'The expectation of life,' says the 1931 British official census report on India is '26.56 for females and 26.91 for males'. The average person born in India could look forward to only twenty-seven years of life.

According to British figures, one hundred and twenty-five million Indians contracted malaria annually and only a few could afford a grain of quinine. Half a million Indians died of tuberculosis each year.[27] [emphasis mine]

Had Gandhi not been assassinated, he would certainly have encountered other illnesses that would not have been caused by 'indulgences'. Personally speaking, I have little doubt he would once again have allowed himself to 'be persuaded' to try out life-saving Western treatment if it were needed.

When he spoke proudly of being willing to be killed by a Bhil's arrow, he was deceiving himself. Gandhi prized his life, even if he did take risks with it in a great cause.

The Mahatma's virulent hatred for the medical profession is such that he argues that the quacks (which is to say doctors without a degree who merely pretend to have knowledge of medicine) are actually better than qualified doctors. Why? Because they charge less. To quote Gandhi: 'The populace in its credulity, and in the hope of ridding itself of some disease, allows itself to be cheated. Are not quacks then, whom we know better than the doctors who put on an air of humaneness?'[28]

While walking about Atta Market close to where I live in Noida, a city not far from New Delhi, I came across a quack's board that spoke of how this unqualified person could cure *swapnadosh*, the 'sin of sleep' or night-time ejaculation while sleeping. In fact, such quackery in India preys upon the guilt of young persons who suffer involuntary seminal discharge at night.

No medical evidence confirms that loss of semen in this manner is in any way unhealthy; indeed, most doctors as well as psychologists would consider it to be healthy. It is nature's own way of getting rid of bodily and sexual tension.

But Gandhi believed otherwise. The Mahatma would not hold this to be quackery but rather words of wisdom. As his biographer writes, Gandhi 'had an almost magical belief in the power of semen: "One who conserves his vital fluid acquires unfailing power," he reportedly said.'[29] It has to be noted that the Mahatma was not expressing an original view—he based it on suggestions made in Ayurveda, the Indian indigenous system of medicine.

Ayurveda is an ancient and great medical system, now undergoing a great revival in India, and it continues to treat millions of patients. It has benefits over the Western allopathic system of medicine, being more reliant on natural herbs. But this is not the place to discuss those advantages. It is not perfect—no system is—and there are some ideas that need to be revised. The importance of conserving semen is one such idea. It is outmoded, with no scientific basis. On this issue, the West has a more scientific and rational attitude.

Chapter 6

GANDHI ON MACHINERY

Machinery is like a snake-hole which may contain from one to a hundred snakes.

—Mahatma Gandhi

It's clear from a reading of *Hind Swaraj* that Gandhi was opposed to the industrialisation of India. Not only did he look upon the railways as epitomising the evil inherent in Western civilisation, he was against machinery in itself.

How else can we interpret the following statement, issued by him in a chapter of *Hind Swaraj* simply titled 'Machinery'?[1] 'It may be considered a heresy,' he writes, 'but I am bound to say that *it were better for us to send money to Manchester and to use flimsy Manchester cloth than to multiply mills in India.*'[2]

In his view, if the entire world wished to get back to the Kingdom of Heaven, it would need to de-industrialise and return to primitive technology. Were it in his power, he would in one fell swoop get rid of trains, cars, aeroplanes, factories, and so forth.

'Machinery has begun to desolate Europe,' he wrote. 'Ruination is now knocking at the English gates. Machinery is the chief symbol of modern civilisation; *it represents a great sin.*'[3]

'*It represents a great sin.*'

No arguments are advanced in support of his views; we only have his conclusion announced.

While Gandhi opposed industrialisation, at the same time he did not hesitate to take money from Indian industrialists, including—paradoxically enough—mill owners. Even the place where he breathed his last was Birla House, a powerful industrialist's residence, which was later converted to Gandhi Smriti, a memorial in the Mahatma's name.[4]

Gandhi was alert to public perception. It would not do to only talk the talk; he needed to walk the talk. If he stayed at Birla House whenever he visited Delhi, people would—despite his dhoti—start talking. He therefore took care to alternate between Bhangi Colony and Birla House.[5] 'Bhangi' was the Indian word for the Dalits who are traditionally employed in the task of sweeping or scavenging, and the residents of the Bhangi Colony were all Dalits.

Yet it was a bit of a farce really, despite the potent symbolism. Poet Sarojini Naidu told Lord Louis Mountbatten about the great expenditure it took to keep Gandhi at the Bhangi Colony. 'My dear Lord Louis,' she said, 'you will never know how much it has cost the Congress Party to keep that old man in poverty.'[6] Ms Naidu went on to explain how twenty or thirty Congress members, all dressed as untouchables, immediately went and occupied the hovels next to Gandhi's.[7]

Ironically enough, Nehru—Gandhi's protégé, and the future PM of India—did not think industry was bad at all. Rather, he thought it was essential for progress.

Post-Independence, he went to work setting up big public sector industries, describing them as 'the temples of Modern India'.

However, Nehru and other Congress leaders understood that they could ignore Gandhi only at the peril of their own political fortunes. Through his dress code, the spiritual aspect of his persona, and various agitations and antics, he had captured the Indian imagination, towering over anyone else on the political firmament.

Did Gandhi seriously think that India would be better off without machines or industry? There is no doubt that he did.

When a questioner asked him how machine-made things are to be eventually given up, this is what he had to say: 'What a few may do, others will copy, and the movement will grow like the coconut of the mathematical problem. *What the leaders do, the populace will gladly do in turn.*'[8]

The questioner points out how there are 'innumerable' machine-made things. Gandhi is not at all disconcerted.

> My answer can be only one. What did India do before these articles were introduced? Precisely the same should be done today. As long as we cannot make pins without machinery, so long will we do without them. The tinsel splendour of glassware we will have nothing to do with, and we will make wicks, as of old, with home grown cotton and use handmade earthen saucers for lamps. So doing, we shall save our eyes and money and will support Swadeshi and so shall we attain Home Rule.[9]

Marx believed that once the 'forces of production' developed, with advanced machinery and new sources of energy, nothing could hold technology back.[10] Not so Gandhi. He was of the view that setting things into reverse gear would not be difficult: 'The matter is neither complicated nor difficult. You and I shall not wait until we can carry others with us.'[11]

If you did not do as Gandhi suggested—that is to say, give up on all the technological progress and go 'back to nature'— you would be either a 'loser' or a 'coward'. He wrote: *Those will be the losers who will not do it*; and those who will not do it, although they appreciate the truth, will deserve to be called cowards.'[12]

'Books,' Gandhi said, 'can be written to demonstrate its [machinery's] evils.'[13] But how those very books would be printed, he does not stop to ask! Through machinery, clearly.

How was *Hind Swaraj* itself printed? Through the machinery that the Mahatma despises.

Gandhi either does not see the contradiction implicit in his statement, or dismisses it as an unworthy argument: 'This is one of those instances which demonstrate that sometimes poison is used to kill poison ...'[14]

When the Mahatma writes *those will be the losers who will not do it*, the reader can detect some optimism. It looks as if Gandhi, at the time of writing *Hind Swaraj*, believed that the world was approaching a sea change in its affairs, when those habituated to the use of technology would be forced to see its evils.

Gandhi was waiting for something to happen—but, alas, nothing did. Western civilisation continued to prosper, newer technological innovations surfaced, more trains ran and more aeroplanes flew, and twenty-one years after Gandhi's death, man journeyed to the moon. It is true that even in his lifetime, Gandhi saw that the world was not changing according to his expectations. Did he change his views? Not at all. In 1945, four-and-a-half decades after *Hind Swaraj* was published, he wrote as follows in a letter to his beloved Nehru:

> It does not frighten me at all that the world seems to be going in the opposite direction. For that matter, when the moth approaches its doom, it whirls around faster and faster till it is burnt up. It is possible that India will not be able to escape this moth-like circling. It is my duty to try, till my last breath, to save India, and through it the world from such a fate.[15]

What about common items such as soap and toothpaste? Was Gandhi averse to using them if they had been manufactured in a factory?

As his niece Manu reported, 'He never used soap for his bath. He used instead a rough stone. This stone had been given to him years ago by Mirabehn.'[16]

One industrial product that Gandhi did use, and which was made in factories, was the watch. There is no record of him having provided an explanation for this or using an alternative such as a stick or a sundial.

If Gandhi is against all advanced technology, it stands to reason that he must also as a matter of course be against all scientific innovation. This is indeed the case. We find him observing, with great satisfaction, how in India 'we have managed with the same kind of plough as existed thousands of years ago'.[17]

There are others in India who hark back to the same golden past of ancient India, but for them, unlike for Gandhi, there is no satisfaction to be derived from arguing that there has been little scientific progress. These right-wing nationalists argue vehemently to the contrary that ancient India was scientifically extremely advanced.

At an Indian Science Congress, all kinds of tall claims were made. A paper presented on ancient Indian aviation technology made the claim that the first human flight took place in Chowpatty, eight years before the Wright brothers flew an aircraft.[18] At the 2019 Indian Science Congress, the vice chancellor of Andhra University claimed that the Kauravas were test tube babies and that our ancestors carried out stem cell research.[19]

What is the motivation behind such false claims? Is it an inferiority complex suffered by some Indians that their civilisation did not produce great advancement in science and technology as happened in the West? Gandhi inverts the entire process. For him, Indian achievement lies in the fact that they continued 'with the same kind of plough as existed thousands of years ago'.[20]

Surprisingly, Gandhi does not make a particular argument that one would expect him to make against machinery and science—that is to say, that modern warfare can be terribly brutal and is, after all, a scientific creation. Even when he is condoning the violence of the Bhil, he does not make the point that medieval violence was in some ways far less brutal than modern warfare. It is rather his contemporary, Tagore, who suggests in his writings that bombs thrown from an aircraft are *far more brutal* than chopping off someone's head on a medieval battleground.

★ ★ ★

In 1888, while on the way to England, we found Gandhi 'unusually attentive to the landscape'.[21] He took care to describe buildings, vegetation and roads. He was especially impressed by the quality of the road in Gibraltar.[22] He marvelled at the

Suez Canal and the 'genius of a man who invented it'.[23] Clearly, at this youthful stage of his life Gandhi was as conventional as they come.

Reading through Gandhi's autobiography, V.S. Naipaul was startled to find that the Mahatma had little, if anything, to say about the physical landscape and environment he found himself in during his stay in England.[24] Naipaul did not, however, stop to ask why this was the case. It was not that the Mahatma was unable to describe these things. Rather, by not describing them he was making a point, for clearly, by that later stage in his life, much water had flowed down the Thames. Mahadev Desai, Gandhi's private secretary, records that the first edition of Gandhi's autobiography was published in two volumes: the first came out in 1927 and the second in 1929.

Gandhi and his views on the world changed radically in the space of more than thirty years. He would no longer have thought of the Suez Canal as a grand achievement, or even praised the architecture of buildings that he found impressive in his youth or the 'bigger and more impressive' railway carriages in Italy.[25] With his new and transformed world view, there was no wish to laud, or even describe, modern technology such as cars, trains, planes and the like. The Mahatma would not have cared to describe these technological creations because for him they all embodied the 'spirit of evil'. His disdain now extended even to buildings constructed after the Industrial Revolution. He seems to have become impervious to their beauty. In the chapter in *Hind Swaraj* titled 'What Is True Civilisation' (Chapter XIII), he approves of the fact that in India 'we have retained the same kind of cottages that we had in former times'.[26] It almost seems as if, for the Mahatma, stagnation is progress.

What Karl Marx classified as the stagnation of Indian rural life, what V.S. Naipaul later referred to as the 'nullity' of Indian villages, Gandhi sees as something entirely glorious. It makes for an original viewpoint, perhaps, but to argue his point he merely uses the tired logic that God gave us two hands and two feet because he did not wish us to be able to cover vast distances within short time frames. Hence the train embodies the spirit of evil, as does the aeroplane. The penicillin injection too represents evil and he would rather risk his wife Kasturba's death than have it administered to her. One could tell Gandhi that by similar logic he shouldn't have been using enemas, for they too constitute the insertion of a foreign substance into a bodily crevice. If God had wished men to use enemas, would he not have created naturally available enemas hanging from trees that man could simply pluck and readily access? As a great user (and giver) of enemas, such logic would possibly have enraged Gandhi, and rightly so—but he would not have seen that it was precisely the same kind of logic that he himself was given to using. At what junction of logic has God ruled the use of the enema permissible and that of the injection prohibited? And was Gandhi too one of those messengers of God who heard His voice more clearly than the rest of us?

Gandhi imagines the lack of innovation and invention in India to be a deliberate and planned strategy by our wise and powerful Indian ancestors, who were in full control of what to change and what not to change. Is he sincere in imagining this, or is it a case of wounded pride and sour grapes, for Gandhi makes his claims with great authority—albeit just like the clever fox who could not jump high enough and claimed that the grapes were sour.

'It was not that we did not know how to invent machinery,' he writes, 'but our forefathers knew, that if we set our hearts after such things, we would become slaves, and lose our moral fibre.'[27]

So it is the English—and more broadly speaking the entire West—that are inferior, because they did not know how to put the brakes on the Industrial Revolution. India, the Mahatma claims, could easily have invented machinery! It's just that in its wisdom it *chose* not to do so.

* * *

Dressed in his hand-spun dhoti, the Mahatma looked not only saintly but also like the true representative and spokesperson of the poorest of the poor in the country. Anyone could be forgiven for simply assuming that he was the one man in the country who truly understood and identified with the poor and wished to alleviate their suffering at any cost.

Machinery potentially represented a great step forward in agriculture, which would make it possible to vastly increase food production. Surely, for the sake of bringing food to the tables of millions of impoverished and starving Indians, the Mahatma would concede that machinery could serve a useful purpose.

By no means. Even if machinery could increase food production and reduce the need for human labour, thus benefitting so many people, and alleviating hunger and preventing starvation, the Mahatma would have none of it. Modern ploughs drawn by tractors are now commonplace in India as elsewhere, but the Mahatma strongly resisted this idea, and instead praised the traditional plough and lack of modernisation. This is what he said at the Kathiawad Political Conference held on 8 January 1925: 'He who eats his food without sacrifice steals it. *By giving up this sacrifice, we become traitors to the country and bang the door in the face of the Goddess of Fortune.*'

* * *

It would have been difficult for Gandhi to directly condemn science (although he recommends that the sciences not be studied), for while the study of history might inflame the passions of those who start to believe that their ancestors were grievously wronged by another community, science is essentially neutral. And yet when he condemns machinery and trains, he implicitly condemns both the entrepreneur and the scientist whose studies made the creation of consumer goods or industrial products possible.

Gandhi finds it difficult to condemn science outright for another reason. His autobiography, *The Story of My Experiments with Truth*, has large sections within it devoted to practical matters, such as eating, the consumption of milk, vegetarianism, defecation, and so forth. He even studies at length the best way to dispose of human excreta.

If the Mahatma was himself conducting such semi-scientific experiments and labelling these as an experiment or search for truth, on what basis could he dismiss those who study the workings of nature as people who have embarked on an evil mission for the Great Satan? He, in fact, sidesteps the issue, avoids making an accusation against science and scientists, and focuses instead on certain end products, namely railways and all manners of machinery.

The other interesting thing is that while the Mahatma attacks factories, he does not directly criticise the Indian businessmen who own them, or others who plan to expand Indian industry, even if he does suggest that they should all abandon profit making and take up the handloom.[28] As early as 1904, before Gandhi wrote *Hind Swaraj*, the representatives of Tata Iron and Steel Company were having meetings in London with John Miller, the managing director of the Bengal–Nagpur Railway Company.[29]

How *could* he have criticised Indian industrialists, when the Congress party was so dependent on them for its funding—and its continued existence? In an interview with his biographer Louis Fischer, the question of party funding was discussed. Gandhi explained how in the beginning he had imagined that if there was a contribution of four annas from each Congress member, it would be conceivable for the party to carry on its activities. He soon realised that this simply wasn't feasible.

There were allegations at the time that Congress was funded by big business and that Gandhi himself was being funded by Bombay mill owners. What truth was there, Fischer asked him, in such assertions?

'Unfortunately, they are true,' Gandhi affirmed. 'Congress hasn't enough money to conduct its work.'

Fischer pressed on. 'What proportion of the Congress budget,' he asked, 'is covered by rich Indians?'

'Practically all of it,' admitted the Mahatma.[30]

The Congress and Gandhi both *had* to depend on contributions from Indian industry. Ghanshyam Das Birla, the textile magnate, was one of their prominent contributors, and Gandhi often stayed at his house when in Delhi. If Birla were to follow Gandhi's advice, he would have to shut down his mills, and if he did so, he would no longer make a profit, and therefore he would be unable to contribute funds to the Congress party.

In 1942, it was starting to become apparent that India would be independent soon. Yet Gandhi refused to concede that post-Independence India will go in for rapid industrialisation when Fischer pressed him on the question. It is highly probable that India will not oppose the advancement of technology, even if it entails (as Gandhi believed) participating in the Devil's work.

'You want to force me into an admission,' he said, 'that we would need rapid industrialisation. I will not be forced into such an admission.'[31]

By sticking to his guns, Gandhi renders himself irrelevant.

Chapter 7

GANDHI ON EDUCATION

To give millions a knowledge of English is to enslave them.
—Mahatma Gandhi

If Gandhi is against industrialisation, machinery and railways, could we really expect him to support the study of the physical sciences, such as the laws of chemistry, physics, and so forth? Should students be reading up on matters such as how a steam engine works, or even for that matter a simpler contraption, the fan—under which Gandhi spent many nights in the hot and humid countryside with his female bed companions?

What were Gandhi's views on electricity, since so many gadgets need electricity in order to run? Did the Mahatma wish to do away with electricity itself?

In an early chapter in his manifesto, Gandhi confirms that it would not be a bad thing to do away with electricity altogether and return to the age of candles with wicks.

Could we expect such a person to support the idea of young girls and boys studying subjects such as physics, chemistry and biology? Probably not. And as we start to read the chapter in the manifesto on education, we see that the Mahatma stays true to form.

'A peasant earns his bread honestly,' Gandhi wrote.[1]

And do scientists not do so? Are all the physicists, chemists and inventers in the service of the Devil?

'He [the peasant] has ordinary knowledge of the world. He knows fairly well how he should behave towards his parents, his wife, his children and his fellow-villagers.'[2] Is this really true? Isn't Gandhi painting a romanticised, idealised image of the peasant? Isn't there a great deal of patriarchy in Indian villages, with wife-beating not being uncommon? As for children, they too receive corporal punishment rather too frequently.[3] And as for behaviour towards 'fellow-villagers' ... unfortunately, all too often the upper-caste peasant knows very well how to treat and oppress those below him in the caste pecking order, not to mention the outcastes—the Dalits.

Gandhi carries on in this fashion, eulogising his mythical peasant: 'He understands and observes the rules of morality. But he cannot write his own name.'[4]

Then almost as if anticipating the Bhutanese king's recommendation, a century later with regard to Gross Domestic Happiness replacing gross domestic product, Gandhi suggests a 'test of contentedness' to silence all who disagree with him. 'What do you propose to do by giving him a knowledge of letters? Will you add an inch to his happiness? Do you wish to make him discontented with his cottage or his lot? And even if you do, he will not need such an education.'[5]

The argument that Gandhi advances is really no different from those advanced by ultra-conservative fathers in Indian villages who do not support the idea that their daughters should receive an education. If the daughter has to grow up to eventually become a housewife, as this argument runs, what use will it be for her to receive an education? Will it not only serve to make her more discontented? Gandhi also makes a bland, unsubstantiated assertion on how happy the peasant is, and produces no empirical evidence to support the view that the peasant is less discontented than an educated man. Also, it must be said that Gandhi at once gets into an analysis of the costs and benefits of education, not considering for a moment that education might be worthwhile in itself: 'Now, let us take higher education. I have learned Geography, Astronomy, Algebra, Geometry, etc. What of that? In what way have I benefited myself or those around me? Why have I learned these things?'[6]

Would the Mahatma have supported Malala Yousafzai's desire to study? It was during a chemistry class that she learned that she had been awarded the Nobel Peace Prize.

Would he ban the study of sciences altogether, for sciences further industrialisation, which promotes evil and takes us away from the Kingdom of God?

And what would have been Gandhi's take on Taliban's point of view? They are, after all, against the education of girls, and favour a religious type of education.

The Mahatma is full of contradictions. He took it upon himself to teach various subjects to his niece Manu. As part of his general inconsistency, he even taught her the sciences, algebra, geometry and mathematics. His views against the teaching of these subjects appear to have mellowed somewhat.

In her memoir, Manu wrote: 'In the Aga Khan Palace I had the good fortune to learn from him various subjects such as Arithmetic, Algebra, Geometry, Geography, History, Science and Sanskrit; but English he never taught me.'[7]

While writing *Hind Swaraj*, Gandhi does not stop to consider that many centuries prior to the arrival of the British, there was the study of science and mathematics, including astronomy, in India too, with famous astronomers such as Aryabhata. Renowned mathematicians in the world today study Vedic mathematics, which was studied and taught in ancient India.

The ascetic in Gandhi goes on to say that we should test so-called education on the anvil of spiritual values. Not such an unreasonable position, one could argue. But then, what *are* those spiritual values according to Gandhi? He speaks of the spiritual value in suppressing the senses, just as he argues in *Hind Swaraj* that God gave humans hands and feet because He did not want them to travel fast using trains and other means of transport. But he does not stop to consider that—assuming we momentarily accept the logic of that argument, even though it is flawed—if God wanted human beings to suppress their senses and passions, He would not have given these things in the first place!

'I must emphatically say,' he wrote, 'that the sciences I have enumerated above, I have never been able to use for controlling my senses.'[8] He probably uses 'senses' here to include 'passion'.

And then in the very next sentence, the hidden patriarch in Gandhi emerges in full force. Education, he wrote, 'does not make men of us. It does not enable us to do our duty.'[9]

With one stroke of his pen, he relegates the cause or worth of education, be it for men or for women. The wording he uses here is also troublesome. Education, he claims, does not make 'men' of us. What about the education of girls—should they not receive education too? Would there be any problem if it did not make 'men' of them?

★ ★ ★

Almost half of the chapter on education in *Hind Swaraj* is devoted to the question of languages, and we come across Gandhi's fierce criticism of Indians learning the English language. After all, if factories, industry, railways and aeroplanes are all devilish creations that were never meant to be, what facilitates their creation and improvement is the study of the sciences; and the study of the sciences is taking place in an evil tongue, the language of the conqueror—English.

The Mahatma does not consider for a moment that India, with its numerous languages and hundreds or even thousands of dialects, needs a common language in which different Indian communities can communicate and converse with one another. He himself wrote *Hind Swaraj* in Gujarati first, but then had it translated into English (before it was translated into all the various other Indian languages) for it to find a wider pan-Indian and global readership.

If Gandhi had been around today and had stuck to his 1909 views, he would without a doubt have hated modern India for its linguistic progress in English, which has in turn enabled it to become one of the leading service providers in the world.

But Gandhi wrote: 'To give millions knowledge of English is to enslave them.'[10] He added, 'It is worth noting that by receiving English education, we have enslaved the nation. Hypocrisy, tyranny, etc., have increased. *English knowing Indians have not hesitated to cheat and strike terror into the people.*'[11]

It is almost saying as if it is not the English who subjugated India, but the Indians who enslaved themselves—by the seemingly innocuous activity of learning the English language; as if on one hand, they enslaved themselves, and on the other, they became English-speaking terrorists.

The Mahatma then goes on to prescribe the fairly narrow circumstances in which the use of the English language might be permitted in his view of the matter. It might be permitted, he wrote, in 'our dealings with the English people, in our dealings with our own people, when we can only correspond with them through that language'—so he does acknowledge its utility as a 'link language' but considers it of limited usefulness. Here's the clincher: '*and for the purpose of knowing how disgusted they [the English] have themselves become with their civilisation, we may use or learn English, as the case may be*'.[12]

Is there space in Gandhi's moral universe for Indian children to start learning English? As far as young children are concerned, not at all. Perhaps, it might be true for the older lot. 'Those who have studied English will have to teach morality to their progeny through their mother tongue, and to teach them another Indian language; *but when they have grown up, they may learn English*, the ultimate aim being that we should not need it.'[13]

There is great irony in Gandhi's condemnation of English, at many levels. When Gandhi left India, he was a vegetarian but could not defend this practice before a friend during his early days in England. It was by reading books written in English, which defended vegetarianism, that he was able to take a stance in favour of his position and even try to convince others to give up meat eating. Had it not been for those readings in English, it is doubtful, as he himself concedes in his autobiography, that he would have been able to defend his eating practices.

There is also the great contradiction that emerges from his own practices in life and what he insists others should do. In his autobiography, he wrote about how he believes English could be a useful language to learn in Pretoria, and he even taught the language there—so, in other words, useful in Pretoria, but best avoided in India.

I saw that very few amongst my audience knew English. As I felt that knowledge of English would be useful in that country, I advised those who had leisure to learn English. I told them that it was possible to learn a language even at an advanced age, and cited cases of people who had done so. I undertook, besides, to teach a class, if one was started, or personally to instruct individuals desiring to learn the language.[14]

Gandhi emphasises the importance of religious education above all other subjects, but he forgets that while he remained in India he was ignorant of the teachings in the Gita, the book he swore by for the rest of his life. It was the books he read in English on the Gita and Hinduism that gave him an understanding of his own religion. In the chapter of his autobiography titled 'Acquaintance with World Religions', he wrote:

> Towards the end of my second year in England, I came across two Theosophists, brothers and both unmarried. They talked to me about the Gita. They were reading Sir Edwin Arnold's translation – *The Song Celestial* – and they invited me to read the original with them. I felt ashamed, as I had read the divine poem neither in Sanskrit nor in Gujarati ...[15]

A little later he continued:

> *The book struck me as being one of priceless worth.* The impression has ever since been growing on me with the result that I regard it today as the book par excellence for the knowledge of Truth. *It has afforded me invaluable help in my moments of gloom. I have read all the English translations of it, and I regard Sir Edwin Arnold's as the best.*[16]

The book struck me as being one of priceless worth.

The Mahatma is talking about the English translation here, not the original Gita (which is of course also priceless).

'It has afforded me invaluable help in my moments of gloom.'

He is again talking about the English translation, not a Gujarati translation of the Gita.

'I have read all the English translations of it, and I regard Sir Edwin Arnold's as the best.'

Gandhi has read *all* the English translations of the Gita, and yet ... he would rather that Indians did not read English. Sir Edwin Arnold's translation provided for the Mahatma 'invaluable help' in his moments of gloom, but he would rather that Indians abjure the learning of the English language. If this is not hypocrisy, double standards and rank paternalism, what is?

★ ★ ★

Gandhi cannot recommend the learning of scientific subjects, since they directly foster the growth of technology and industry. Indeed, in Chapter XVIII, he wrote disparagingly: 'We should abandon the pretension of learning many sciences.'[17]

If we rule out the sciences, history and mathematics, what is left are the arts, languages and religious studies. Now, it must be said that Gandhi was a man with a limited aesthetic sense. He saw beauty in nature, but not in art or architecture. He was utilitarian, in a narrow sense of the term. He could not see how those who had studied the sciences could benefit the common man. And as for the arts, his extreme utilitarian perspective (not 'education for education's sake') made him conclude that little was to be gained from a study of those subjects. For this reason, there is practically no discussion in *Hind Swaraj* on the importance of studying literature, drama, painting, sculpture, and so forth. So what are Gandhi's views on the study of languages—and of religion?

He starts off by asserting somewhat vaguely: 'I think we have to improve all our languages.'[18] But can languages be improved by us? Or do they grow and thrive organically over the centuries?

In the next line, he reveals his confusion over what languages can be used to teach, if we are not to be learning only the languages themselves. He has already stated that we should not waste time learning the sciences and history: 'What subjects we should learn through them need not be elaborated here.'[19]

In *Hind Swaraj*, Gandhi suggests that all Indians should learn Hindi, but in later years he was to change his ideas, and shift his insistence from Hindi to Hindustani. At that stage, he was unfairly accused by right-wing Hindu nationalists of having given in to Muslim pressure.[20] As a matter of fact, more people understood Hindustani than Hindi, and therefore the decision was a fair and logical one.

* * *

In *Hind Swaraj*, Gandhi is clearly opposed to Western education. Although he is utilitarian in a sense, since he does not value education for its own sake, his utilitarianism is cast in an ethical mould, so let's call it an ethical utilitarianism. In other words, he will agree to recommend a subject for study, once he is convinced that learning it will work to the overall benefit of society. The learning of the physical sciences will not prove advantageous to the health or well-being of society as he sees it; rather, it will indirectly advance technology and 'machinery'. At the same time, the learning of the arts too does not benefit the common man. The Mahatma is not an aesthete like his great contemporary, India's first Nobel laureate, Rabindranath Tagore.

In *Hind Swaraj*, Gandhi also argues against the teaching of history. He much prefers to have stories from religion with a moral content. It is unlikely that Gandhi would recommend literature for reading, since so much of Western literature at the time was already replete with references to the modern age. He might have recommended reading Charles Dickens's *Hard Times*, because it speaks of the evils of factories. On the whole, therefore, he might have decided that Western literature was best ignored. On the other hand, most novelists, playwrights and short-story writers, whether from the West or the East, consider that a morality tale lowers the art form, and is something best avoided. Oscar Wilde famously said: 'There is no such thing as a moral or an immoral book. Books are well written or badly written. That is all.' The Mahatma would have had difficulty comprehending such an objection. Morality tales, in his view, were the best of all, especially if they were sourced from religion.

With the physical sciences, mathematics, history, geography and a great deal of literature ruled out, much has been culled from the teaching syllabus that the Mahatma would design.

In almost Talibani style (though content is another matter), he makes the following pronouncement on what is the most important subject to be taught. No surprises here.

'Religious, that is ethical, education will occupy the first place,' he said.[21] Religion is of such importance, so his argument seems to run here, that the language in which the original texts of a religion were written down must also be mastered by students. And so, he wrote, 'every cultured Indian will know in addition to his own provincial language, if a Hindu, Sanskrit; if a Mohammedan, Arabic; if a Parsee, Persian and all Hindi'. Lest he be accused of creating watertight compartments, he hastens to add that '[s]ome Hindus should know Arabic and Persian; some Mohammedans and Parsees, Sanskrit'.[22]

In later years, when Gandhi spent time teaching his niece Manu, he focused on religious instruction. He asked her to read the Gita and taught her his own interpretations of that sacred Hindu text. He also taught her Sanskrit.

The dictator within him kept asserting itself, however. One cannot help but conclude that he called Manu away from Karachi for his own selfish needs, even though he lectured her on the importance of selflessness.

Manu wrote about what the Mahatma told her: 'He is a thief who spends even a moment without sacrifice. We all must perform this incessant sacrifice …'[23]

As regards the Mahatma's selfishness in seeking Manu to be with him, he probably thought it was his right as an elder to make this demand upon her, and did not change his mind even when he came to know of her feelings. She wrote:

> Although Bapu thus looked after my studies, I complained to him at times that he had made me give up my education, since he called me away from Karachi, where I was going to school. I wanted to pass examinations, and had a fascination for degrees like girls of today. I am grateful to God, however, for His having saved me from that delusion.[24]

Although in the end it appears that the Mahatma convinced Manu that there was no need for her to have a degree, the mind of a young girl was pitted against a mature and accomplished mind. What chance did she have?

Gandhi had gone overseas at great personal cost to his family. Despite the long connection that the Gandhis had with the kingdom of Porbandar, the British official, Sir Frederic Lely, who administered the territory (while the ruler lived in Bombay), flatly refused to help.[25] Gandhi's elder brother helped raise the money.[26] The family jewellery was pawned to make up the shortfall.[27] Gandhi made no objections to the sacrifices of his family: he was raring to go. So, was he in any moral position to exhort others to abandon formal studies against their will?

It wasn't even the case that Gandhi was a particularly deserving student. In the preparatory exam for Grade VII, the highest grade in the school young Gandhi was admitted to in 1886, he scored an average of 31.8 per cent in five subjects.[28] Not an outstanding performance by any measure! In the matriculation, Gandhi's performance was a modest 40 per cent. He was midway in terms of ranking: out of 824 students who had qualified, he was ranked 404 in the province.[29] Could it be that his own poor performance in so many subjects led him later to criticise formal education so severely? Whatever the case, it was on account of his family's sacrifices that he was able to go overseas. His performance did not *deserve* a scholarship; one cannot blame Sir Frederic for refusing to help him.

Was it fair of Gandhi to ignore Manu's wishes, *even if he thought they were misplaced*? Could he not understand that she would have liked the company of children her age, and to have a chance to make friends and compete with them in examinations? Did she not have the right to pursue a career of her choice—and what careers would have been possible for her without educational qualifications? Even if one were to concede for a moment that the Mahatma was right, did she not have the right to make her own mistakes? After all, Gandhi himself dismissed the advice of his father's friend, a Sheth from the merchant community, who dissuaded him from travelling overseas when he decided to become a barrister.[30]

Gandhi believed that learning various Indian languages would help in communication and promote unity. 'Several Northerners and Westerners [he means the Indians to the west of the country here, and not the foreigners] *should learn Tamil*,' he wrote. But English should be avoided in this context, and resorted to only when absolutely necessary. We are to assume, naturally, that the publication of *Hind Swaraj* in English was one such 'absolutely necessary' occasion.

Why Tamil? India has so many languages (there were fourteen scheduled languages listed when the Constitution was first promulgated; in 2024 there are twenty-two), so why did the Mahatma single out Tamil and not Manipuri or Bengali? The choice appears to be ad hoc, and the answer lies in the Mahatma's own life history. It's unfair to try to impose one's own dietary preferences on others, one's own use of the enema on the rest of the ashram, and one's own wish to learn another language on the rest of the country—but this is exactly what Gandhi does in *Hind Swaraj*. This is not the first time that he tries to impose his own leanings and preferences in this way. He wrote in his autobiography about his experiences on a ship while returning to India from South Africa in 1896: 'The ship's doctor gave me a *Tamil Self-Teacher* which I began to study. My experience in Natal had shown me that I should acquire a knowledge of Urdu to get into closer contact with the Musalmans, and of Tamil to get into closer touch with the Madras Indians ...'[31]

A little further on, he ruminates: 'I still feel what a handicap this ignorance of Tamil or Telugu has been. The affection that the Dravidians in South Africa showered on me remains a cherished memory.'[32]

The teaching of religion is given huge importance. However, he soon moves into extremely troubled waters.

Gandhi tried to synthesise the core of all world religions by taking a bit from here and a bit from there. His intentions cannot be faulted, but although he tried to combine something from Islam, something from the Gita and something from the Bible in his own speeches and sermons, at the same time he knew that he could not tell the mullahs how to teach Islam or for that matter Christian priests how to teach Christianity. The priests and mullahs would revolt and turn against him. Who is Gandhi to speak on Islam or Christianity, the non-Hindu religious leaders would legitimately ask, especially since he pronounces himself a Hindu?

And so while he states, in the chapter on education in *Hind Swaraj*, that religion is the most important subject to study, we find him for the first time conceding in the context of religious instruction that 'the task is indeed difficult'.[33]

> My head begins to turn as I think of religious education. Our religious teachers are hypocritical and selfish; they will have to be approached. The Mullahs, the Dasturs and the Brahmins hold the key in their hands, but if they will not have the good sense, the energy that we have derived from English education will have to be devoted to religious education.[34]

'*... the energy that we have derived from English education will have to be devoted to religious education.*'

Is this a Freudian slip of the tongue, or something lost in translation? Given the previous content, it would have appeared more natural if Gandhi had said that the energy *expended* thus far on Western education will have to be devoted to religious education. He appears to have inadvertently conceded that Indians have derived energy from Western education. So is it really so terrible after all?

Chapter 8

GANDHI ON AHIMSA

An eye for an eye only ends up making the whole world blind.
— Mahatma Gandhi

Hind Swaraj doesn't have a chapter specifically on 'ahimsa', which one might have expected, but there are two chapters that focus on the issue: one titled 'Brute Force' (Chapter XVI) and the other titled 'Passive Resistance' (Chapter XVII). Gandhi also touches briefly on the subject in a chapter titled 'Italy and India' (Chapter XV).

It may be that he chose to write a chapter on passive resistance because the term is much better known to a foreign readership than is ahimsa or satyagraha—the latter an expression that most Indians are familiar with today but was coined by Gandhi in 1907,[1] two years before the publication of *Hind Swaraj*.

In later years, Gandhi distinguished between the two terms. In a letter sent in 1920, he wrote:

I have drawn the distinction between passive resistance as understood and practised in the West and satyagraha before I had evolved the doctrine of the latter to its full logical and spiritual extent. I often used 'passive resistance' and 'satyagraha' as synonymous terms: but as the doctrine of satyagraha developed, the expression 'passive resistance' ceases even to be synonymous, as passive resistance has admitted of violence as in the case of the suffragettes and has been universally acknowledged to be a weapon of the weak. Moreover passive resistance does not necessarily involve complete adherence to truth under every circumstance. Therefore it is different from satyagraha in three essentials: Satyagraha is a weapon of the strong; it admits of no violence under any circumstance whatsoever; and it ever insists upon truth.[2]

These two chapters are the most rational and powerful within *Hind Swaraj*, and it is possibly for this reason that Leo Tolstoy, in a short letter to Gandhi, confined his remarks to the importance of 'passive resistance'.

On 4 April 1910, Gandhi had sent a copy of *Hind Swaraj* to the great Russian writer, seeking his approval. 'As your very devoted adherent,' he wrote, 'I send you together with this letter, a little book I have compiled in which I have translated my own writings from Gujarati.' Clearly, he was looking for an endorsement from Tolstoy, not so very differently from how today first-time novelists seek endorsements from established and bestselling authors. Tolstoy replied to Gandhi the following month. In his letter dated 8 May 1910, he wrote: 'I have read the book with great interest, for I consider the question there dealt with—Passive Resistance—to be of very great importance.'[3] In effect, he ignored the rest of the book, although in his letter he promised to write again. Gandhi waited a full three months, and then in his usual persistent but polite manner raised the issue once more. On 15 August 1910, he wrote:

> Count Tolstoy – I am much obliged to you for your encouraging and cordial letter of the 6th of May. I very much value your *general approval* of my booklet, Indian Home Rule. And if you have the time, I shall look forward to your detailed criticism of the work, which you have been so good as to promise in your letter.

That letter and the broader endorsement that Gandhi was hoping for never came. And yet Gandhi presumed upon Tolstoy's approval when he wrote 'I very much value your general approval of my booklet'. Tolstoy did very much appreciate the work Gandhi was carrying on. The Russian writer had his own rather outlandish views on several things, but he wasn't about to go ahead and endorse someone else's outlandish ideas of the evils of trains, doctors and lawyers.

In the chapter titled 'Brute Force' in *Hind Swaraj*, the questioner poses an interesting question, which Gandhi responds to with extreme lucidity and deep conviction.

The questioner asks: 'Shall I think of the means when I have to deal with a thief in the house? My duty is to drive him out anyhow.'[4]

Gandhi's response is both complex and eloquent:

> I do not agree with you that the thief may be driven out by any means. If it is my father who has come to steal, I shall use one kind of means. If it is an acquaintance, I shall use another and in the case of a perfect stranger I shall use a third. If it is a white man, you will perhaps say you will use means different from those you will adopt with an Indian thief. If it is a weakling, the means

will be different from those to be adopted for dealing with an equal in physical strength; and if the thief is armed from top to toe, I shall simply remain quiet.[5]

This is Gandhi at his practical and strategic best, although with his plan to 'simply remain quiet' in the presence of an armed thief, some people might accuse him of cowardice.

'I fancy,' he further wrote, 'that I should pretend to be sleeping whether the thief was my father or that strong armed man.'[6]

At this point, a reader of the manifesto might imagine that Gandhi would pretend to be sleeping in the instance of his father, owing to the traditional Indian reverence for the elderly. How distressing it would be to find one's own father a thief! This is not at all what the Mahatma means to say, however.

'The reason for this,' he wrote, with unintentional humour, 'is that my father would also be armed.'[7]

What, then, is the difference between the two scenarios? Why not just say 'armed man' and be done with it? Is there a difference?

Evidently there is, for Gandhi points to how differently he would react.

'The strength of my father,' he wrote, 'would make me weep with pity,' whereas 'the strength of the armed man would rouse in me anger.'[8]

Gandhi reiterates that the means will be different for each situation. 'You will also have seen,' he wrote, 'that any means will not avail to drive away the thief. You will have to adopt means to fit each case.'[9]

He then dwells on the situation where the thief is a strong, armed man, and presents two conflicting scenarios: one that his view leads to an escalation in conflict, and another that aim to transform the moral being of the thief. This is what Gandhi has elsewhere referred to as *hridaya parivartan*, the conversion or transformation of someone's heart through moral force.

It is worth reproducing at some length here Gandhi's writing on how different approaches will lead to different consequences, for this lies at the heart of his theory of non-violence. He makes his points with truth and eloquence.

Let us proceed a little further. The well-armed man has stolen your property; you have harboured the thought of his act, you are filled with anger; you argue that you want to punish that rogue, not for your own sake, but for the good of your neighbours; you have collected a number of armed men, you want to take his house by assault, he is duly informed of it, he runs away, he too is incensed. He collects his brother robbers and sends you a defiant message that he will commit robbery in broad daylight. You are strong, you do not fear him, you are prepared to receive him. Meanwhile the robber pesters your neighbours. They complain before you. You reply that you are doing all for their sake, you do not mind that your own goods have been stolen. Your neighbours reply that the robber never pestered them before, and that he commenced his depredations only after you declared hostilities against him. You are between Scylla and Charybdis. You are full of pity for the poor man. What they say is true. What are you to do? You will be disgraced if you now leave the robber alone. You therefore tell the poor men: 'Never mind. Come, my wealth is yours. I will give you arms. I will teach you how to use them; you should belabour the rogue; don't leave him alone.' And so the battle grows; the robbers increase in numbers; your neighbours have deliberately put themselves to inconvenience. *Thus the result of wanting to take revenge upon the robber is that you have disturbed your own peace, you are in perpetual fear of being robbed and assaulted, your courage has given place to cowardice. If you will patiently examine the argument, you will see that I have not overdrawn the picture.* This is one of the means. Now, let us examine the other. You set this armed robber down as an ignorant brother; you intend to reason with him at a suitable opportunity; you argue that he is, after all, a fellow-man; you do not know what prompted him to steal. You, therefore, decide that, when you can, you will destroy the man's motive for stealing. Whilst you are thus reasoning with yourself, the man comes again to steal. Instead of being angry with him, you take pity on him. You think that this stealing habit must be a disease with him. Henceforth, you therefore keep your doors and windows open, you change your sleeping place, and you keep your things in a manner most accessible to him. The robber comes again and is confused as all this is new to him, nevertheless he takes away your things. But his mind is agitated. He enquires about you in the village, he comes to learn about your broad and loving heart, he repents, he begs your pardon, returns you your things, and leaves off the stealing habit. He becomes your servant, and you find for him honourable employment. This is the second method. Thus, you see, different means have brought about totally different results.[10]

It is easy enough to critique and dismiss the simple example the Mahatma has given here, but he is on far surer footing than in the rest of *Hind Swaraj*.

It could be argued, for instance, that the robber, sensing weakness on the part of the victim of the robbery, might out of meanness commit yet another robbery soon enough. *Hridaya parivartan,* which means bringing about a change of heart in others through one's own good behaviour, is not for everyone.

And what would Gandhi do if the robber decided to assault his wife or daughter? Why has Gandhi not chosen to give that example? What use would hridaya parivartan be of in those instances?

Could Gandhi have converted the heart of Winston Churchill, who famously asked: 'Why isn't Gandhi dead yet?'[11]

(It could be said in a lighter vein that the two were like a Tom and Jerry duo, with Gandhi being Jerry, the mouse who would tease the big cat and run away. Tom never thought Jerry was up to any good whatsoever. In 1920, Churchill astonished guests at a dinner by suggesting that he would 'have Gandhi bound hand and foot at the gates of Delhi, and let the Viceroy sit on the back of a giant elephant and trample the Mahatma into the dirt'.)

Despite such failings, Gandhi is saying something important here. He himself acknowledges that his 'policy' of heart conversion will not work in all instances.

> I do not wish to deduce from this that robbers will act in the above manner or that all will have the same pity and love like you. But I only wish to show that fair means alone can produce fair results, and that, at least in the majority of cases, if not indeed in all, the force of love and

pity is infinitely greater than the force of arms. There is harm in the exercise of brute force, never in that of pity.[12]

He goes on to develop his theme of converting the heart of the enemy in the context of appealing to the colonial power in India through petitions.

> A petition of an equal is a sign of courtesy, a petition from a slave is a symbol of his slavery. A petition backed by force is a petition from an equal and, when he transmits his demand in the form of a petition, it testifies to his nobility. Two kinds of force can back petitions. 'We shall hurt you if you do not give this' is one kind of force; it is the force of arms, whose evil results we have already examined. The second kind of force can thus be stated: 'If you do not concede our demand, we shall be no longer your petitioners. You can govern us only so long as we remain the governed; we shall no longer have any dealings with you.' The force implied in this may be described as love force, soul force, or more popularly, but less accurately, passive resistance. This force is indestructible. He who uses it perfectly understands his position. We have an ancient proverb which literally means, 'One negative cures thirty-six diseases.' The force of arms is powerless when matched against the force of love or the soul.[13]

Gandhi's example is brilliant, showing the power of mediation, negotiation and how overlooking faults in the 'other' can be crucial to continued peaceful coexistence. When first reading *Hind Swaraj*—a book that angered me very much—I could sense wisdom shining through, and the clear perception of a great truth.

Gandhi adopted 'passive resistance', a great tactic within the Indian historical context. Indeed, it can be persuasively argued that the transition from being a subject people to being independent citizens was achieved with reduced loss of life than would have been the case had another approach been adopted.

In the chapter of *Hind Swaraj* titled 'Passive Resistance' the questioner asks 'if there is any historical evidence as to the success of what you have called soul-force or truth-force? No instance seems to have happened of any nation having risen through *rakshasha*. I still think that the evil-doers will not cease doing evil without physical punishment.'[14]

Gandhi is not at all enamoured with the study of history. He prefers myths and legends, so his response is true to form.

'It is, therefore, necessary,' he writes, 'to know what history means. The Gujarati equivalent means: "It so happened!" If that is the meaning of history, it is possible to give copious evidence.'[15]

Although he doesn't say so, it can be fairly assumed that the Mahatma thinks it would be an excellent idea to extract morality tales from Hindu scriptures and possibly other religions to show the victory of good over evil, and of transforming 'hearts' through the force of love. Consider, for instance, the story of how the evil ogre or *rakhsasa*, Angulimal, underwent hridaya parivartan following his encounter with the Buddha.

'But if it [history] means,' the Mahatma goes on to add, 'the doings of the kings and the emperors, there can be no evidence of soul-force or passive resistance in such history.'[16]

A little further on in the chapter, Gandhi reminisces: 'I remember an incident when, in a small principality, the villagers were offended by some command issued by the prince. The former immediately began vacating the village. The prince became nervous, apologized to his subjects, and withdrew his command. Many such instances can be found in India.'[17]

'... *the villagers were offended by some command issued by the prince.*'

An interesting tale, but too politely worded in traditional Gandhian-speak. The villagers were 'offended'—it is not that they felt persecuted, not that some terrible new tax had been imposed upon them, not that something had happened that they could not bear. It was 'some command' and they were 'offended'. Gandhi writes as if it were a tea party, and the guests were offended and walked out.

'... *the former immediately began vacating the village.*'

No context is provided. Who were these villagers, how much land did they own, were they not primarily a farming community, and if they did start vacating their village—presumably leaving their lands and houses behind—where did they go, where did they plan to live henceforth, and how did they plan to earn their livelihood? No such detail is given. The story, legend, or myth is an uninteresting tale, having not been embellished with proper facts. The Mahatma imposes upon the reader here by asking him to suspend not only his intellect but all basic curiosity. And he casually adds that while this is not the history of kings and queens, many such instances can be found in India.

Although Gandhi writes with feeling and conviction on the subject of ahimsa, his one-size-fits-all theory is not entirely convincing. What does he have to say of massacres throughout history? He does not deny that they took place but suggests that they could have been prevented by using 'soul-force' or passive resistance. He thus explains away the massacres of American Indians, the genocide of Australian indigenous peoples, and the various mass killings that have taken place as having happened because ... there was no 'soul-force' in opposition.

'Those people who have been warred against have disappeared,' he writes, 'as, for instance, the natives of Australia of whom hardly a man was left alive by the intruders. Mark please that these natives did not use soul-force in self-defense, and it does not require much foresight to know that *the Australians will share the same fate as their victims.*'[18]

'*... it does not require much foresight to know that the Australians will share the same fate as their victims.*'

Such facile language. 'It does not require *much* foresight'— but surely, this would be evident to anyone with even a small amount of foresight and common sense. A century has gone by since Gandhi wrote those words, and the children of the white Australians that perpetrated the massacres are still very much around, and in far greater numbers. Is it divine retribution that the Mahatma speaks of here, albeit of a delayed variety? Do we detect in these words a desire for revenge for the killings of the indigenous people? Surely not!

'*... the Australians will share the same fate as their victims.*'

The Mahatma does not say 'may' but uses the word 'will' as if this is bound to be the case. And by 'the same fate', does he mean that they will also die, or does it mean that they too will be massacred by a superior force?

Will God punish them for their sins, by wreaking some terrible calamity on them, such that the entire white population of Australia will be exterminated? Even though Gandhi is a religious man, surely this cannot be the meaning of his words.

But possibly this *is* exactly what he means. On 15 January 1934, a terrible earthquake devastated a part of Bihar. As could be expected, Gandhi made a tour of the area, trying to organise help for the suffering. What was unexpected, however, was his statement spelling out the reasons for the earthquake. 'This earthquake,' he told the public, 'is a chastisement for your sins,' mainly 'the sin of untouchability.'[19] Such an unscientific approach angered the great poet Rabindranath, who pleaded that such words from the mouth of the Mahatma had the potential to spread unreason and superstition among people. The Mahatma did not budge and stuck stubbornly to his statement, drawing a connection between the spiritual world and material phenomena. 'The connection between cosmic phenomena and human behavior is a living faith,' he argued, 'that draws me closer to God.'[20]

But the Australians who committed the massacres are long gone. For decades now, the Australian people and government have been apologetic about what happened in the past. Are we to assume that Gandhi believes the sins of the fathers will be visited upon their sons? And if so, is it fair?

And as far as the massacres of indigenous peoples in Australia and presumably those of the Native Indians in the Americas are concerned, Gandhi appears to suggest that they could have been averted if only these populations had used 'soul-force'. How can Gandhi, a man who disputes the uses of history, categorically assert that the exterminated peoples did not use any 'soul-force'? He was not there to be able to testify to this. It is what we would call an *ex post facto* conclusion without any basis.

It's almost as if he is condemning the indigenous peoples for not using 'soul-force' and thinking of ahimsa as a universal power that can withstand all kinds of brute force. The same attitude emerges even with regard to the most notorious massacre of his own countrymen.

In the context of Jallianwala Bagh massacre, historian Alex von Tunzelmann wrote on how 'perhaps the most surprising response of all came from Mohandas Gandhi, the leader of the formerly peaceful campaign which had ended in such carnage'.[21] Even a large section of British society was horrified at the atrocity,[22] and therefore it was all the more astonishing that, as author Patrick French states, Gandhi concluded that the victims of the massacre carried out by General Dyer were 'definitely not heroic martyrs' and criticised them for 'having taken to their heels' rather than face death calmly.[23] On balance, we should consider that it was indeed shameful that Gandhi thus condemned the innocent dead (those in Jallianwala Bagh, as well as the massacred indigenous peoples in Australia) even as he announced his faith that the British would see that justice was done.[24] He may himself have been a man of great courage, but he displays an arrogance here that is especially shocking given the compassion that is generally attributed to him. He also seems to presume, with a marked lack of wisdom and introspection, that he would himself always remain calm in the face of death. If he was in fact so calm, why did he consent to take quinine for the treatment of his malaria, while disallowing the use of penicillin for his wife when she lay on her deathbed? The truly brave and compassionate do not so easily allege cowardice on the part of others. As the Bible says, judge not, lest ye be judged.

At this stage in his life, it also appears that he had a one-point formula for combating violence, that of always confronting the perpetrator with passive resistance. My way is the only right way, he seems to be saying all too often. It wasn't even that he always succeeded in confronting the person perpetrating violence.

In 1896, when he returned to South Africa with his family, for twenty-three days, the port supervisors did not allow his ship to dock. When Gandhi eventually disembarked, he was attacked by a white mob who threw stones, eggs and bricks at him. They then set upon him with blows and kicks. It was only because of the intervention of the police superintendent's wife, who put herself in between the mob and Gandhi's family, that they were saved. Later that same day, a mob surrounded the house where the family were hiding—they were fully prepared to lynch him.[25]

Gandhi did not foolishly confront them. He would certainly have put his family at grave risk had he done so. How insensitive of him, then, to say that the Jallianwala Bagh protesters had 'turned heel'. There were women with children among them. Did he honestly expect mothers to turn their children's faces towards those who would fire at them?

In the incident in South Africa, Gandhi was persuaded to disguise himself as a policeman, with a tin pan under his turban, and in this fashion he made his way to the local police station.

Gandhi behaved sensibly here. But the latter-day Mahatma would possibly have accused the younger Gandhi of 'turning heel' and of failing to confront the perpetrators of violence courageously.

The award-winning film *Gandhi* (1982) focuses on the incident when the Mahatma was thrown out of a railway compartment in Pietermaritzburg.[26] The event in Durban was equally significant, though is less well known. Whereas he suffered no physical harm in the train incident, he was beaten black and blue in Durban after leaving the ship.

There is a strange paradox: on one hand, there is Gandhi's insensitive, callous and completely unacceptable response to Jallianwala Bagh massacre; and on the other, he does have interesting and important things to say on the theme of non-violent protests.

It all comes down to Gandhi's assessment of the nature of evil, of human brutality and ultimately of human conscience.

He assumes that all of us have a conscience, even those who are perpetrating crimes of unspeakable brutality, and that all that is really needed is a jolt to the conscience, powerful enough to awaken it and transform the heart of darkness.

This, he believes, can be accomplished using 'soul-force'.

Certainly, the conscience of a nation can be shocked. To give a contemporary example, it's certainly true that the pictures of torture in Abu Ghraib prison shocked the conscience of the American people as well as the rest of the world. In today's world, no government can afford to ignore public opinion.

What Gandhi is really saying is that the shock to an individual tyrant's conscience as well as to an oppressor nation is greater when the victim behaves (a) with strength, (b) with non-violence and (c) without hatred.

It's true that passive resistance can be more dramatic than the regular form of resistance that we are all used to. It is also true that it requires a considerable amount of courage.

Gandhi explains this quite beautifully. 'What do you think?' he wrote:

> Wherein is courage required—in blowing others to pieces from behind a cannon, or with a smiling face to approach a cannon and to be blown to pieces? Who is the true warrior—he, who keeps death always as a bosom-friend, or he who controls the death of others? Believe me that a man devoid of courage and manhood can never be a passive resister.[27]

Although the Mahatma is opposed to cities, industry, machinery, and so forth, and regards the village community as his ideal, we never see him waxing eloquent on the beauties of nature in the manner of his contemporary, Rabindranath Tagore.

And yet in the context of describing the meaning and virtue of 'passive resistance', Gandhi turns poetic, almost Shakespearean: 'Passive resistance is an all-sided sword, it can be used anyhow; it blesses him who uses it and him against whom it is used. Without drawing a drop of blood, it produces far-reaching results. It never rusts and cannot be stolen.'[28]

'... *it blesses him that uses it and him against whom it is used.*'

It was Shakespeare who wrote of mercy, saying 'it blesseth him that gives and him that takes'.[29] Now the Mahatma is saying something similar about passive resistance, possibly influenced by the Bard.

Humour apart, Gandhi does display an understanding of the psychology of a tyrant. It is his argument, perhaps, that a man who beats his wife is more likely to be brought to his senses if she resists using non-violence. As the social historian Khilnani wrote, in stark contrast to the macho style of the khaki-shorts-wearing right-wing Hindus, Gandhi feminised the display of courage to great political advantage. The Mahatma himself never acknowledges that he is doing anything of the kind; I counted the use of the word 'manhood' several times in the chapter in the manifesto on passive resistance.

The mystic Osho (who claims to have met Gandhi as a child) remarks that Gandhi simply adopted the age-old technique used by Indian women to get their husbands to accede to their demands. After the demand for, say, a saree has been raised politely a few times, with no action taken on it, the wife decides to go on a hunger fast. The husband tells himself: 'Big Deal! Let's see how long she can last.' A few days later, not only does the wife stop eating but she stops cooking as well! Passive resistance is taken one step further. The husband can possibly manage to eat away from home for a few days, but for how long? And what about the children? He also notices that his wife is turning pale. He begins to worry. Who is going to look after the family if something happens to her? In a great panic, he rushes to the market and buys the saree. He learns to listen to his wife more attentively in the future.

If we compare this technique with that of a wife who is simply fighting, the latter behaviour can possibly lead to a flare-up, with the husband assaulting her and cowing her into submission. However, in the case where the wife is on a fast in protest and not displaying any anger or hate towards him but only displaying steely resolve and determination, he slowly comes to realise that he cannot simply beat her into submission.

In his younger days, Gandhi was a jealous and possessive husband. He was also consumed with his self-assumed importance as a husband, and decided that his wife Kasturba could not leave the house without his permission. Like other Indian women, Kasturba knew she could not openly disobey her husband. When her mother-in-law asked her to accompany her to the temple, she went along despite Gandhi's instructions. She returned home to find a furious Gandhi, and they had their first major fight—which Gandhi lost by the sheer power of logic. He was forced to remove his restrictions. As Tunzelmann wrote: 'All Gandhi's famous tactics—passive resistance, civil disobedience, logical argument, non-violence in the face of violence, emotional blackmail—had come from Kasturba's influence.'[30]

The Mahatma himself conceded this. 'I learnt the lessons of non-violence from my wife,' he admitted.[31]

Explaining the true meaning of passive resistance, Gandhi wrote: 'The real meaning of the statement that we are a law-abiding nation is that we are passive resisters. When we do not like certain laws, we do not break the heads of lawgivers but we suffer and do not submit to the laws.'[32]

So far so good, but then the Mahatma who disavows the lessons of history goes on to assert: 'That we should obey laws whether good or bad is a newfangled notion. There was no such thing in former days. The people disregarded those laws they did not like, and suffered the penalties for their breach. *It is contrary to our manhood if we obey laws repugnant to our conscience.*'[33]

'There was no such thing in former days.'

It is too much to expect Gandhi to provide us with facts and figures, dates and years. We, the readers of *Hind Swaraj*, are simply expected to accept his statements as unvarnished truth.

He goes on to suggest that he does not believe in the separation of state and religion: 'A man who has realized his manhood, who fears only God, will fear no one else. Manmade laws are not necessarily binding on him.'[34]

Some of Gandhi's ideas on passive resistance are profound and expressed beautifully and convincingly, but he ruins this chapter of *Hind Swaraj* by veering off on to sermons on chastity towards the end.

This is what the great, but repressed, Mahatma had to say to his followers: 'Chastity is one of the greatest disciplines without which the mind cannot attain requisite firmness. A man who is unchaste loses stamina, becomes emasculated and cowardly.'[35]

Again, no proof is offered, just bald assertions. Since the Mahatma does not believe in research, he could simply have given his own example. He took his chastity vow fairly late in life. Did he do so because he had lost stamina and become emasculated and cowardly as a consequence?

There is no medical evidence to support Gandhi's conclusions, but then he has already made clear what he thinks of the medical profession. Yet here he is issuing pronouncements that are certainly medical or at least quasi-medical in nature.

And what about women? What are the consequences for them if they are not chaste? Gandhi does not specify.

The Mahatma insists that chastity is an absolute must for him who wishes to become a passive warrior—or even, for that matter, an active, armed warrior: 'Let there be no mistake, as those who want to train themselves in the use of arms are also obliged to have these qualities more or less. Everybody does not become a warrior for the wish. A would-be warrior would have to observe chastity and to be satisfied with poverty as his lot.'[36]

The sermonising streak is present in Gandhi together with a severe distaste for being questioned. 'Yours is not to ask why,' he seems to be saying.

It is not only pre-marital sex that the Mahatma is opposed to; that, at least, could have been reasonably comprehended even by his critics. As regards chastity, Gandhi does not make any exceptions even for married men. It does not matter whether you are married or not, you have to observe chastity. Sex appears to be, for the Mahatma, almost like an evil that could be compared, in his mind at least, with devilish machinery and railways.

He does not mince words in the context of sex and the married man: 'What then is a married man to do is the question that arises naturally, and yet it need not. *When a husband and wife gratify the passions, it is no less an animal indulgence on that account. Such an indulgence except for perpetuating the race is strictly prohibited.*'[37]

And yet this is not all. Gandhi knows his people very well. There may be many among his youthful followers who could use the desire to have children as a justification for sex.

'The thing is Mahatma-ji,' such a male follower could say to Gandhi, 'my wife and I are trying to have a child—and this is really the reason we have sex. She is not getting pregnant despite our frequent intercourse. Anyhow, we will keep trying and once she is pregnant, I will embrace celibacy.'

Although Gandhi despises lawyers, he has himself been one—and a clever one at that—for far too long for him not to spot that loophole. So he cleverly seals it up by adding the following:

> But a passive resister has to avoid *even that limited indulgence* because he can have no desire for progeny. A married man, therefore, can observe perfect chastity. This subject is not capable of being treated at greater length. Several questions arise: How is one to carry one's wife with one? What are her rights, and other such questions? Yet those who wish to take part in a great work are bound to solve these puzzles.[38]

'*This subject is not capable of being treated at greater length.*'

The subject is perfectly capable. It is the Mahatma who does not wish to discuss it at further length. Why? For several reasons. For one, it would not appear to behove someone with his stature to go into more detail on such issues. Secondly, he would be getting into muddy waters here—and he might suspect that whatever answer he gave with respect to wives' rights would be found offensive by wives themselves. The politician inside him would not have wished to alienate that constituency. And finally, if he did provide some guidance in these matters, there would be bound to be yet further questions that would arise. It would all become rather endless and eventually bog him down.

'*How is one to carry one's wife with one?*'

Gandhi asks, and this question itself *raises a presumption* that after all the man is the decision maker and the woman or wife is not a co-equal. The alternative question that never occurs to him is: 'How is one to carry one's husband?'

Chapter 9

THE SAINT'S COMMANDMENTS

If a doctor, he will give up medicine, and understand that rather than mending bodies, he should mend souls.

— Mahatma Gandhi

The last chapter of *Hind Swaraj* is as much a call for action as it is a set of moral prescriptions. The commandments are addressed, in the main, to three kinds of Indians: lawyers, doctors and the so-called 'wealthy Indians' who contributed so much to the Congress party's coffers.

Gandhi was a strange man in many ways. One of these was the way in which he combined strokes of practical genius with long-winded and impractical 'idealism'. In other words, there was a part of Gandhi that was highly aware of the world of realpolitik, where he could even be rightly considered a political genius. The famous Dandi march to protest against the salt tax, the idea of non-violent resistance, the Swadeshi campaign—these were part of 'Genius Gandhi'.[1] There was another misguided and absurd side to him as well, which formed a part of his psyche and persona. This was the Gandhi that combined a hatred for all things modern, including most manifestations of industrial society, such as trains, aircraft and machines, in general. This was also the Gandhi who discouraged education in physics, chemistry, biology, medicine, geography, history and the English language. This was the Gandhi who hated the injection but loved the enema, and who believed that moral and religious teaching should have primacy over all other subjects. It was also the Gandhi who carried out bizarre experiments, in bathing and sleeping with young women..

But let us now come to the problematic aspects of the last chapter of his manifesto. There are problems here, even before the Mahatma begins on his commandments.

Consider, for example, his acceptance that there would be skirmishes between religious communities post-Independence. The communities are not named, but clearly he would have been referring to the two main religious groups, the Hindu majority and the large Muslim minority, of undivided India. There seems to be a kind of practical acceptance, but is this really the case? Gandhi wrote:

If the English vacated India, bag and baggage, it must not be supposed that she would be widowed. It is possible that those who are forced to observe peace under their pressure would fight after their withdrawal. *There can be no advantage in suppressing an eruption; it must have its vent.* If, therefore, before we can remain in peace, we must fight amongst ourselves, it is better that we do so.[2]

When Partition happened, the scale of arson, rapes and killings that took place shook Gandhi. He had never anticipated this. He did not blame the British for failing to preserve the peace. There were, I suspect, several reasons for this.

First, it was in a sense not their fault, or, to be more accurate, not entirely their fault. Yes, there was British culpability in as much as the partition of the country was rushed through; that was clearly a blunder of Himalayan proportions, as were the hastily drawn borders, but the Congress too had been caught napping.

Secondly, Gandhi had been saying all along in his manifesto—and one imagines he remained consistent in this view even though Independence was not to happen until several decades later—that there was no need for the British to protect the weak. He may have meant this in the context of minor skirmishes and killings (a few hundred deaths only?), but surely he would not have extended his comments to apply to the communal slaughter of hundreds of thousands of Hindus and Muslims grasping at each other's throats. This is what he writes: 'If, therefore, before we can remain in peace, we must fight amongst ourselves, it is better that we do so. There is no occasion for a third party to protect the weak. It is this so-called protection which has unnerved us. Such protection can only make the weak weaker.'[3]

With such views, articulated again and again, how could Gandhi have then blamed the British? And this brings us to the third reason why Gandhi could not. He blamed *himself* for what happened, and he *was* to blame, in a sense.

Although generally active and dynamic, Gandhi became too passive once it was clear to everyone that Partition was inevitable. The death of his dream of an undivided India may have been responsible for that inertia, for he was a fighter to the core. For so many years, he had steadfastly clung on to the idea of an undivided India—even proposing plans as unrealistic as making Jinnah the PM. He never stopped to consider that a partition of the country could take place and that a Plan B was needed for that eventuality.

There are many who believe that the bloodletting that followed Partition was completely unpredictable. An alternative argument can, however, be advanced: that it *was* foreseeable, and that there should have been planning and preparation to diminish the bloodletting that took place. Gandhi, and the Congress under his leadership, should have carefully considered what B.R. Ambedkar had proposed, if they hadn't studied or thought over the matter themselves.

In the nineteen 'commandments', or moral prescriptions, that Gandhi gives in the last chapter, he maintains strange balance of thoughts that are brilliant, practical and effective, and some that are vague, incoherent and impractical..

Using nineteen separately stated points, he follows a strange logic in advising those Indians who are imbued with 'real love' for the nation. Many of these commandments could easily have been integrated—as will become evident as we move along. It almost appears that the Mahatma wished to have an impressive number of commandments, so rather than integrating them, he issued separate commandments to lawyers, doctors, and so on. Was it the case that after making his recommendations—for instance, abolishing the railways and aircraft, getting rid of all machinery, and not studying any of these subjects—in earlier chapters, he realised that they were mostly negative in character. In the end, he found himself at a bit of a loss when it came to making concrete recommendations to help realise his manifesto. It is also strange that lawyers receive such prominence in terms of the commandments because the manifesto itself has only a single chapter devoted to them. In order to demonstrate the hollowness or meaninglessness of these commandments it may be useful to dissect them as below:

1.   'He will only on rare occasions make use of the English language.'[4]

Naturally, this injunction is so important that it is the very first commandment for all Indians. Legend has it that the Native

American Indians did not trust the white man, telling each other that 'the white man speaks with a forked tongue'. For Gandhi, not only was the white man's tongue forked but the tongue, meaning the language, was itself evil.

The next four commandments are directed at lawyers, already discussed in an earlier chapter.

The best thing for a lawyer to do is to give up his profession entirely, Gandhi advises.

2.   'If a lawyer, he will give up his profession and take up a hand-loom.'[5]

What can such a lawyer do instead, assuming that 'taking up the handloom' is not meant to be a new career option? Were a lawyer to fall under the Mahatma's spell (a not completely unlikely eventuality given his stature in the country) and ask if he could work as a judge instead, Gandhi's answer would have been a resolute 'No'. Indeed, anticipating such a question, the fifth commandment specifically makes it clear that becoming a judge is just as bad.

5.   'If a lawyer, he will refuse to be a judge, as he will give up his profession.'[6]

A lawyer who continues to practise law is not eligible to be a judge. In order to qualify to be a judge, he will have to perforce give up practising as a lawyer. This particular commandment is therefore poorly formulated, and appears vague, contradictory and incoherent.

What if our imaginary obedient lawyer asked Gandhi if he could become a train driver instead? A definite 'No' would have again been the answer. If Gandhi could have employed archaic biblical speech, he would have counter-questioned such a lawyer: 'Wilt thou give up the pernicious practice of law only to become a driver then of the engine of evil?'

What about a job as a station master at the railway station? Not as bad as being a driver, but still indirectly supportive of evil!

What about training and working as an airline pilot, even if such an option did exist for Indians? It is practically certain that Gandhi would have considered the profession to be abominable. Columnist Richard Grenier wrote on how '… he happened to be in England when Louis Bleriot, the great French aviation pioneer first flew across the English Channel—an event which at the time stirred as much excitement as Lindbergh's later flight across the Atlantic—and Gandhi was in a positive fury that giant crowds were acclaiming such an insignificant event.'[7]

What if our hypothetical lawyer thought of working in a factory as a legal adviser or a consultant? Gandhi has already announced earlier in his manifesto that in his view factories are evil. All industry was evil, save homespun traditional handicrafts. So no factory employment for the gentleman who at Gandhi's behest has given up the practice of law.

What about working as an electrician? Or if that is beneath the lawyer's dignity, what about teaching law, or English, history, geography or the sciences?

I could go on and on, but I need not labour the point further. It is just as well that Gandhi only asked our resigning lawyer to 'take up a handloom' and didn't proffer any further advice on how the lawyer was to earn money to support his family.

As an aside, it may be mentioned here that Indian communists have wondered why Gandhi never thought of fighting on behalf of factory workers to ensure that they received a fair wage and worked in safe and hygienic conditions. The answer is quite simple. It was not that Gandhi didn't feel any sympathy or empathy for factory workers, but the much greater issue for him was the abolition of the factories themselves!

3.   'If a lawyer, he will devote his knowledge to enlightening both his people and the English.'[8]

The lawyer in Gandhi finds an excuse here for the very many lawyers who play a leadership role in the Congress party; otherwise, he could be accused of hypocrisy. He concedes that lawyers have 'knowledge', and presumably the lawyers within the Congress were using their knowledge in enlightening the people and the English. What about men like Jawaharlal Nehru's father, who might be said to be doing both—practising law, as well as 'enlightening' the people and the English? Gandhi does not speak of those who straddle both these worlds, but there must have been many, for membership of the party alone would not keep the kitchen fires burning. The professional politician who swings deals, works as a 'fixer' and doesn't need to work for a living had yet to emerge in India.

4.   'If a lawyer, he will not meddle with the quarrels between parties, but will give up the courts and from his experience induce the people to do likewise.'[9]

Let us read this again.

If a lawyer, he will not meddle with the quarrels between parties (and how will he be a lawyer then?) *but will give up the courts* (this point was already made in the second commandment, so why repeat it?), *and from his experience* (how can the Mahatma presume what experience will teach people?) *induce the people* (one can assume he means the litigants here) *to do likewise.*

Gandhi does not propose any alternative to the courts. He earlier spoke of how he does not believe in third-party mediation. The parties themselves know who is right. So are quarrels simply going to disappear? All that needs to happen, in his view, is for the lawyers to give up practice and convince parties not to waste their time in the courts. This is Gandhi indulging in wishful thinking, and at his most vague and obscure.

* * *

Thus far, we have dealt with the first five commandments. The next three are directed at doctors, whom Gandhi considers to be as pernicious as lawyers. Bodies do not need to be 'repaired'; it is souls that need mending.

6.   'If a doctor, he will give up medicine, and understand that rather than mending bodies, he should mend souls.'[10]

Gandhi was lucky that he did not himself suffer any serious illness at the time; if he had, he would in all probability have reconsidered this piece of advice. To those who would vouch for the Mahatma's sincere intentions—that he would not advise others to do what he would not do himself—we can suggest they look at what the he did in real life. He allowed his wife, Kasturba, to pass away rather than receive a penicillin injection, but not long thereafter allowed himself to be persuaded to take quinine to cure his malaria. After Kasturba's death, would he ever have regretted his decision to not allow her to be treated? It is doubtful.

He even tells the doctors—who have taken the Hippocratic oath—not to be concerned if the patient who does not receive treatment were to die. Here it is in his own words: the eighth commandment (we will examine the seventh commandment shortly).

8.   'Although a doctor, he will take up a hand-loom, and if any patients come to him, will tell them the cause of their

diseases, and will advise them to remove the cause rather than pamper them by giving useless drugs; …'

So drugs are useless, and they 'pamper' the patients, like sweets for children? Now here comes the clincher in the second part of the eighth commandment.

'… *he will understand that if by not taking drugs, perchance the patient dies, the world will not come to grief and that he will have been really merciful to him.*'[11]

Doctors, then, who have studied Western medicine, should in Gandhi's view simply forget about the Hippocratic oath they have taken to save the lives of patients. What about religious teachings on the sanctity of human life and the duty to save human life at all costs? All religions teach this; in modern times, the Catholic religion even forbids the use of contraception and abortion on this account. How does Gandhi reconcile the eighth commandment with advice in the scriptures of different religions that all speak of the sanctity and importance of human life?

The seventh commandment addresses this issue. Gandhi has studied all the world religions and pronounces that his views are quite in sync with all religions—although the truth of the matter is that many leaders, priests, mullahs and pundits of those religions might strongly disagree and support the 'vivisection' that could potentially save lives. This commandment might appear, at first glance, to be simply a regurgitation of the other two commandments addressed to doctors, but in fact it is not.

7. 'If a doctor, he will understand that *no matter to what religion he belongs*, it is better that bodies remain diseased rather than that they are cured through the instrumentality of the diabolical vivisection that is practised in European schools of medicine.'[12]

Gandhi would be at one with tribes in Afghanistan who do not allow their womenfolk to receive medical treatment at the hands of male Western doctors. He would even perhaps go a step further and say that men too should stop receiving such treatment.

Would Gandhi have modified his commandments had there been an epidemic causing hundreds of thousands, or even millions, to die and a vaccine or cure was available by using Western medicine? He does not answer this question in *Hind Swaraj* (or rather he does not pose it to himself), but probably he would not.

Although Gandhi was opposed to doctors and Western medicine, he had his strong views on medicine published in *A Guide to Health*. This is what he says specifically on the issue of vaccination: 'Vaccination is a barbarous practice, and it is one of the most fatal of all delusions current in our time not to be found even among the so-called savage races of the world.'[13]

A little later he adds a few words about how disgusting it is.

Moreover, vaccination is a very dirty process, for the serum which is introduced into the human body includes not only that of the cow, but also of the actual small-pox patient. An average man would even vomit at the mere sight of this stuff. If the hand happens to touch it, it is always washed with soap. The mere suggestion of tasting it fills us with indignation and disgust. But how few of those who get themselves vaccinated realise that they are in effect eating this filthy stuff![14]

Of course, Gandhi suggests his own remedy, the 'wet sheet pack'. It does not matter that most doctors consider it to be 'sheer quackery', for as he has already let us know in *Hind*

Swaraj, quacks are often far better than doctors. Although the above remarks are made in the context of smallpox, lest he be misunderstood, the Mahatma hastens to add that they apply more or less to the case of chickenpox as well: 'We do not dread chicken-pox so much as its elder sister, since it is not so fatal, and does not cause disfigurement and the like. It is, however, exactly the same as small-pox in other respects, and should therefore be dealt with in the same way.'[15]

It is Gandhi's considered view that mankind should allow epidemics to rage on and kill hundreds of thousands, if not millions of human beings, rather than have recourse to this abhorrent stuff, namely the constituent elements of a vaccine, for the principle is the same. I am not putting words into the Mahatma's mouth. Read him directly.

> I cannot also help feeling that vaccination is a violation of the dictates of religion and morality. The drinking of the blood of even dead animals is looked upon with horror even by habitual meat-eaters. Yet, what is vaccination but the taking in of the poisoned blood of an innocent living animal? *Better far were it for God-fearing men that they should a thousand times become the victims of small-pox and even die a terrible death than that they should be guilty of such an act of sacrilege.*[16]

It was not only vaccines he was against, but even inoculation for plague.

> Bubonic Plague is a terrible disease, and has accounted for the death of millions of our people since the year 1896, when it first made its real entry into our land. The doctors, in spite of all their investigations, have not yet been able to invent a sure remedy for it. Now-a-days

the practice of inoculation has come into vogue, and the belief has gained ground that an attack of plague may be obviated by it. *But inoculation for plague is as bad and as sinful as vaccination for small-pox.*[17]

The Mahatma does not lose the opportunity to lecture mankind on morality even in his small booklet on health. He offers a hellfire sermon, no less.

Hell itself would be preferable to the body which is the slave of vice, which is constantly filled with decaying matter and which emits filthy odours, whose hands and feet are employed in unworthy deeds, whose tongue is employed in eating things that ought not to be eaten or in uttering language that ought not to be uttered, whose eyes are employed in seeing things that ought not to be seen, whose ears are employed in the hearing of things that ought not to be heard, and whose nose is employed in the smelling of things that ought not to be smelt.[18]

And finally:

[O]ur attempt in these pages has been to teach the great truth that perfect health can be attained only by living in obedience to the laws of God, and defying the power of Satan. True happiness is impossible without true health, and true health is impossible without a rigid control of the palate. All the other senses will automatically come under our control when the palate has been brought under control.[19]

The nine commandments that now follow are all directed at 'wealthy men' and 'others'. The ninth and tenth commandments are directed exclusively at the 'wealthy man', with the ninth exhorting him to 'speak out his mind, and fear no one' despite his wealth.

9.   'Although a wealthy man, yet regardless of his wealth, he will speak out his mind and fear no one.'[20]

The assumption here is that wealth produces cowardice. There is nothing wrong with the commandment per se, but it seems to suggest, erroneously, that poor men have less to fear than wealthy men. It also ignores the vested interest and greed that sometimes gag the mouths of wealthy men, and speaks only of their fear.

One cannot help but contrast the prosaic and dull nature of the Mahatma's commandment with what his contemporary, Rabindranath Tagore, famously wrote on a similar theme.

> Where the mind is without fear and the head is held high
> Where knowledge is free
> Where the world has not been broken up into fragments
> By narrow domestic walls
> Where words come out of the depth of truth[21]

Gandhi may have railed against lawyers, but he is himself not unlike lawyers—for the most part prosaic and matter-of-fact rather than poetic.

The tenth commandment recalls the handloom theme.

10.   'If a wealthy man, he will devote his money to establishing hand-looms, and encourage others to use hand-made goods by wearing them himself.'[22]

While repeating the handloom theme, it is interesting what Gandhi chooses *not* to say here to wealthy Indians. In line with the philosophy of *Hind Swaraj*, if he were specifically addressing rich Indians, he should have exhorted them to shut down their factories and mills. He chooses to say this not directly but obliquely, when he suggests that they establish hand-looms. As a great believer in religion, the Mahatma could never have supported the communists; and the communists also supported the development of industry, which Gandhi does not. At the same time, while Gandhi condemns British industry, he chooses not to directly condemn Indian industry, or to issue a disparaging statement against those wealthy men who have made money by copying Western industries.

We now come to the remaining nine commandments. Gandhi uses a strange way to phrase these remaining nine commandments, or moral imperatives—call them what you will—which in their phrasing appear disrespectful of the common man. Let me explain. These nine commandments are directed at the wealthy man but include all other Indians too by beginning with either 'Like every other Indian' or 'Like others'.

An obvious question one feels impelled to ask is why he does not simply direct these nine commandments towards *all* Indians, in which the rich and wealthy would automatically get included.

The next nine commandments are general in nature. Many are simple exhortations, with the eleventh commandment being one such generic sample of the 'rise and shine' variety. When he speaks of 'repentance, expiation and mourning', these are vague, similar sounding words, an exhortation without clarity.

11. 'Like every other Indian, *he* [the wealthy Indian] *will know* that this is a time for repentance, expiation and mourning.'[23]

Two expressions that recur in the last nine moral instructions are 'he will know' and 'he will understand'. If the wealthy man, and the 'others', will either 'know' or 'understand' all the moral imperatives that follow, it is reasonable to ask what is the point of Gandhi telling them these things. Hence, these serve as classic examples of the famous Gandhian politeness and doublespeak.

Gandhi introduces small variations in the seven commandments, sometimes using 'Like every other Indian' or 'Like others', as well as 'he will understand' and 'he will know', in the hope that they do not sound too repetitive—but alas, they do still sound repetitive. Would Gandhi approve of his commandments being recited, or rather chanted like a mantra, by Indian children in schools across the land? We don't know the answer to that question but can easily imagine children reciting the commandments in a sing-song way in a class designed to build character, in a school that will not be teaching history, geography, physics, chemistry, biology and much else besides.

The twelfth and seventeenth commandments are cast in the over-forgiving saintly mode. The aggressor is not to blame; the victim is possibly equally to blame. One wonders whether these are another part of the Gandhi doublespeak! Is he here trying to exonerate the British by taking the stance that the victim must have in some way allowed or been responsible for the actions of the aggressor? On the surface he appears to be doing so, but it is possible he may actually be trying to shame the British by playing the 'noble victim' card.

12. 'Like every other Indian, he will know that to blame the English is useless, that they came because of us, and remain also for the same reason, and that they will either go or change their nature only when we reform ourselves.'[24]

The seventeenth commandment uses similar language. We are also guilty for having encouraged the sinner!

17. 'Like others, he will understand that deportation for life to the Andamans *is not enough expiation* for the sin of encouraging European civilisation.'[25]

Is this demagoguery or once again rhetoric? The rich man, like others, will understand that 'deportation for life' is still not enough punishment for the sin of encouraging European civilisation. A few simple questions reveal the lack of thought behind this commandment.

Who were the people who were being sent to the Andamans at the time? Obviously, they were those who were either dangerous criminals or who were fighting for Indian self-rule, independence or Hind Swaraj. Gandhi does not laud the contributions of those patriots who were incarcerated for fighting the English. Rather he blames wealthy men and others in India, from whom, incidentally, he does not hesitate to take funds. How have these people encouraged European civilisation, even if we deem it to be the evil that Gandhi has determined it to be? He imposes collective guilt on the entire population of India for having committed the sin of encouraging European civilisation. And what of the rest of the colonised world? Are they too similarly guilty? And what of the American Indians and Australian indigenous people? Are they also guilty? If 'deportation for life' is not sufficient? punishment (as determined by Gandhi), will death by hanging be sufficient? Or will that too be insufficient? Gandhi remains silent on this unposed question.

Being sent off to jail is specially recommended for the wealthy Indian, even if he is the least likely to choose to be jailed. The thirteenth commandment reads as follows:

13. 'Like others, he [the rich man] will understand that at a time of mourning there can be no indulgence, and that,

whilst we are in a fallen state to be in gaol or banishment is much the best.'[26]

Did Gandhi in some sense save the best for last? The sixteenth commandment is almost Christian in content (though it also evokes masochistic elements that exist in the Jain religion) in almost exalting 'suffering' and asceticism as an ideal. Suffering is also referred to in sixteenth and eighteenth commandments.

16. 'Like others, he will understand that we will become free only through suffering.'[27]

This is quite simply worded. At one level, it states that Indians have to make sacrifices to attain freedom. At another level, by emphasising our own suffering (namely the suffering of Indians), Gandhi connects with a broader theme in the rest of the manifesto that explicitly steers clear of causing 'suffering' to the enemy—the colonising British.

The eighteenth commandment makes this clear.

18. 'Like others, he will know that no nation has risen without suffering; that even in physical warfare, the true test is suffering and not the killing of others, much more so in the warfare of passive resistance.'[28]

The words 'no nation has risen without suffering' is an oft-used platitude unworthy of Gandhi's original, if skewed, thinking. What does it really mean to say that 'no nation has risen without suffering'? Who will measure the quantity of suffering that a nation needs to suffer in order to rise? And why does Gandhi not embellish his statement with some historical examples? The thing is that he doesn't like to read history and doesn't recommend that anyone else read it either.

In the nineteenth commandment, he compares the experience of suffering to the savouring of a rare delicacy.

19. 'Like others he will know that it is an idle excuse to say that we shall do a thing when the others also do it; that we should do what we know to be right, and that others will do it when they see the way that when I fancy a particular delicacy, I do not wait till others taste it; that to make a national effort and to suffer are in the nature of delicacies; and that to suffer under pressure is no suffering.'[29]

***

Surprisingly, Gandhi's manifesto does not discuss the issue of caste and caste discrimination, which represent an evil that persists to this day. Although not discussed in the manifesto, it may be worthwhile to briefly discuss Gandhi's views on the matter.

Throughout *Hind Swaraj*, Gandhi lauds ancient civilisation, but his version of ancient India is not truly ancient India but more of a flawed medieval version. Why do I say this? Because Gandhi remained wedded to the idea of caste as something progressive for very many years.

B.R. Ambedkar, the Dalit leader, discussed the transition in Gandhi's thinking. To begin with, he utterly and completely believed in the caste system, and later shifted position to argue not in favour of rigidity within sub-castes anymore but in favour of a system of the broader *varna* category referring to the four main castes of Brahmin, Kshatriya, Vaisya and Sudra. Social hierarchy still remained important in the Mahatma's world view. It appears that he had not fully overcome some of the prejudice that he held in South Africa. In that country, he was pro-Indian but against many of the other races. In this regard it is worthwhile to quote the author Gary Beene, who points out how Gandhi's enigmatic attitude towards race became evident in a letter he wrote on 15 February 1905 to Dr Charles Porter, medical officer of health for Johannesburg.

> Why, of all places in Johannesburg, the Indian location should be chosen for dumping down all Kaffirs of the town, passes my comprehension. Of course, under my suggestion, the Town Council must withdraw the Kaffirs from the location. About the mixing of the Kaffirs with the Indians, I must confess I feel most strongly. I think it is very unfair to the Indian population, and it is an unfair tax on even the proverbial patience of my countrymen.[30]

The term 'kaffir' did not mean infidel (as it does from an Islamic perspective in the subcontinent). Rather the term was an ethnic slur used to identify certain groups such as the Zulu, Sotho, Tswana, Xhosa among others.[31]

That this letter to Dr Porter is not a random statement but represents Gandhi's ambiguous attitude towards certain African communities is further illustrated in other correspondence.

In the context of a court decision in June 1906 (the year of the Zulu uprising in which Gandhi participated as a commander of an Indian unit), he wrote as follows in the *Indian Opinion*.

> You say that the magistrate's decision is unsatisfactory, because it would enable a person, howsoever unclean, to travel by tram, and that even the Kaffirs would be able to do so. But the magistrate's decision is quite different. The Court declared that the Kaffirs have no legal right to travel by tram. And according to tram regulations those in an unclean dress or in a drunken state are prohibited from boarding a tram. Thanks to

the Court's decision, only clean Indians or coloured people other than Kaffirs can now travel in the trams.[32]

Gandhi also wished the Indians to have greater privileges than the local population in South Africa in the carrying of arms. In another piece published in the *Indian Opinion,* he wrote:

> In this instance of the firearms, the Asiatic has been most improperly bracketed with the natives. The British Indian does not need any such restrictions as are imposed by the Bill on the natives regarding the carrying of firearms. The prominent race can remain so by preventing the native from arming himself. Is there a slightest vestige of justification for so preventing the British Indian?[33]

A year before the Mahatma penned his manifesto, he was incarcerated in a South African prison. There he disparaged his fellow inmates in a way not unlike that in which a prejudiced upper-caste Hindu might view untouchables: 'Kaffirs are as a rule uncivilised—the convicts even more so. They are troublesome, very dirty and live almost like animals.'[34]

Although Gandhi modified his views on caste, it was a long time before that happened. In 1922, thirteen years after the publication of *Hind Swaraj,* he wrote at considerable length and with great confidence and aplomb on the issue of caste in the Gujarati journal *Navajivan.*[35]

1. I believe that if Hindu society has been able to stand, it is because it is founded on the caste system;
2. The seeds of Swaraj are to be found in the caste system. Different castes are like different sections of military division. Each division is working for the good of the whole.

'*Different castes are like different sections of military division.*'

Pacifists might be surprised at what might be perceived as an indirect compliment to the military. Clearly, this line has something to do with the Mahatma's fond recall of time spent working with the British army in various African conflicts. He continued:

3. A community which can create the caste system must be said to possess unique powers of organisation.

4. Caste has a readymade means for spreading primary education. Every caste can take the responsibility for the education of the children of the caste. Caste has a political basis. It can work as an electorate for a representative body. Caste can perform judicial functions by electing persons to act as judges to decide disputes among members of the same caste. With castes it is easy to raise a defence force by requiring each caste to raise a brigade.

We may be left speechless while reading paragraph 4. It is a lot to digest all at once.

'*Every caste can take the responsibility for the education of the children of the caste.*'

At the time Gandhi does not appear to realise that there are hundreds of sub-castes in the country. Shall each sub-caste have its own school? Will this promote integration of the country, and help in nation-building? Is this kind of nation-building even important?

'*Caste can perform judicial functions by electing persons to act as judges to decide disputes among members of the same caste.*'

Gandhi has made it clear that he is against the Western model of justice, and while he despises lawyers and judges in general, he is happy to have a folksy kind of justice rendered.

This is not all. Gandhi makes it clear that he supports the ban on inter-caste dining. He doesn't support the idea of two people from different castes getting married despite being in love with each other—he supports the ban on marriage between a boy and girl from different castes.

> I believe that inter-dining or intermarriage is not necessary for promoting national unity. *That dining together creates friendship is contrary to experience. If this was true, there would have been no war in Europe. Taking food is as dirty an act as answering the call of nature. The only difference is that after answering a call of nature we get peace while after eating food we get discomfort. Just as we perform the act of answering the call of nature in seclusion so also the act of taking food must also be done in seclusion.*[36]

The Mahatma does not even enjoy eating food and considers it something 'dirty', and bizarrely enough ranks the pleasures of defecation at a higher level!

In a clip from a BBC interview that I watched on YouTube recently, B.R. Ambedkar accuses the Mahatma of only paying lip service to the cause of the untouchables (as well as to democracy).[37] Gandhi, he states, was really an orthodox Hindu. The views the Mahatma expressed in English and which would be received by an international audience were at sharp variance with the views he expressed in Gujarati journals.

Certainly, what Gandhi wrote in the Gujarati journal remains both shocking and nonsensical: 'I believe that inter-dining or intermarriage is not necessary for promoting national unity.'

Does the Mahatma believe then, to the contrary, that the graded system of castes promotes national unity? When he extols the virtues of the Indian village, the reader of his writings in English imagines that he has some ideal village in mind where the divisions of caste do not exist. Attempts at breaking the caste hierarchy are brutally punished by village communities. Shaving the person's head and having him parade through the village square is one of the common but lighter punishments. Khap Panchayats often tie couples who have fallen in love to trees and beat them to death. It is unlikely that Gandhi would have approved of the harsher punishments, but shaving a person's head seemed to him to be an entirely apposite penalty for, say, the crime of an 'unlawful' embrace.

Gandhi welcomes the rigidity of the caste system and refers to it as an eternal principle. The fact is, though, that he extols that caste was probably never as rigid in the very ancient India as it subsequently became. However, the Mahatma does not hesitate to attribute 'eternal' qualities to something completely temporal.

> To destroy caste system and adopt Western European social system means that Hindus must give up the principle of hereditary occupation which is the soul of the caste system. Hereditary principle is an eternal principle. To change it is to create disorder. I have no use for a Brahmin if I cannot call him a Brahmin for my life. It will be a chaos if every day a Brahmin is to be changed into a Shudra and a Shudra is to be changed into a Brahmin.[38]

Anyhow, in order not to persist with a patently untenable position, in 1925 he changed his stance. It was not caste he was defending now, but the varna system—the four big caste groupings within which all the sub-castes fell.

Clarifying his earlier stated position regarding caste, on 3 February 1925, Gandhi explained:

I gave support to caste because it stands for restraint. But at present caste does not mean restraint, it means limitations. Restraint is glorious and helps to achieve freedom. But limitation is like chain. It binds. There is nothing commendable in castes as they exist today. They are contrary to the tenets of the shastras. The number of castes is infinite and there is a bar against intermarriage. This is not a condition of elevation. It is a state of fall.[39]

The Mahatma has come round to an extent, but only to an extent. He no longer supports the existence of a multitude of castes but continues to defend the varna system. When asked what the way forward is, Gandhi opines that 'the best remedy is that small castes should fuse themselves into one big caste. There should be four such big castes, so that we may reproduce the old system of four *varnas*.'[40]

Chapter 10

IN CONCLUSION

Whether the person who helps you with the enema is a man or a woman, it should make, and I am sure it will make, no difference to you at all[1]

— Mahatma Gandhi

In some ways this is an easy chapter to write and in other ways it is extremely difficult. A question often asked in India is whether Gandhi is relevant today.

It is answered with an almost deafening 'Yes!' by politicians of all hues (otherwise you are in danger of being branded as a communist, or an extreme right-winger). The 'Yes' is expected from the politician seeking public approval. Even within the intelligentsia, there is very little dissension. When someone like Arundhati Roy writes questioning the Mahatma's views and his action taken on caste, a cry goes up. 'Oh, she's crazy, isn't she?' is a not-so-uncommon reaction among middle-class Indians and, to be fair to them, Roy does sometimes take rather extreme and very-shrill positions. The other people who deny Gandhi's continued relevance are extreme right-wing nationalists who accuse him of having been anti-Hindu and never relevant in the first place. Among this group are supporters of Nathuram Godse, the man who assassinated the Mahatma; some of them even wish to build a memorial to honour the assassin,[2] who is a hero in their eyes. Also among this right-wing group are those who hold that the title of 'Father of the Nation' is unwarranted.[3]

There are not many voices questioning the Mahatma's continued relevance, let alone his legacy (or not that are heard loudly enough, at any rate). Why is this the case? Part of the reason, I suspect, has to be a colonial mindset, and part of it is to do with the mindset that many Indians have—one not-sufficiently-critical of great people. These two reasons are interconnected.

The world recognises the Mahatma's greatness. The 1982 film *Gandhi* had won eight Oscars. Whenever an eminent foreign dignitary comes to India, he does not return to his home country before paying his respects at Shanti Van, the memorial that exists in the Mahatma's name in New Delhi.[4] Can the whole world be mistaken in attributing to Gandhi such greatness? The poor man dressed so simply, lived so simply, and he died at the hands of an assassin for what—for trying to bring about communal amity and peace in the country. If we ourselves were to question the greatness and the relevance of the Mahatma in contemporary times, this line of reasoning goes, how stupid that would be. The world these days is already ablaze with conflict, with so many wars and other hostilities around the globe. How can we even think of saying that Gandhi is not relevant anymore?

Such rhetorical questions do not, in my view, truly address the issue of the Mahatma's relevance. The proper questions to ask are (a) what was the *full content* of his message, views and teachings; and (b) *how much of that* continues to be relevant, if it was ever relevant?

No one can question Gandhi's teachings on the importance of non-violence or his message on communal amity and peace. As Naipaul wrote in *India: A Wounded Civilisation*, Gandhi was also one of the first Indians to raise the question of cleanliness and underline its importance, and this too was a hugely significant contribution from both an aesthetic and a public health perspective.

That being said, in the context of the Mahatma's continued relevance, we also need to ask the following questions.

How relevant was the Mahatma's sexual experimentation? What great truths emerged from this? Is it of continued relevance for ageing and young Indians? The brahmacharya message, it may be noted, was not the Mahatma's original contribution. This issues of the practice of brahmacharya and his recommended use of the enema are not raised in *Hind Swaraj*, but it deserves a mention here. The Mahatma emphasised the importance of the enema. Was this really so important?

There are also very many outlandish, bizarre and superstitious views expressed by the Mahatma in *Hind Swaraj*— the subject of this book—that are clearly *not* relevant and *should not* be relevant. These views need to be discarded.

But, the Mahatma's apologists will argue that all this is not important. What we need to consider, they will say, are Gandhi's contributions to the freedom of the country without any unnecessary bloodshed, and to the general cause of non-violent protest and civil disobedience in progressive movements across the world.

This argument is not fair. After all, we need to judge Gandhi *on his own terms*, and he did consider all his other, quite absurd ideas on factories, machinery, the dispensability of lawyers and doctors, the importance (or lack of importance) of English language literacy for Indians, of the rule of law, and so on to be extremely significant.

And it is on the basis of all these various ideas that Gandhi is no longer relevant. Yes, his contribution to the cause of Indian independence was undoubtedly huge, despite valid arguments that others such as Subhas Chandra Bose did not receive the recognition they deserved. Indian independence was a non-violent revolution for which Gandhi can be lauded, but he does have to take at least some of the blame (together with the Congress and the British) for the orgy of violence and bloodletting that followed Partition.

Several other summations and conclusions may be formed.

India, and indeed the world, misunderstood the true nature of the Mahatma's costume. Gandhi spoke and wrote excellent English; he was a qualified barrister, and he had acquired a reputation for himself as the spokesperson and representative of oppressed Indians in South Africa. These were not small achievements for an Indian at that time, and therefore when he donned the poor man's symbol, it was naturally assumed that he did so to symbolise his stance against British imperialism and simultaneously declare his own identification with the poorest of the poor in India.

There was much more to the costume—and it is that 'much more' that people the world over, including Indians, either chose to ignore or misunderstood. Gandhi had started to believe that all machinery was evil, that industry and factories were Satan's handiwork, that the railways were the instrument of the Devil. So when he donned that ancient homespun costume, he was not only identifying with the poorest of the poor; while the dress was an important symbolic and politically astute gesture against the British, it was equally a gesture against the manufacture of cloth in mills and factories. He railed not only against machinery and railways but also against doctors, lawyers, engineers, politicians, and so forth. We ignored these astounding but strongly held beliefs for two reasons: first, the Mahatma had all the *other* stupendous achievements; and secondly, we liked to imagine that he did not literally mean what he said and wrote, because we knew him to be a great believer in symbolism.

It was Gandhi's simple attire and campaign and his ideas of non-violent resistance against the British that won him his global reputation and the admiration of men like Einstein, who famously remarked: 'Generations to come, it may well be, will scarce believe that such a man as this one, ever in flesh and blood, walked upon this earth.'

As regards Gandhi's sartorial replacement of Western-style dress with the simple dhoti, one may observe that Gandhi was a man addicted to stylish Western attire for many years, as he himself noted in his autobiography.[5] When he first took his family with him to South Africa, he pondered how he should make them dress. After careful deliberation, he decided that the way the Parsis dressed was the most sophisticated.[6] It may have been his encounter in England with the simply attired writer Narayan Hemchandra that influenced him with respect to adopting the dhoti, though that decision was taken decades later. Hemchandra once came to Gandhi's house dressed in a shirt and dhoti. Gandhi's landlord announced that some 'madcap' had come to see him. Conscious of how Western people would react to the dhoti, Gandhi asked his friend if the children had not teased him. 'Well, they ran after me,' his friend replied, 'but I did not mind them, and they were quiet.'[7]

Hemchandra planned on going to the US. When Gandhi questioned him about how he would be able to afford it, he chided Gandhi on his extravagant ways and expensive dress, and explained that he had very limited requirements.

Puritan-minded Gandhi had his own eccentricities, but approved of and adopted the markedly off-centre and odd views of some of his contemporaries. For instance, he remarks approvingly of Tolstoy's views on tobacco. 'Tobacco, he [Tolstoy] argued, was the worst of all intoxicants, inasmuch as a man addicted to it was tempted to commit crimes which a drunkard never dared to do; liquor made a man mad, but tobacco clouded his intellect, and made him build castles in the air.'[8]

Now, tobacco is certainly a scourge as far as health is concerned, and more so than alcohol, but few would hold today that its chief demerit lies in the fact that men under its influence start to commit crimes or build castles in the air. At the age of twelve, Gandhi himself smoked cigarettes with a young relative, first by picking up stubs and then after stealing money from elders to buy the same[9]. So it wasn't that he didn't know what tobacco was all about.

He even allows Tolstoy's views to affect his perception of the Eiffel Tower. In his younger days, Gandhi loved the architecture of churches in Paris, but one cannot help suspecting that the fact that they were religious monuments contributed to his perception of their beauty. He agrees with Tolstoy that the Eiffel Tower was possibly the creation of a man under the influence of tobacco. 'I do not know what purpose it serves today,' he wrote, denying that it is in any way artistic.[10] Had there been a Holy Cross mounted at the very top of that tower, there is a chance that Gandhi might have changed his mind.

One can safely assume that even Einstein, who greatly admired Gandhi, would have been shocked by the Mahatma's views on science and his obsession with religious myths and legends. The physicist himself was rather dismissive of both Christianity and Judaism, as revealed in a letter sold at an auction in 2008.[11] In this letter, written as a response to the philosopher

Eric Gutkind, he stated how 'the word God is for me nothing more than the expression and product of human weaknesses, the Bible a collection of honourable, but still primitive legends which are nevertheless pretty childish'.[12]

* * *

Although Gandhi swore by the assertions made in *Hind Swaraj* many years after it was written, his life throughout was one of inconsistency, in terms of his attitude towards caste, the English language, the use of trains, the donations the Congress received from men who owned factories and towards much else.

Apart from going on a fast every time the Congress or the people did not listen to him, Gandhi was also dictatorial within his own family. It is easier to adjust to a dictator who is at least consistent, but Gandhi changed his mind over the years and expected others to follow suit. In his younger days, he insisted that everybody in the family learn to eat with forks and knives, but later, when his infatuation with these affectations wore away, he asked them all to give up the practice as part of the unnecessary 'tinsel of civilisation'.[13]

Many admirers of Gandhi are of the view that he cannot be accused of nepotism. Not only did he not favour his children, he practically disfavoured them. This may be true in a sense, but the nepotism charge cannot be entirely dismissed, for while he did not favour his children, he did help out his nephews. So— extended nepotism? The irony is that the Gandhi name remained a dynastic symbol for decades after the Mahatma's death, although this was because of a fortuitous marriage between Nehru's daughter Indira and a man named Feroze Gandhi.[14]

The conflicts that Gandhi had with his alcoholic son Harilal are well known. A much-acclaimed play directed by

Feroz Khan, titled *Mahatma vs Gandhi*, and a film by the same director, *Gandhi, My Father* (2007), further explore this theme.[15]

To the world he might have seemed a kindly old soul who wouldn't harm anyone, but this was far from the truth. He meted out harsh punishments for minor transgressions. He used to bathe with a stone instead of soap (this may have been because most soap is manufactured in factories). During the pre-Partition riots in Noakhali, his niece accidentally left that stone at a weaver's house. He sent her back at once for it. Fearful for her safety, for it was night-time and there was no telling what might happen, she asked if someone could accompany her. The Mahatma refused. She records her fearful tale of fetching the stone. It would appear that such punishments were routine with Gandhi.[16] In Johannesburg, his son Manilal once left a pair of glasses behind. No forgiveness. Poor Manilal was made to walk 32 kilometres to get them back.[17]

Not only did Gandhi try to rule his family with an iron hand, he even allowed his close friends to join in the supervision. Arun Gandhi wrote how his father Manilal Gandhi, who was tasked by the Mahatma to edit *Indian Opinion*, was often assailed from all sides.

> He was not allowed to flourish. He had too many fathers and mothers. And if he wrote something in *Indian Opinion*, Bapuji would criticise him and Kallenbach would criticise him and everybody would criticise him and nobody would appreciate what he was doing. So with all these—Miss Schelesin, Hannaben and Kallenbach and Bapuji, and everybody sitting and judging him, he felt oppressed by it.[18]

The Mahatma the world knows is possibly vastly different from the man he really was.

AFTERWORD

In my critique of Gandhi's *Hind Swaraj*, I have tried to shed light on the gaps in the Mahatma's vision for his country and his overall world view. It has been my endeavour to connect Gandhi's writing to lesser-known facets of the man himself, and to do so in a manner that has not been attempted before. In the course of writing this book, I have examined one of Gandhi's most seminal works, exposing its flaws, together with numerous contradictions and misogyny evident in the manifesto page after page. While the great man's powerful teachings on non-violence resonate with everyone across the world to this day, he also held and expressed unequivocally a host of other unsavoury and extraordinary views, such as his fierce opposition to vaccines, which he considered to be barbaric. Some of those views, which this book scrutinizes closely, are akin to those espoused by the Taliban.

In respect of Gandhi, hagiographies from Indian and Western historians are all too common. Moving away from such attempts, I believe that this book has offered up an impartial critique of Gandhi's manifesto against Western, industrial civilisation, in which the Mahatma expressed occasionally super-rational, but more often than not bizarre and outlandish views on democracy, industrialisation, machinery, railways, education, caste, lawyers, doctors and modern medicine. It is my hope that a sharp and unforgettable psychological profile of the Mahatma emerges for the reader after reading this book.

ENDNOTES

Preface

1. Author's note: The most authoritative source for Gandhi's original English translation of *Hind Swaraj* is currently to be found in Anthony J. Parel's edited version of *'Hind Swaraj' and Other Writings*, published by Cambridge University Press in 2018. I have used the centenary edition of this volume as my primary reference source to what Gandhi wrote. One of the many useful things in Parel's book from my point of view is that Gandhi's text starts on page 1; for the previous seventy or so pages that comprise the editor's introduction and other preliminary material, Roman numerals are used.

2. The authors of the three reviews cited were Sudhir Mishra, Ankit Singh and Mayank Chaudhury.

3. The reviewer's name is Nitin Arora.

4. Stefan Simanowitz, 'New Cash for Honours Revelations Should Speed Reform of House of Lords', *New Statesman*, 24 November 2014, https://tinyurl.com/tsj8tp35.

5. Jad Adams, 'Thrill of the Chaste: The Truth About Gandhi's Sex Life', *The Independent*, 7 April 2010.

6. Srikant Prasoon, ed., *My Letters: M.K. Gandhi* (Cedar Books, 2013), 177.

7. Gandhi, *Hind Swaraj and Other Writings*, ed. Anthony J. Parel, (Cambridge University Press Centenary Edition, 2018), 6.

8. Ramachandra Guha, *Gandhi before India* (Penguin Books, 2014), 366.

9. Jad Adams, 'Thrill of the Chaste: The Truth About Gandhi's Sex Life', *The Independent*, 7 April 2010.

10. Ramachandra Guha, *Gandhi before India* (Penguin Books, 2014), 362.

11. B.R. Ambedkar, *What Congress and Gandhi Have Done to the Untouchables* (New Delhi: Kalpaz Publications, 2017).

12. Srikant Prasoon, ed. *My Letters: M.K. Gandhi* (Cedar Books, 2013), 71.

13. Suresh Sharma and Tripud Suhrud, *M. K. Gandhi's Hind Swaraj* (Orient Blackswan, 2010).

14. Ibid.

15. Ibid., 19.

16. Winston S. Churchill, *India: Speeches and an Introduction* (London: Thornton Butterworth Ltd, 1931), 75.

17. Louis Fischer, *The Life of Mahatma Gandhi* (Jonathan Cape, 1951), 37.

18. M.J. Akbar, *Nehru: The Making of India* (New Delhi: Roli Books, 2002), 34.

19. Louis Fischer, *The Life of Mahatma Gandhi* (Jonathan Cape, 1951), 460.

20. M.K. Gandhi, 'A Word of Explanation', *Young India*, January 1921, Bombay Sarvodaya Mandal and Gandhi Research Foundation, 8 November 2024, https://tinyurl.com/bp8v6suv.

21. Gandhi, *Hind Swaraj and Other Writings*, ed. Anthony J. Parel (Cambridge University Press Centenary Edition, 2018), 5.

22. Ibid., 6.

23. Ibid., 8.

24. Ramachandra Guha, *Gandhi Before India* (Penguin Books, 2014), 366.

25. Gandhi, *Hind Swaraj and Other Writings*, ed. Anthony J. Parel (Cambridge University Press Centenary Edition, 2018), 39.

Chronology

1. Louis Fischer, *The Life of Mahatma Gandhi* (Jonathan Cape, 1951).

2. Jad Adams, 'Thrill of the Chaste: The Truth About Gandhi's Sex Life', *The Independent*, 7 April 2010.

3. Ibid.

4. Ibid.

5. Louis Fischer, *The Life of Mahatma Gandhi* (Jonathan Cape, 1951).

6. Ibid.

7. Gary Beene, *The Seeds We Sow: Kindness That Fed a Hungry World* (Sunstone Press, 2010), 272.

8. Louis Fischer, *The Life of Mahatma Gandhi* (Jonathan Cape, 1951).

9. Jad Adams, 'Thrill of the Chaste: The Truth About Gandhi's Sex Life', *The Independent*, 7 April 2010.

10. Suresh Sharma and Tripud Suhrud, *M. K. Gandhi's Hind Swaraj* (Orient Blackswan, 2010), 35.

11. Ibid., ix.

Chapter 1: Gandhi on the British Parliament

1. Gandhi, *Hind Swaraj and Other Writings*, ed. Anthony J. Parel (Cambridge University Press Centenary Edition, 2018), p. 11.

2. Ibid., 6.

3. Ibid., 29.

4. Ibid., 30.

5. Ibid., 31.

6. Ibid.

7. Ibid.

8. Sunil Khilnani, *The Idea of India* (Penguin India, 1997), 27.

9. Tapati Dasgupta, *Social Thought of Rabindranath Tagore: A Historical Analysis* (Abhinav Publications, 1993), 188.

10. Sandip Rai, 'Nehru Got Netaji Executed: Swamy', *The Times of India*, 23 January 2015, https://tinyurl.com/mme5jn9s. Accessed on 2 November 2024.

11. Marshall J. Getz, *Subhas Chandra Bose: A Biography* (Jefferson: MacFarland and Company, 2002).

12. Sunil Khilnani, *The Idea of India* (Penguin India, 1997), 27.

13. Louis Fischer, *The Life of Mahatma Gandhi* (Jonathan Cape Ltd, 1951), 472.

14. M. Brecher, *Nehru: A Political Biography* (Oxford University Press, 1959), 65.

15. Rajmohan Gandhi, *Patel: A Life* (Navjivan Publishing House, 1990), 370.

16. Maulana Abul Kalam Azad, *India Wins Freedom* (Orient Blackswan, 1988), 162.

17. Ibid. 377.

18. Ibid. 371.

19. Winston S. Churchill, 'Parliament Bill', House of Commons, 11 November 1947, https://tinyurl.com/yc8x69ct. Accessed on 2 December 2024.

20. Gandhi, *Hind Swaraj and Other Writings*, ed. Anthony J. Parel (Cambridge University Press Centenary Edition, 2018), 31–32.

21. Ibid., 32.

22. Ibid.

23. Ibid.

24. Rabindranath Tagore, *Gitanajali,* 'Introduction by W.B. Yeats' (Simon & Schuster, 1997).

25. Gandhi, *Hind Swaraj and Other Writings,* ed. Anthony J. Parel (Cambridge University Press Centenary Edition, 2018), 16–17.

Chapter 2: Gandhi on Civilisation

1. *Gandhi, Hind Swaraj and other Writings,* ed. Anthony J. Parel (Cambridge University Press Centenary Edition, 2018).

2. Ibid., 7.

3. Ibid.

4. Ibid., 79.

5. Ibid., 37.

6. Ibid., 35.

7. Ibid., 35–36.

8. Ibid.

9. Ibid., 36.

10. Jad Adams, *Gandhi: Naked Ambition* (Quercus Publications, 2011).

11. Mahatma Gandhi, *My Experiments with Truth: An Autobiography* (Jaico Publishing, 2008), 268.

12. Ibid., 269.

13. Ibid.

14. Hanne Nabintu Herland, *How the West Lost Its Greatness and Was Weakened from Within* (Christian Publishing House, 2017).

15. 'Understand That Norwegian Men Want Thai Wives', Dagbladet, 15 November 2016, https://tinyurl.com/mrycuwaa. Accessed on 2 December 2024.

16. Gandhi, *Hind Swaraj and Other Writings,* ed. Anthony J. Parel (Cambridge University Press Centenary Edition, 2018), 36.

17. Manubehn Gandhi, *Bapu: My Mother* (Navjivan Publishing House, 1947), 7.

18. Gandhi, *Hind Swaraj and other Writings*, ed. Anthony J. Parel (Cambridge University Press Centenary Edition, 2018), 15.

19. Dadabhai Naoroji, *Poverty and Un-British Rule in India*, Nabu Press, 2013.

20. Gandhi, *Hind Swaraj and Other Writings*, ed. Anthony J. Parel (Cambridge University Press Centenary Edition, 2018), Chapter 9.

21. Ibid., 45.

22. Ibid., 46.

23. Stuart Hilton, *The Grand Experiment: The Birth of the Railway Age* (Ian Allan Publishing, 2007).

24. Aruna Awasthi, *History and Development of Railways in India* (Deep and Deep Publications, 1994).

25. Gandhi, *Hind Swaraj and Other Writings*, ed. Anthony J. Parel (Cambridge University Press Centenary Edition, 2018), p. 46.

26. Ibid.

27. Ibid.

28. Ibid., 48.

29. Ibid., 46.

30. Ibid.

31. Ibid.

32. Ibid.

33. Salman Rushdie, 'Magic in Service of Truth', *New York Times*, 21 April 2014.

34. Robert Persig, *Zen and the Art of Motorcycle Maintenance: An Inquiry into Values* (India: Vintage, 2014).

35. Shankaranand Shastri, *My Memories and Experiences of Babasaheb Dr. Ambedkar* (New Delhi: Samyak Prakashan, 2021), 91.

36. Louis Fischer, *The Life of Mahatma Gandhi* (Jonathan Cape, 1951), 461.

37. Ibid., 466.

38. Gandhi, *Hind Swaraj and Other Writings*, ed. Anthony J. Parel, (Cambridge University Press Centenary Edition, 2018), 49.

39. Ibid.

40. Ibid.; expression used by Gandhi.

41. Although Chapter 10 of *Hind Swaraj* is mostly on Hindu–Muslim relations, he makes this comment on all forms of transport in this chapter.

42. Gandhi, *Hind Swaraj and Other Writings*, ed. Anthony J. Parel (Cambridge University Press Centenary Edition, 2018), 49.

43. Ibid.

44. Mahatma Gandhi, *My Experiments with Truth: An Autobiography* (Jaico Publishing, 2008), 45.

45. Gandhi, *Hind Swaraj and Other Writings*, ed. Anthony J. Parel (Cambridge University Press Centenary Edition, 2018), 43.

46. Ibid.

47. Ibid., 108.

48. Ibid., 68.

49. Ibid.

50. Ibid., 64.

Chapter 3: Gandhi on Hindu–Muslim Relations

1. John J. Mearsheimer, *Why Leaders Lie: The Truth about Lying in International Politics* (New York: Oxford University Press, 2011), 54.

2. In his book *Why Leaders Lie*, Prof. John Mearsheimer provides as an example the strategic lie during the Cuban missile crisis when President Kennedy had a deal with the Soviets to withdraw missiles from Turkey in exchange for the Russians withdrawing missiles from Cuba. To his domestic audience, Kennedy continued to deny that there had been any such deal. Ibid., 82.

3. Gandhi, *Hind Swaraj and Other Writings,* ed. Anthony J. Parel, (Cambridge University Press Centenary Edition, 2018), p. 51.

4. Ibid.

5. B.R. Ambedkar, 'Chapter II: A Nation Calling for a Home' and 'Chapter XII: National Frustration', in *Pakistan, or the Partition of India* (New Delhi: Samyak Prakashan, 2013).

6. Some readers may feel that I should have quoted from communal speeches given by Hindu leaders as well. These undoubtedly exist, but the purpose of this quote is to reveal some fears within the Muslim community, not to argue that the Hindus were better.

7. B.R. Ambedkar, 'Chapter X: Social Stagnation' in *Pakistan, or the Partition of India* (New Delhi: Samyak Prakashan, 2013).

8. Timur Kuran and Anantdeep Singh, Economic Modernization in Late British India, *Chicago Journal,* 2013.

9. Nathuram Godse, *Why I Assassinated Gandhi* (Foresight Publishers and Distributors, 2014), 55.

10. Gandhi, *Hind Swaraj and Other Writings,* ed. Anthony J. Parel (Cambridge University Press Centenary Edition, 2018), 54.

11. Sunil Khilnani, *The Idea of India* (Penguin India, 1997), 164.

12. Ibid., 165.

13. Ibid.; quoted by Khilnani; original source not identified.

14. Cited in B. R. Ambedkar, 'Chapter II: A Nation Calling for a Home', in *Pakistan, or the Partition of India* (New Delhi: Samyak Prakashan, 2013).

15. Ibid.

16. Gandhi, *Hind Swaraj and Other Writings,* ed. Anthony J. Parel (Cambridge University Press Centenary Edition, 2018), 55.

17. Nirad C. Chaudhuri, *The Autobiography of an Unknown Indian* (London: Macmillan and Company, 1951), 61.

18. B.R. Ambedkar, 'Chapter II: A Nation Calling for a Home', in *Pakistan, or the Partition of India* (New Delhi: Samyak Prakashan, 2013).

19. Ibid.

20. Ibid.

21. Ibid.

22. Ibid.

23. Ibid., Chapter VI, 'Pakistan and Communal Peace'.

24. Ibid.

25. Ibid.

26. Ibid.

27. Ibid.

Chapter 4: Gandhi on Lawyers and Lawyering

1. Debbie Vogel, '"Kill the Lawyers" – A Line Misinterpreted', *New York Times*, 17 June 1990.

2. Gandhi, *Hind Swaraj and Other Writings,* ed. Anthony J. Parel, (Cambridge University Press Centenary Edition, 2018), p. 59.

3. Ibid., 56.

4. Manubehn Gandhi, *Bapu: My Mother*, Navjivan Publishing House, 1947, p. 12.

5. Gandhi, *Hind Swaraj and Other Writings,* ed. Anthony J. Parel, (Cambridge University Press Centenary Edition, 2018), 57.

6. Ibid., 56–57.

7. Ibid., 56.

8. Sukla Das, *Crime and Punishment in Ancient India*, Abhinav Publications, 1990, p. 104.

9. Ibid.

10. Gandhi, *Hind Swaraj and Other Writings,* ed. Anthony J. Parel, (Cambridge University Press Centenary Edition, 2018), 57.

11. Ibid.

12. Barry Bearak, 'In India the Wheels of Justice Hardly Move', *New York Times*, 1 June 2000.

13. Gandhi, *Hind Swaraj and Other Writings*, ed. Anthony J. Parel, (Cambridge University Press Centenary Edition, 2018), 59.

14. Ibid.

15. Ibid.

16. Ibid.

17. Ibid.

18. Ibid.

19. Ibid.

20. Ibid., 67.

21. Louis Fischer, *The Life of Mahatma Gandhi* (Jonathan Cape, 1951).

22. Peter Conn, *Pearl S. Buck: A Cultural Biography* (Cambridge University Press, 1998).

23. Mahatma Gandhi, *My Experiments with Truth: An Autobiography* (Jaico Publishing, 2008), 58.

24. Ibid.

25. Ibid., 59.

26. Ibid., 60.

27. Yogesh Chadha, *Gandhi: A Life* (John Wiley and Sons, 1998), 37.

28. Louis Fischer, *The Life of Mahatma Gandhi* (Jonathan Cape Ltd, 1951), 162.

29. Yogesh Chadha, *Gandhi: A Life* (John Wiley and Sons, 1998), 47.

30. Ramachandra Guha, *Gandhi before India* (Penguin Books, 2014), 91.

31. Report from the *Natal Mercury*, cited in Burnett Britton, *Gandhi Arrives in South Africa* (Greenleaf Books, 2000), notes section, p. xviii.

32. Ramachandra Guha, *Gandhi before India* (Penguin Books, 2014), 91.

Chapter 5: Gandhi on the Medical Profession

1. Jad Adams, 'Thrill of the Chaste: The Truth about Gandhi's Sex Life', *The Independent*, 7 April 2010.

2. Ibid.

3. Mahatma Gandhi, *My Experiments with Truth: An Autobiography* (Jaico Publishing, 2008), 195.

4. Louis Fischer, *The Life of Mahatma Gandhi* (Jonathan Cape Ltd, 1951)., 81.

5. 'All Life Is One', Bombay Sarvodaya Mandal and Gandhi Research Foundation, https://tinyurl.com/2s4aph2d. Accessed on 2 December 2024.

6. Mahatma Gandhi, *My Experiments with Truth: An Autobiography* (Jaico Publishing, 2008), 35.

7. Gandhi, 'Chapter XX: Conclusion' in *Hind Swaraj and Other Writings*, ed. Anthony J. Parel (Cambridge University Press Centenary Edition, 2018).

8. Ibid., 60.

9. Ibid., 61.

10. Ibid.

11. Ibid., 147.

12. Ibid., 61.

13. Thomas Pakenham, *The Boer War* (New York: Random House, 1979).

14. Gary Beene, *The Seeds We Sow: Kindness That Fed a Hungry World* (Sunstone Press, 2010), 271.

15. Ibid.

16. Mahatma Gandhi, *My Experiments with Truth: An Autobiography* (Jaico Publishing, 2008), 167.

17. 'The Truth About Gandhi', *Harvard Crimson*, 7 March, 1983, quoting Richard Grenier in 'The Gandhi Nobody Knows', *Commentary*, 3 January 1983.

18. Robert Bud, *Penicillin: Triumph and Tragedy* (Oxford University Press, 2009).

19. Yogesh Chadha, *Gandhi: A Life* (John Wiley and Sons, 1998), 40.

20. Ibid.

21. Eleanor Morton, *The Women in Gandhi's Life* (New York: Dodd, Mead & Co., 1953), 78.

22. Manubehn Gandhi, *Bapu: My Mother* (Navjivan Publishing House, 1947), 4.

23. Ibid., 40–41.

24. Yogesh Chadha, *Gandhi: A Life* (John Wiley and Sons, 1998), 71.

25. Ibid.

26. Uma Dhupelia-Mesthrie, 'Writing the life of Manilal Mohandas Gandhi', *Journal of Natal and Zulu History*, 24–25 (2006–2007): 193.

27. Louis Fischer, *The Life of Mahatma Gandhi* (HarperCollins Publishers, 2012), 455.

28. Gandhi, *Hind Swaraj and Other Writings*, ed. Anthony J. Parel (Cambridge University Press Centenary Edition, 2018), 63.

29. Jad Adams, 'Thrill of the Chaste: The Truth About Gandhi's Sex Life', *The Independent*, 7 April 2010.

Chapter 6: Gandhi on Machinery

1. Gandhi, 'Chapter XIX: Machinery' in *Hind Swaraj and Other Writings*, ed. Anthony J. Parel (Cambridge University Press Centenary Edition, 2018).

2. Ibid., 106.

3. Ibid.

4. M.M. Juneja, *The Mahatma and the Millionaire: A Study in Gandhi-Birla Relations* (Hissar: Modern Publishers, 1993), 223.

5. Ibid., 230.

6. Ibid., 231.

7. Ibid.

8. Gandhi, *Hind Swaraj and Other Writings,* ed. Anthony J. Parel (Cambridge University Press Centenary Edition, 2018), 108.

9. Ibid., 107–08.

10. William Dugger and Howard J. Sherman, *Reclaiming Evolution* (Routledge, 2000), 37.

11. Gandhi, *Hind Swaraj and Other Writings,* ed. Anthony J. Parel (Cambridge University Press Centenary Edition, 2018), 107–08.

12. Ibid., 108.

13. Ibid., 109.

14. Ibid.

15. Srikant Prasoon, ed., *My Letters: M.K. Gandhi* (Cedar Books, 2013), p. 71.

16. Manubehn Gandhi, *Bapu: My Mother* (Navjivan Publishing House, 1947), 20.

17. Gandhi, *Hind Swaraj and Other Writings,* ed. Anthony J. Parel (Cambridge University Press Centenary Edition, 2018), 66.

18. Snehai Rebello, 'Big Claims on Ancient Aviation, Surgery at ISC', *Hindustan Times,* 5 January 2015, https://tinyurl.com/b57te3rj. Accessed on 2 December 2024.

19. Sumeet Kaul, 'What's Science Got to Do With It', *The Times of India,* 9 January 2019.

20. Gandhi, *Hind Swaraj and Other Writings,* ed. Anthony J. Parel (Cambridge University Press Centenary Edition, 2018), 66.

21. Ramachandra Guha, *Gandhi before India* (Penguin Books, 2014), 37.

22. Ibid.

23. Ibid.

24. V.S. Naipaul, *An Area of Darkness* (Pan Macmillan, 2010), 62.

25. Ramachandra Guha, *Gandhi before India* (Penguin Books, 2014), 37.

26. Gandhi, *Hind Swaraj and Other Writings*, ed. Anthony J. Parel, (Cambridge University Press Centenary Edition, 2018), 66.

27. Ibid., 66–67.

28. *What Congress and Gandhi Have Done to the Untouchables* (New Delhi: Kalpaz Publications, 2017).

29. Gandhi, 'Chapter XX: Conclusion' in *Hind Swaraj and Other Writings*, ed. Anthony J. Parel, (Cambridge University Press Centenary Edition, 2018).

30. 1904–05 Tata Central Archives, File No.108, TISCO, 1904–16; cited in David Lockwood, *The Indian Bourgeoisie: A Political History of the Indian Capitalist Class* (I.B. Tauris, 2012).

31. Louis Fischer, *The Life of Mahatma Gandhi* (Jonathan Cape Ltd, 1951), 466.

32. Ibid., 472.

Chapter 7: Gandhi On Education

1. Gandhi, *Hind Swaraj and Other Writings*, ed. Anthony J. Parel (Cambridge University Press Centenary Edition, 2018), 99.

2. Ibid.

3. It is another matter that Western society sometimes tilts to the other extreme.

4. Gandhi, *Hind Swaraj and Other Writings*, ed. Anthony J. Parel (Cambridge University Press Centenary Edition, 2018), 99.

5. Ibid.

6. Ibid.

7. Manubehn Gandhi, *Bapu: My Mother* (Navjivan Publishing House, 1947), 10.

8. Gandhi, *Hind Swaraj and Other Writings*, ed. Anthony J. Parel (Cambridge University Press Centenary Edition, 2018), 100.

9. Ibid.

10. Ibid., 101.

11. Ibid., 102.

12. Ibid.

13. Ibid., 102–03.

14. Mahatma Gandhi, *My Experiments with Truth: An Autobiography* (Jaico Publishing, 2008), 121–22.

15. Ibid., 64.

16. Ibid., 65.

17. Gandhi, *Hind Swaraj and Other Writings*, ed. Anthony J. Parel (Cambridge University Press Centenary Edition, 2018), 103.

18. Ibid.

19. Ibid.

20. Gandhi's assassin, Godse, writes in his statement as to why he killed Gandhi: 'in his desire to please the Muslims, he insisted that Hindustani alone should be the national language of India'. See Nathuram Godse, *Why I Assassinated Gandhi* (Foresight Publishers and Distributors, 2014), 71.

21. Gandhi, *Hind Swaraj and Other Writings*, ed. Anthony J. Parel (Cambridge University Press Centenary Edition, 2018), 103.

22. Ibid.

23. Manubehn Gandhi, *Bapu: My Mother* (Navjivan Publishing House, 1947), 11.

24. Ibid.

25. Ramachandra Guha, *Gandhi before India* (Penguin Books, 2014), 34.

26. Ibid.

27. Ibid.

28. Ibid., 30.

29. Ibid.

30. Mahatma Gandhi, *My Experiments with Truth: An Autobiography* (Jaico Publishing, 2008), 39.

31. Ibid., 159.

32. Ibid.

33. Gandhi, *Hind Swaraj and Other Writings*, ed. Anthony J. Parel (Cambridge University Press Centenary Edition, 2018), 104.

34. Ibid.

Chapter 8: Gandhi on Ahimsa

1. Alex von Tunzelmann, *Indian Summer: The Secret History of the End of an Empire*, Simon & Schuster, 2007, 28.

2. Gandhi M.K., 'Letter to Mr.—', 25 January 1920, in *The Collected Works of Mahatma Gandhi*, 19, 350.

3. Gandhi, *Hind Swaraj and Other Writings*, ed. Anthony J. Parel (Cambridge University Press Centenary Edition, 2018), 139.

4. Ibid., 78.

5. Ibid., 80.

6. Ibid.

7. Ibid.

8. Ibid.

9. Ibid., 81.

10. Ibid.

11. Alex von Tunzelmann, *Indian Summer: The Secret History of the End of an Empire* (Simon & Schuster, 2007), 56.

12. Gandhi, *Hind Swaraj and Other Writings*, ed. Anthony J. Parel (Cambridge University Press Centenary Edition, 2018), 82.

13. Ibid., 82–83.

14. Ibid., 86.

15. Ibid., 87.

16. Ibid.

17. Ibid., 93.

18. Ibid., 87.

19. Louis Fischer, *The Life of Mahatma Gandhi* (Jonathan Cape Ltd, 1951), 405.

20. Ibid.

21. Alex von Tunzelmann, *Indian Summer: The Secret History of the End of an Empire* (Simon & Schuster, 2007), 49.

22. Nigel Collett, *The Butcher of Amritsar: General Reginald Dyer* (London and New York: Hambledon Continuum, 2005), 101.

23. Patrick French, *Liberty or Death: India's Journey to Independence and Division* (London: Flamingo, 1998), 20.

24. S.R. Singh, 'Gandhi and the Jallianwala Bagh Tragedy: A Turning Point in the Indian Nationalist Movement', in V. N. Datta and S. Settar, eds, *Jallianwalan Bagh Massacre* (Delhi: Pragati Publications, 2000), 196–199.

25. Alex von Tunzelmann, *Indian Summer: The Secret History of the End of an Empire* (Simon & Schuster, 2007), 26; Louis Fischer, *The Life of Mahatma Gandhi* (Jonathan Cape, 1951), 67; Erik H. Erikson, *Gandhi's Truth: On the Origins of Militant Non-Violence* (London: Faber and Faber Limited, 1970), 179.

26. Ramachandra Guha, *Gandhi before India* (Penguin Books, 2014), 123.

27. Gandhi, *Hind Swaraj and Other Writings*, ed. Anthony J. Parel (Cambridge University Press Centenary Edition, 2018), 91–92.

28. Ibid., p. 92.

29. Portia's famous speech in *The Merchant of Venice* (Act IV, Scene 1) by William Shakespeare.

30. Alex von Tunzelmann, *Indian Summer: The Secret History of the End of an Empire* (Simon & Schuster, 2007), 23.

31. Arun Gandhi, *Daughter of Midnight: The Child Bride of Gandhi* (Blake Publishing Limited, 1996), 212.

32. Gandhi, *Hind Swaraj and Other Writings*, ed. Anthony J. Parel (Cambridge University Press Centenary Edition, 2018), 89.

33. Ibid., 89–90.

34. Ibid., 90.

35. Ibid., 95.

36. Ibid., 97.

37. Ibid., 95.

38. Ibid.

Chapter 9: The Saint's Commandments

1. Dennis Dalton, *Mahatma Gandhi: Nonviolent Power in Action* (New York: Columbia University Press, 1991), 154.

2. Gandhi, *Hind Swaraj and Other Writings,* ed. Anthony J. Parel, (Cambridge University Press Centenary Edition, 2018), 111.

3. Ibid.

4. Ibid., 114.

5. Ibid.

6. Ibid.

7. Richard Grenier, 'The Gandhi Nobody Knows', *Commentary,* March 1983.

8. Gandhi, *Hind Swaraj and Other Writings,* ed. Anthony J. Parel, (Cambridge University Press Centenary Edition, 2018), 114.

9. Ibid.

10. Ibid., 115.

11. Ibid.

12. Ibid.

13. Mahatma Gandhi, *A Guide to Health* (Prabhat Prakashan, 2016), 106.

14. Ibid., 107.

15. Ibid., 113.

16. Ibid., 108.

17. Ibid., 113.

18. Ibid., 146.

19. Ibid., 147.

20. Gandhi, *Hind Swaraj and Other Writings*, ed. Anthony J. Parel (Cambridge University Press Centenary Edition, 2018), 115.

21. Rabindranath Tagore, *Gitanjali: A Collection of Poems* (Simon & Schuster, 1992).

22. Gandhi, *Hind Swaraj and Other Writings*, ed. Anthony J. Parel (Cambridge University Press Centenary Edition, 2018), 115.

23. Ibid.

24. Ibid., 115.

25. Ibid., 116.

26. Ibid.

27. Ibid.

28. Ibid.

29. Ibid.

30. Gary Beene, *The Seeds We Sow: Kindness That Fed a Hungry World* (Sunstone Press, 2010), 271–72.

31. Ibid.

32. Ibid.

33. Ibid.

34. Ibid.

35. B.R. Ambedkar, 'Chapter XI: Gandhism: The Doom of the Untouchables' in *What Congress and Gandhi Have Done to the Untouchables* (New Delhi: Kalpaz Publications, 2017).

36. Ibid.

37. BBC News India, 'Bhimrao Ambedkar's Iconic Interview from 1955 | Archives', *YouTube*, 17 March 2023, https://tinyurl.com/4k7pwb2m. Accessed on 5 November 2024.

38. *What Congress and Gandhi Have Done to the Untouchables* (New Delhi: Kalpaz Publications, 2017).

39. Ibid.

40. Ibid.

Chapter 10: In Conclusion

1. Gandhi quoted in Vinay Lal, 'Nakedness, Non-violence and Brahmcharya', *Journal of the History of Sexuality*, 2000.

2. A. Subramani, 'Madras HC dismisses PIL on Godse Memorial in Chennai', *The Times of India*, 27 January 2015.

3. 'Father of Nation Title to Gandhi Was Unwarranted', *The Financial Express*, 11 February 2014.

4. Barack Obama, who visited in 2015, took care to visit Gandhi's samadhi.

5. Mahatma Gandhi, *My Experiments with Truth: An Autobiography* (Jaico Publishing, 2008), 50.

6. Ibid., 94.

7. Ibid., 73.

8. Ibid., 75.

9. Louis Fischer, *The Life of Mahatma Gandhi* (Jonathan Cape Ltd, 1951), 27.

10. Mahatma Gandhi, *My Experiments with Truth: An Autobiography* (Jaico Publishing, 2008), 75.

11. 'Childish Superstition: Einstein's Letter Makes View of Religion Relatively Clear', *The Guardian*, 13 May 2008.

12. Ibid.

13. Mahatma Gandhi, *My Experiments with Truth: An Autobiography* (Jaico Publishing, 2008), 189.

14. Jad Adams and Phillip Whitehead, *The Dynasty: The Nehru-Gandhi Story* (London: Penguin Books and BBC Books, 1997), 14.

15. Uma Dhupelia-Mesthrie, 'Writing the Life of Manilal Mohandas Gandhi', *Journal of Natal and Zulu History*, 24–25 (2006–07), 190.

16. Manubehn Gandhi, *Bapu: My Mother* (Navjivan Publishing House, 1947), 33.

17. Uma Dhupelia-Mesthrie, 'Writing the Life of Manilal Mohandas Gandhi', *Journal of Natal and Zulu History*, 24–25 (2006–07), 194.

18. Letter to Uma Mesthrie from Arun Gandhi, dated 29 February 1980; cited by Uma Dhupelia-Mesthrie in 'Writing the Life of Manilal Mohandas Gandhi', *Journal of Natal and Zulu History*, 24–25 (2006–07), 206.

BIBLIOGRAPHY

Adams, Jad, and Phillip Whitehead. *The Dynasty: The Nehru-Gandhi Story*. London: Penguin Books and BBC Books, 1997.

Akbar, M.J. *Nehru: The Making of India*. New Delhi: Roli Books, 2002.

Ambedkar, B.R. *Pakistan, or the Partition of India*. New Delhi: Samyak Prakashan, 2013.

———, *What Congress and Gandhi Have Done to the Untouchables*. New Delhi: Kalpaz Publications, 2017.

Awasthi, Aruna. *History and Development of Railways in India*. New Delhi, India: Deep and Deep Publications, 1994.

Azad, Maulana Abul Kalam. *India Wins Freedom*. Hyderabad: Orient Blackswan, 1988.

Beene, Gary. *The Seeds We Sow: Kindness That Fed a Hungry World*. USA: Sunstone Press, 2010.

Brecher, Michael. *Nehru: A Political Biography*. New Delhi, India: Oxford University Press, 1959.

Britton, Burnett. *Gandhi Arrives in South Africa*. Texas, USA: Greenleaf Books, 2000.

Bud, Robert. *Penicillin: Triumph and Tragedy*. Oxford, UK: Oxford University Press, 2009.

Chadha, Yogesh. *Gandhi: A Life*. USA: John Wiley and Sons, 1998.

Chaudhuri, Nirad C. *The Autobiography of an Unknown Indian.* London: Macmillan and Company, 1951.

Churchill, Winston S. *India: Speeches and an Introduction.* London: Thornton Butterworth Ltd, 1931.

Collett, Nigel. *The Butcher of Amritsar: General Reginald Dyer.* London and New York: Hambledon Continuum, 2005.

Conn, Peter J. *Pearl S. Buck: A Cultural Biography.* UK: Cambridge University Press, 1998.

Dalton, Dennis. *Mahatma Gandhi: Nonviolent Power in Action.* New York: Columbia University Press, 1991.

Das, Sukla. *Crime and Punishment in Ancient India.* New Delhi, India: Abhinav Publications, 1990.

Dasgupta, Tapati. *Social Thought of Rabindranath Tagore: A Historical Analysis.* New Delhi, India: Abhinav Publications, 1993.

Datta, V.N., and S. Settar (eds) *Jallianwalan Bagh Massacre.* New Delhi, India: Pragati Publications, 2000.

Dugger, William, and Howard J. Sherman. *Reclaiming Evolution.* Oxfordshire, United Kingdom: Routledge, 2000.

Erikson, Erik H. *Gandhi's Truth: On the Origins of Militant Non-Violence.* London: Faber and Faber Limited, 1970.

Fischer, Louis. *The Life of Mahatma Gandhi.* London, UK: Jonathan Cape, 1951.

French, Patrick. *Liberty or Death: India's Journey to Independence and Division.* London: Flamingo, 1998.

Gandhi, Arun. *Daughter of Midnight: The Child Bride of Gandhi.* Blake Publishing Limited, 1996.

Gandhi, Hind Swaraj and other Writings, ed. Anthony J. Parel, (Cambridge University Press Centenary Edition, 2018).

Gandhi, Mahatma. *A Guide to Health.* Prabhat Prakashan, 2016.

Gandhi, Mahatma. *My Experiments with Truth: An Autobiography.* Mumbai, India: Jaico Publishing, 2008.

Gandhi, Manubehn. *Bapu: My Mother*. Ahmedabad, India: Navjivan Publishing House, 1947.

Gandhi, Rajmohan. *Patel: A Life*. Ahmedabad, India: Navjivan Publishing House, 1990.

Getz, Marshall J. *Subhash Chandra Bose: A Biography*. Jefferson: MacFarland and Company, 2002.

Godse, Nathuram. *Why I Assassinated Gandhi*. Foresight Publishers and Distributors, 2014.

Guha, Ramachandra. *Gandhi before India*. India: Penguin, 2014.

Hilton, Stuart. *The Grand Experiment: The Birth of the Railway Age*. London, UK: Ian Allan Publishing, 2007.

Juneja, M. M. *The Mahatma and the Millionaire: A Study in Gandhi-Birla Relations*. Hissar: Modern Publishers, 1993.

Khilnani, Sunil. *The Idea of India*. Penguin India, 1997.

Lockwood, David. *The Indian Bourgeoisie: A Political History of the Indian Capitalist Class*. London, UK: I.B. Taurus, 2012.

Mearsheimer, John J. *Why Leaders Lie: The Truth about Lying in International Politics*. New York: Oxford University Press, 2011.

Morton, Eleanor. *The Women in Gandhi's Life*. New York, US: Dodd, Mead & Co., 1953.

Naipaul, V. S. *An Area of Darkness*. India: Pan Macmillan, 2010.

Naoroji, Dadabhai. *Poverty and Un-British Rule in India*. Charleston, USA: Nabu Press, 2013.

Packenham, Thomas. *The Boer War*. New York: Random House, 1979.

Parel, Anthony, ed. *Hind Swaraj and Other Writings*. New Delhi: Cambridge University Press, 2018.

Persig, Robert. *Zen and the Art of Motorcycle Maintenance*. India: Vintage, 2014.

Prasoon, Srikant (ed.) *My Letters: M. K. Gandhi*. India: Cedar Books, 2013.

Sharma, Suresh, and Tripud Suhrud. *M. K. Gandhi's Hind Swaraj*. Hyderabad, India: Orient Blackswan, 2010.

Shastri, Shankaranand. *My Memories and Experiences of Babasaheb Dr. Ambedkar*. New Delhi, India: Samyak Prakashan, 2021.

Tagore, Rabindranath. *Gitanjali: A Collection of Poems*. India: Simon & Schuster, 1992.

Tunzelmann, Alex von. *Indian Summer: The Secret History of the End of an Empire*. USA: Simon & Schuster, 2007.

ACKNOWLEDGEMENTS

A book such as the present one benefits from discussions and brainstorming. Over the past couple of years, I discussed my critique with classmates, deans, professors and lecturers from universities and institutions where I have previously studied. Too numerous to name individually, these include Nasser Zakr, my class fellow from Harvard and colleague at the United Nations; a few classmates from the Judge Business School, University of Cambridge, who would prefer not to be acknowledged individually; Yves del Monaco, who worked in war-torn Kosovo during the same years that I was there and was my classmate, both at the London School of Journalism and at the University of Oxford; the erudite historian and author, Professor Shama Mitra Chenoy; Professor Manjula Batra, former dean at the Department of Law, Jamia Millia Islamia; and Narendra Laljani, former dean at Ashridge, UK, who was my classmate at Hindu College, University of Delhi.

The book also benefited greatly from brainstorming sessions that I held with out-of-the-box thinker and friend Pradipto Mitro, who works and lives in California. Intense discussions over endless cups of tea with Praveen Kumar, India-based educator and motivator who works with young children across the globe, were particularly useful. Special thanks are also due to Lipika Bhushan who helped with taking this project forward. A special word of thanks for Wendy Toole, one of my editors, who did an excellent edit but also made very many valuable suggestions. I would also like to thank Sakschi Verma who carried out a further painstaking and meticulous edit. And finally, I would like to thank Shantanu Ray Chaudhuri, editor-in-chief at Om Books International, for fast-tracking this project, and taking it out in record time with excellent production values.

Hind Swaraj or Indian Home Rule

Mohandas Karamchand Gandhi

To the Reader

I would like to say to the diligent reader of my writings and to others who are interested in them that I am not at all concerned with appearing to be consistent. In my search after Truth I have discarded many ideas and learnt many new things. Old as I am in age, I have no feeling that I have ceased to grow inwardly or that my growth will stop at the dissolution of the flesh. What I am concerned, with is my readiness to obey the call of Truth, my God, from moment to moment, and, therefore, when anybody finds any inconsistency between any two writings of mine, if he has still faith in my sanity, he would do well to choose the later of the two on the same subject.

M. K. GANDHI
Harijan, 29-4-1933, P. 2

Table of Contents

A Word of Explanation

It is certainly my good fortune that this booklet of mine is receiving wide attention. The original is in Gujarati. It has a chequered career. It was first published in the columns of the *Indian Opinion* of South Africa. It was written in 1908 during my return voyage from London to South Africa in answer to the Indian school of violence and its prototype in South Africa. I came in contact with every known Indian anarchist in London. Their bravery impressed me, but I felt that their zeal was misguided. I felt that violence was no remedy for India's ills, and that her civilization required the use of a different and higher weapon for self-protection. The Satyagraha of South Africa was still an infant hardly two years old. But it had developed sufficiently to permit me to write of it with some degree of confidence. What I wrote was so much appreciated that it was published as a booklet. It attracted some attention in India. The Bombay Government prohibited its circulation. I replied by publishing its translation. I thought it was due to my English friends that they should know its contents.

In my opinion it is a book which can be put into the hands of a child. It teaches the gospel of love in place of that of hate. It replaces violence with self-sacrifice. It pits soul force against brute force. It has gone through several editions and I commend it to those who would care to read it. I withdraw nothing except one word of it, and that in deference to a lady friend.

The booklet is a severe condemnation of 'modern civilization'. It was written in 1908. My conviction is deeper today than ever. I feel that if India will discard 'modern civilization', she can only gain by doing so.

But I would warn the reader against thinking that I am today aiming at the Swaraj described therein. I know that India is not ripe for it. It may seem an impertinence to say so. But such is my conviction. I am individually working for the self-rule pictured therein. But today my corporate activity is undoubtedly devoted to the attainment of Parliamentary Swaraj in accordance with the wishes of the people of India. I am not aiming at destroying railways or hospitals, though I would certainly welcome their natural destruction. Neither Railways nor hospitals are a test of a high and pure civilisation. After the stormy thirty years through which I have since passed I have seen nothing to make me alter the view expounded in it. Let the reader bear in mind that it is a faithful record of conversations I had with workers, one of whom was an avowed anarchist. He should also know that it stopped the rot that was about to set in among some Indians in South Africa. The reader may balance against this the opinion of a dear friend, who alas! is no more, that it was the production of a fool.[1]

Segaon, July 14th,1938

M. K. Gandhi

---

1. Reproduced from the *Aryan Path-Special Hind Swaraj Number*, published in September, 1938.

⚭ Chapter 1 ⚭

The Congress and Its Officials

Reader: Just at present there is a Home Rule wave passing over India. All our countrymen appear to be pining for National Independence. A similar spirit pervades them even in South Africa. Indians seem to be eager to acquire rights. Will you explain your views in this matter?

Editor: You have put the question well, but the answer is not easy. One of the objects of a newspaper is to understand popular feeling and to give expression to it; another is to arouse among the people certain desirable sentiments; and the third is fearlessly to expose popular defects. The exercise of all these three functions is involved in answering your question. To a certain extent the people's will has to be expressed; certain sentiments will need to be fostered and defects will have to be brought to light. But, as you have asked the question, it is my duty to answer it.

Reader: Do you then consider that a desire for Home Rule has been created among us?

Editor: That desire gave rise to the National Congress. The choice of the word "National" implies it.

Reader: That surely, is not the case. Young India seems to ignore the Congress. It is considered to be an instrument for perpetuating British Rule.

Editor: That opinion is not justified. Had not the Grand Old Man of India prepared the soil, our young men could not have even spoken about Home Rule. How can we forget what Mr. Hume has written, how he has lashed us into action, and with what effort he has awakened us, in order to achieve the objects of the Congress?

Sir William Wedderburn has given his body, mind and money to the same cause. His writings are worthy of perusal to this day. Professor Gokhale in order to prepare the nation, embraced poverty and gave twenty years of his life. Even now, he is living in poverty. The late Justice Budruddin Tyebji was also one of those who, through the Congress, sowed the seed of Home Rule. Similarly, in Bengal, Madras, the Punjab and other places, there have been lovers of India and members of the Congress, both Indian and English.

Reader: Stay, stay; you are going too far, you are straying away from my question. I have asked you about Home- or Self-Rule; you are discussing foreign rule. I do not desire to hear English names, and you are giving me such names. In these circumstances, I do not think we can ever meet. I shall be pleased if you will confine yourself to Home Rule. All other talk will not satisfy me.

Editor: You are impatient. I cannot afford to be likewise. If you will bear with me for a while, I think you will find that you will obtain what you want. Remember the old proverb that the tree does not grow in one day. The fact that you have checked me and that you do not want to hear about the well-wishers of India shows that, for you at any rate, Home Rule is yet far away. If we had many like you, we would never make any advance. This thought is worthy of your attention.

Reader: It seems to me that you simply want to put me off by talking round and round. Those whom you consider to be well-wishers of India are not such in my estimation. Why, then, should I listen to your discourse on such people? What has he whom you consider to be the Father of the Nation done for it? He says that the English Governors will do justice and that we should co-operate with them.

Editor: I must tell you, with all gentleness that it must be a matter of shame for us that you should speak about that great man in terms of disrespect. Just look at his work. He has dedicated his life to the service of India. We have learned what we know from him. It was the respected Dadabhai who taught us that the English had sucked our life-blood. What does it matter that, today, his trust is still in the English nation? Is Dadabhai less to be honoured because, in the exuberance of youth, we are prepared to go a step further? Are we, on that account, wiser than he? It is a mark of wisdom not to kick away the very step from which we have risen higher. The removal of a step from a staircase brings down the whole of it. When, out of infancy, we grow into youth, we do not despise infancy, but, on the contrary, we recall with affection the days of our childhood. If, after many years of study, a teacher were to teach me something, and if I were to build a little more on the foundation laid by that teacher, I would not, on that account, be considered wiser than the teacher. He would always command my respect. Such is the case with the Grand Old Man of India. We must admit that he is the author of nationalism.

Reader: You have spoken well. I can now understand that we must look upon Mr. Dadabhai with respect. Without him and men like him, we should probably not have the spirit that fires us. How can the same be said of Professor Gokhale? He has constituted himself a great friend of the English; he says that we have to learn a great deal from them, that we have to learn their political wisdom, before we can talk of Home Rule. I am tired of reading his speeches.

Editor: If you are tired, it only betrays your impatience. We believe that those, who are discontented with the slowness of their parents and are angry because the parents would not run with their children, are considered disrespectful to their parents. Professor Gokhale occupies the place of a parent. What does it matter if he cannot run with us? A nation that is desirous of securing Home Rule cannot afford to despise its ancestors. We shall become useless, if we lack respect for our elders. Only men with mature thoughts are capable of ruling themselves and not the hasty-tempered. Moreover, how many Indians were there like Professor Gokhale, when he gave himself to Indian education? I verily believe that whatever Professor Gokhale does, he does with pure motives and with a view to serving India. His devotion to the Motherland is so great that he would give his life for it, if necessary. Whatever he says is said not to flatter anyone but because he believes it to be true. We are bound, therefore, to entertain the highest regard for him.

Reader: Are we, then, to follow him in every respect?

Editor: I never said any such thing. If we conscientiously differed from him, the learned Professor himself would advise us to follow the dictates of our conscience rather than him.

Our chief purpose is not to decry his work, but to believe that he is infinitely greater than we are, and to feel assured that compared with his work for India, ours is infinitesimal. Several newspapers write disrespectfully of him. It is our duty to protest against such writings. We should consider men like Professor Gokhale to be the pillars of Home Rule. It is bad habit to say that another man's thoughts are bad and ours only are good and that those holding different views from ours are the enemies of the country.

Reader: I now begin to understand somewhat your meaning. I shall have to think the matter over. But what you say about Mr. Hume and Sir William Wedderburn is beyond my comprehension.

Editor: The same rule holds good for the English as for the Indians. I can never subscribe to the statement that all Englishmen are bad. Many Englishmen desire Home Rule for India. That the English people are somewhat more selfish than others is true, but that does not prove that every Englishman is bad. We who seek justice will have to do justice to others. Sir William does not wish ill to India—that should be enough for us. As we proceed, you will see that, if we act justly, India will be sooner free. You will see, too, that if we shun every Englishman as an enemy, Home Rule will be delayed. But if we are just to them, we shall receive their support in our progress towards the goal.

Reader: All this seems to me at present to be simply nonsensical. English support and the obtaining of Home Rule are two contradictory things. How can the English people tolerate Home Rule for us? But I do not want you to decide this question for me just yet. To spend time over it is useless.

When you have shown how we can have Home Rule, perhaps I shall understand your views. You have prejudiced me against you by discoursing on English help. I would, therefore, beseech you not to continue this subject.

Editor: I have no desire to do so. That you are prejudiced against me is not a matter for much anxiety. It is well that I should say unpleasant things at the commencement. It is my duty patiently to try to remove your prejudice.

Reader: I like that last statement. It emboldens me to say what I like. One thing still puzzles me. I do not understand how the Congress laid the foundation of Home Rule.

Editor: Let us see. The Congress brought together Indians from different parts of India, and enthused us with the idea of nationality. The Government used to look upon it with disfavour. The Congress has always insisted that the Nation should control revenue and expenditure. It has always desired self-government after the Canadian model. Whether we can get it or not, whether we desire it or not, and whether there is not something more desirable, are different questions. All I have to show is that the Congress gave us a foretaste of Home Rule. To deprive it of the honour is not proper, and for us to do so would not only be ungrateful, but retard the fulfillment of our object. To treat the Congress as an institution inimical to our growth as a nation would disable us from using that body.

꧁   Chapter 2   ꧂

The Partition of Bengal

Reader: Considering the matter as you put it, it seems proper to say that the foundation of Home Rule was laid by the Congress. But you will admit that this cannot be considered a real awakening. When and how did the real awakening take place?

Editor: The seed is never seen. It works underneath the ground, is itself destroyed, and the tree which rises above the ground is alone seen. Such is the case with the Congress. Yet, what you call the real awakening took place after the Partition of Bengal. For this we have to be thankful to Lord Curzon. At the time of the Partition, the people of Bengal reasoned with Lord Curzon, but in the pride of power he disregarded all their prayers. He took it for granted that Indians could only prattle, that they could never take any effective steps. He used insulting language, and in the teeth of all opposition partitioned Bengal. That day may be considered to be the day of the partition of the British Empire. The shock the British power received through the

Partition has never been equalled by any other act. This does not mean that the other injustices done to India are less glaring than that done by the Partition. The salt-tax is not a small injustice. We shall see many such things later on. But the people were ready to resist the Partition. At that time feeling ran high. Many leading Bengalis were ready to lose their all. They knew their power; hence the conflagration. It is now well-nigh unquenchable; it is not necessary to quench it either. The Partition will go, Bengal will be reunited, but the rift in the English barque will remain; it must daily widen. India awakened is not likely to fall asleep. The demand for the abrogation of the Partition is tantamount to a demand for Home Rule. Leaders in Bengal know this. British officials realize it. That is why the Partition still remains. As time passes, the Nation is being forged. Nations are not formed in a day; the formation requires years.

Reader: What, in your opinion, are the results of the Partition?

Editor: Hitherto we have considered that for redress of grievances we must approach the throne, and if we get no redress we must sit still, except that we may still petition. After the Partition, people saw that petitions must be backed up by force, and that they must be capable of suffering. This new spirit must be considered to be the chief result of the Partition. That spirit was seen in the outspoken writings in the Press. That which the people said tremblingly and in secret began to be said and to be written publicly. The Swadeshi movement was inaugurated. People, young and old, used to run away at the sight of an English face; it now no longer awes them. They do not fear even a row, or being imprisoned. Some of the best sons of India are at present in banishment. This is something different from mere petitioning. Thus are the people moved.

The spirit generated in Bengal has spread in the north to the Punjab, and in the south to Cape Comorin.

Reader: Do you suggest any other striking result?

Editor: The Partition has not only made a rift in the English ship but has made it in ours also. Great events always produce great results. Our leaders are divided into two parties: the Moderates and the Extremists. These may be considered as the slow party and the impatient party. Some call the Moderates the timid party, and the Extremists the bold party. All interpret the two words according to their preconceptions. This much is certain—that there has arisen an enmity between the two. The one distrusts the other and imputes motives. At the time of the Surat Congress there was almost a fight. I think that this division is not a good thing for the country, but I think also that such divisions will not last long. It all depends upon the leaders how long they will last.

Chapter 3

Discontent and Unrest

Reader: Then you consider the Partition to be a cause of the awakening? Do you welcome the unrest which has resulted from it?

Editor: When a man rises from sleep, he twists his limbs and is restless. It takes some time before he is entirely awakened. Similarly, although the Partition has caused an awakening, the comatose condition has not yet disappeared. We are still twisting our limbs and are still restless, and just as the state between sleep and awakening must be considered to be necessary, so may the present unrest in India be considered a necessary and therefore, a proper state. The knowledge that there is unrest will, it is highly probable, enable us to outgrow it. Rising from sleep, we do not continue in a comatose state, but according to our ability, sooner or later, we are completely restored to our senses. So shall we be free from the present unrest which no one likes.

Reader: What is the other form of unrest?

Editor: Unrest is, in reality, discontent. The latter is only now described as unrest. During the Congress period it was labelled discontent. Mr. Hume always said that the spread of discontent in India was necessary. This discontent is a very useful thing. As long as a man is contented with his present lot, so long is it difficult to persuade him to come out of it. Therefore it is that every reform must be preceded by discontent. We throw away things we have, only when we cease to like them. Such discontent has been produced among us after reading the great works of Indians and Englishmen. Discontent has led to unrest, and the latter has brought about many deaths, many imprisonments, many banishments. Such a state of things will still continue. It must be so. All these may be considered good signs but they may also lead to bad results.

Chapter 4

What Is Swaraj?

Reader: I have now learnt what the Congress has done to make India one nation, how the Partition has caused an awakening, and how discontent and unrest have spread through the land. I would now like to know your views on Swaraj. I fear that our interpretation is not the same as yours.

Editor: It is quite possible that we do not attach the same meaning to the term. You and I and all Indians are impatient to obtain Swaraj, but we are certainly not decided as to what it is. To drive the English out of India is a thought heard from many mouths, but it does not seem that many have properly considered why it should be so. I must ask you a question. Do not think that it is necessary to drive away the English, if we get all we want?

Reader: I should ask of them only one thing, that is: "Please leave our country." If, after they have complied with this request, their withdrawal from India means that they are still in India. I should have no objection. Then we would understand that, in their language, the word "gone" is equivalent to "remained".

Editor: Well then, let us suppose that the English have retired. What will you do then?

Reader: That question cannot be answered at this stage. The state after withdrawal will depend largely upon the manner of it. If, as you assume, they retire, it seems to me we shall still keep their constitution and shall carry on the Government. If they simply retire for the asking we should have an army, etc., ready at hand. We should, therefore, have no difficulty in carrying on the Government.

Editor: You may think so; I do not. But I will not discuss the matter just now. I have to answer your question, and that I can do well by asking you several questions. Why do you want to drive away the English?

Reader: Because India has become impoverished by their Government. They take away our money from year to year. The most important posts are reserved for themselves. We are kept in a state of slavery. They behave insolently towards us and disregard our feelings.

Editor: If they do not take our money away, become gentle, and give us responsible posts, would you still consider their presence to be harmful?

Reader: That question is useless. It is similar to the question whether there is any harm in associating with a tiger if he changes his nature. Such a question is sheer waste of time. When a tiger changes his nature, Englishmen will change theirs. This is not possible, and to believe it to be possible is contrary to human experience.

Editor: Supposing we get Self-Government similar to what the Canadians and the South Africans have, will it be good enough?

Reader: That question also is useless. We may get it when we have the same powers; we shall then hoist our own flag. As is Japan, so must India be. We must own our navy, our army, and we must have our own splendour, and then will India's voice ring through the world.

Editor: You have drawn the picture well. In effect it means this: that we want English rule without the Englishman. You want the tiger's nature, but not the tiger; that is to say, you would make India English. And when it becomes English, it will be called not Hindustan but *Englistan*. This is not the Swaraj that I want.

Reader: I have placed before you my idea of Swaraj as I think it should be. If the education we have received be of any use, if the works of Spencer, Mill and others be of any importance, and if the English Parliament be the Mother of Parliaments, I certainly think that we should copy the English people, and this to such an extent that, just as they do not allow others to obtain a footing in their country, so we should not allow them or others to obtain it in ours. What they have done in their own country has not been done in any other country. It is, therefore, proper for us to import their institutions. But now I want to know your views.

Editor: There is need for patience. My views will develop of themselves in the course of this discourse. It is as difficult for me to understand the true nature of Swaraj as it seems to you to be easy. I shall, therefore, for the time being, content myself with endeavouring to show that what you call Swaraj is not truly Swaraj.

∽ **Chapter 5** ∽

The Condition of England

Reader: Then from your statement I deduce that the Government of England is not desirable and not worth copying by us.

Editor: Your deduction is justified. The condition of England at present is pitiable. I pray to God that India may never be in that plight. That which you consider to be the Mother of Parliaments is like a sterile woman and a prostitute. Both these are harsh terms, but exactly fit the case. That Parliament has not yet, of its own accord, done a single good thing. Hence I have compared it to a sterile woman. The natural condition of that Parliament is such that, without outside pressure, it can do nothing. It is like a prostitute because it is under the control of ministers who change from time to time. Today it is under Mr. Asquith, tomorrow it may be under Mr. Balfour.

Reader: You have said this sarcastically. The term "sterile woman" is not applicable. The Parliament, being elected by the people, must work under public pressure. This is its quality.

Editor: You are mistaken. Let us examine it a little more closely. The best men are supposed to be elected by the people. The members serve without pay and therefore, it must be assumed, only for the public weal. The electors are considered to be educated and therefore we should assume that they would not generally make mistakes in their choice. Such a Parliament should not need the spur of petitions or any other pressure. Its work should be so smooth that its effects would be more apparent day by day. But, as a matter of fact, it is generally acknowledged that the members are hypocritical and selfish. Each thinks of his own little interest. It is fear that is the guiding motive. What is done today may be undone tomorrow. *It is not possible to recall a single instance in which finality can be predicted for its work.* When the greatest questions are debated, its members have been seen to stretch themselves and to doze. Sometimes the members talk away until the listeners are disgusted. Carlyle has called it the "talking shop of the world". Members vote for their party without a thought. Their so-called discipline binds them to it. If any member, by way of exception, gives an independent vote, he is considered a renegade. If the money and the time wasted by Parliament were entrusted to a few good men, the English nation would be occupying today a much higher platform. Parliament is simply a costly toy of the nation. These views are by no means peculiar to me. Some great English thinkers have expressed them. One of the members of that Parliament recently said that a true Christian could not become a member of it. Another said that it was a baby. And if it has remained a baby after an existence of seven hundred years, when will it outgrow its babyhood?

Reader: You have set me thinking; you do not expect me to accept at once all you say. You give me entirely novel views.

I shall have to digest them. Will you now explain the epithet "prostitute"?

Editor: That you cannot accept my views at once is only right. If you will read the literature on this subject, you will have some idea of it. Parliament is without a real master. Under the Prime Minister, its movement is not steady but it is buffeted about like a prostitute. The Prime Minister is more concerned about his power than about the welfare of Parliament. His energy is concentrated upon securing the success of his party. His care is not always that Parliament shall do right. Prime Ministers are known to have made Parliament do things merely for party advantage. All this is worth thinking over.

Reader: Then you are really attacking the very men whom we have hitherto considered to be patriotic and honest?

Editor: Yes, that is true; I can have nothing against Prime Ministers, but what I have seen leads me to think that they cannot be considered really patriotic. If they are to be considered honest because they do not take what are generally known as bribes, let them be so considered, but they are open to subtler influences. In order to gain their ends, they certainly bribe people with honours. I do not hesitate to say that they have neither real honesty nor a living conscience.

Reader: As you express these views about Parliament, I would like to hear you on the English people, so that I may have your view of their Government.

Editor: To the English voters their newspaper is their Bible. They take their cue from their newspapers which are often dishonest. The same fact is differently interpreted by different newspapers, according to the party in whose interests they are edited. One newspaper would consider a great Englishman to be a paragon of honesty, another would consider him dishonest. What must be the condition of the people whose newspapers are of this type?

Reader: You shall describe it.

Editor: These people change their views frequently. It is said that they change them every seven years. These views swing like the pendulum of a clock and are never steadfast. The people would follow a powerful orator or a man who gives them parties, receptions, etc. As are the people, so is their Parliament. They have certainly one quality very strongly developed. They will never allow their country to be lost. If any person were to cast an evil eye on it, they would pluck out his eyes. But that does not mean that the nation possesses every other virtue or that it should be imitated. If India copies England, it is my firm conviction that she will be ruined.

Reader: To what do you ascribe this state of England?

Editor: It is not due to any peculiar fault of the English people, but the condition is due to modern civilization. It is a civilization only in name. Under it the nations of Europe are becoming degraded and ruined day by day.

❧ Chapter 6 ❧

Civilization

Reader: Now you will have to explain what you mean by civilization.

Editor: It is not a question of what I mean. Several English writers refuse to call that civilization which passes under that name. Many books have been written upon that subject. Societies have been formed to cure the nation of the evils of civilization. A great English writer has written a work called *Civilization: Its Cause and Cure*. Therein he has called it a disease.

Reader: Why do we not know this generally?

Editor: The answer is very simple. We rarely find people arguing against themselves. Those who are intoxicated by modern civilization are not likely to write against it. Their care will be to find out facts and arguments in support of it, and this they do unconsciously, believing it to be true. A man whilst he is dreaming, believes in his dream; he is undeceived only when he is awakened from his sleep. A man labouring under the bane of civilization is like a dreaming man. What we usually read are the works of defenders of modern civilization, which undoubtedly claims among its votaries very brilliant and even some very good men. Their writings hypnotize us. And so, one by one, we are drawn into the vortex.

Reader: This seems to be very plausible. Now will you tell me something of what you have read and thought of this civilization?

Editor: Let us first consider what state of things is described by the word "civilization". Its true test lies in the fact that people living in it make bodily welfare the object of life. We will take some examples. The people of Europe today live in better-built houses than they did a hundred years ago. This is considered an emblem of civilization, and this is also a matter to promote bodily happiness. Formerly, they wore skins, and used spears as their weapons. Now, they wear long trousers, and, for embellishing their bodies, they wear a variety of clothing, and, instead of spears, they carry with them revolvers containing five or more chambers. If people of a certain country, who have hitherto not been in the habit of wearing much clothing, boots, etc., adopt European clothing, they are supposed to have become civilized out of savagery. Formerly, in Europe, people ploughed their lands mainly by manual labour. Now, one man can plough a vast tract by means of steam engines and can thus amass great wealth. This is called a sign of civilization. Formerly, only a few men wrote valuable books. Now, anybody writes and prints anything he likes and poisons people's minds. Formerly, men travelled in wagons. Now, they fly through the air in trains at the rate of four hundred and more miles per day. This is considered the height of civilization. It has been stated that, as men progress, they shall be able to travel in airship and reach any part of the world in a few hours. Men will not need the use of their hands and feet. They will press a button, and they will have their clothing by their side. They will press another button, and they will have their newspaper. A third, and a motor-car will be in waiting for them. They will have a variety of delicately dished up food. Everything will be done by machinery. Formerly, when people wanted to fight with one another, they measured between them their bodily strength; now it is possible to take away thousands of lives by one man working behind a gun from a hill. This is civilization. Formerly, men worked in the open air only as much as they liked. Now thousands of workmen meet together and for the sake of maintenance work in factories or mines. Their condition is worse than that of beasts. They are obliged to work, at the risk of their lives, at most dangerous occupations, for the sake of millionaires. Formerly, men were made slaves under physical compulsion. Now they are enslaved by temptation of money and of the luxuries that money can buy. There are now diseases of which people never dreamt before, and an army of doctors is engaged in finding out their cures, and so hospitals have increased. This is a test of civilization. Formerly, special messengers were required and much expense was incurred in order to send letters; today, anyone can abuse his fellow by means of a letter for one penny. True, at the same cost, one can send one's thanks also. Formerly, people had two or three meals consisting of home-made bread and vegetables; now, they require something to eat every two hours so that they have hardly leisure for anything else. What more need I say? All this you can ascertain from several authoritative books. These are all true tests of civilization. And if anyone speaks to the contrary, know that he is ignorant. This civilization takes note neither of morality nor of religion. Its votaries calmly state that their business is not to teach religion. Some even consider it to be a superstitious growth. Others put on the cloak of religion, and prate about morality. But, after twenty years' experience, I have come to the conclusion that immorality is often taught in the name of morality. Even a child can understand that in all I have described above there can be no inducement to morality. Civilization seeks to increase bodily comforts, and it fails miserably even in doing so.

This civilization is irreligion, and it has taken such a hold on the people in Europe that those who are in it appear to be half mad. They lack real physical strength or courage. They keep up their energy by intoxication. They can hardly be happy in solitude. Women, who should be the queens of households, wander in the streets or they slave away in factories. For the sake of a pittance, half a million women in England alone are labouring under trying circumstances in factories or similar institutions. This awful fact is one of the causes of the daily growing suffragette movement.

This civilization is such that one has only to be patient and it will be self-destroyed. According to the teaching of Mahommed this would be considered a Satanic Civilization. Hinduism calls it the Black Age. I cannot give you an adequate conception of it. It is eating into the vitals of the English nation. It must be shunned. Parliaments are really emblems of slavery. If you will sufficiently think over this, you will entertain the same opinion and cease to blame the English. They rather deserve our sympathy. They are a shrewd nation and I therefore believe that they will cast off the evil. They are enterprising and industrious, and their mode of thought is not inherently immoral. Neither are they bad at heart. I therefore respect them. Civilization is not an incurable disease, but it should never be forgotten that the English people are at present afflicted by it.

❦ **Chapter 7** ❦

Why Was India lost?

Reader: You have said much about civilization—enough to make me ponder over it. I do not now know what I should adopt and what I should avoid from the nations of Europe, but one question comes to my lips immediately. If civilization is a disease and if it has attacked England, why has she been able to take India, and why is she able to retain it?

Editor: Your question is not very difficult to answer, and we shall presently be able to examine the true nature of Swaraj; for I am aware that I have still to answer that question. I will, however, take up your previous question. The English have not taken India; we have given it to them. They are not in India because of their strength, but because we keep them. Let us now see whether these propositions can be sustained. They came to our country originally for purposes of trade. Recall the Company Bahadur. Who made it Bahadur? They had not the slightest intention at the time of establishing a kingdom. Who assisted the Company's officers? Who was tempted at the sight of their silver? Who bought their goods? History testifies that we did all this. In order to become rich all at once we welcomed the Company's officers with open arms. We assisted them. If I am in the habit of drinking *bhang* and a seller thereof sells it to me, am I to blame him or myself? By blaming the seller, shall I be able to avoid the habit? And, if a particular retailer is driven away, will not another take his place? A true servant of India will have to go to the root of the matter. If an excess of food has caused me indigestion, I shall certainly not avoid it by blaming water. He is a true physician who probes the cause of disease, and if you pose as a physician for the disease of India, you will have to find out its true cause.

Reader: You are right. Now I think you will not have to argue much with me to drive your conclusions home. I am impatient to know your further views. We are now on a most interesting topic. I shall, therefore, endeavour to follow your thought, and stop you when I am in doubt.

Editor: I am afraid that, in spite of your enthusiasm, as we proceed further, we shall have differences of opinion. Nevertheless, I shall argue only when you stop me. We have already seen that the English merchants were able to get a footing in India because we encouraged them. When our Princes fought among themselves, they sought the assistance of Company Bahadur. That corporation was versed alike in commerce and war. It was unhampered by questions of morality. Its object was to increase its commerce and to make money. It accepted our assistance, and increased the number of its warehouses. To protect the latter it employed an army which was utilized by us also. Is it not then useless to blame the English for what we did at that time? The Hindus and the Mahomedans were at daggers drawn. This, too, gave the Company its opportunity and thus we created the circumstances that gave the Company its control over India. Hence it is truer to say that we gave India to the English than that India was lost.

Reader: Will you now tell me how they are able to retain India?

Editor: The causes that gave them India enable them to retain it. Some Englishmen state that they took and they hold India by the sword. Both these statements are wrong. The sword is entirely useless for holding India. We alone keep them. Napolean is said to have described the English as a nation of shopkeepers. It is a fitting description. They hold whatever dominions they have for the sake of their commerce. Their army and their navy are intended to protect it. When the Transvaal offered no such attractions, the late Mr. Gladstone discovered that it was not right for the English to hold it. When it became a paying proposition, resistance led to war. Mr. Chamberlain soon discovered that England enjoyed a suzerainty over the Transvaal. It is related that someone asked the late President Kruger whether there was gold in the moon. He replied that it was highly unlikely because, if there were, the English would have annexed it. Many problems can be solved by remembering that money is their God. Then it follows that we keep the English in India for our base self-interest. We like their commerce; they please us by their subtle methods and get what they want from us. To blame them for this is to perpetuate their power. We further strengthen their hold by quarrelling amongst ourselves. If you accept the above statements, it is proved that the English entered India for the purposes of trade. They remain in it for the same purpose and we help them to do so. Their arms and ammunition are perfectly useless. In this connection I remind you that it is the British flag which is waving in Japan and not the Japanese. The

English have a treaty with Japan for the sake of their commerce, and you will see that if they can manage it their commerce will greatly expand in that country. They wish to convert the whole world into a vast market for their goods. That they cannot do so is true, but the blame will not be theirs. They will leave no stone unturned to reach the goal.

❧ Chapter 8 ☙

The Condition of India

Reader: I now understand why the English hold India. I should like to know your views about the condition of our country.

Editor: It is a sad condition. In thinking of it my eyes water and my throat gets parched. I have grave doubts whether I shall be able sufficiently to explain what is in my heart. It is my deliberate opinion that India is being ground down, not under the English heel, but under that of modern civilization. It is groaning under the monster's terrible weight. There is yet time to escape it, but every day makes it more and more difficult. Religion is dear to me and my first complaint is that India is becoming irreligious. Here I am not thinking of the Hindu or the Mahomedan or the Zoroastrian religion but of that religion which underlies all religions. We are turning away from God.

Reader: How so?

Editor: There is a charge laid against us that we are a lazy people and that Europeans are industrious and enterprising. We have accepted the charge and we therefore wish to change our condition. Hinduism, Islam, Zoroastrianism, Christianity and all other religions teach that we should remain passive about worldly pursuits and active about godly pursuits, that we should set a limit to our worldly ambition and that our religious ambition should be illimitable. Our activity should be directed into the latter channel.

Reader: You seem to be encouraging religious charlatanism. Many a cheat has, by talking in a similar strain, led the people astray.

Editor: You are bringing an unlawful charge against religion. Humbug there undoubtedly is about all religions. Where there is light, there is also shadow. I am prepared to maintain that humbugs in worldly matters are far worse than the humbugs in religion. The humbug of civilization that I am endeavouring to show to you is not to be found in religion.

Reader: How can you say that? In the name of religion Hindus and Mahomedans fought against one another. For the same cause Christians fought Christians. Thousands of innocent men have been murdered, thousands have been burned and tortured in its name. Surely, this is much worse than any civilization.

Editor: I certainly submit that the above hardships are far more bearable than those of civilization. Everybody understands that the cruelties you have named are not part of religion although they have been practised in its name; therefore there is no aftermath to these cruelties. They will always happen so long as there are to be found ignorant and credulous people. But there is no end to the victims destroyed in the fire of civilization. Its deadly effect is that people come under its scorching flames believing it to be all good. They become utterly irreligious and, in reality, derive little advantage from the world. Civilization is like a mouse gnawing while it is soothing us. When its full effect is realized, we shall see that religious superstition is harmless compared to that of modern civilization. I am not pleading for a continuance of religious superstitions. We shall certainly fight them tooth and nail, but we can never do so by disregarding religion. We can only do so by appreciating and conserving the latter.

Reader: Then you will contend that the Pax Britannica is a useless encumbrance?

Editor: You may see peace if you like; I see none.

Reader: You make light of the terror that the Thugs, the Pindaris and the Bhils were to the country.

Editor: If you give the matter some thought, you will see that the terror was by no means such a mighty thing. If it had been a very substantial thing, the other people would have died away before the English advent. Moreover, the present peace is only nominal, for by it we have become emasculated and cowardly. We are not to assume that the English have changed the nature of the Pindaris and the Bhils. It is, therefore, better to suffer the Pindari peril than that someone else should protect us from it and thus render us effeminate. I should prefer to be killed by the arrow of a Bhil than to seek unmanly protection. India without such protection was an India full of valour. Macaulay betrayed gross ignorance when he libelled Indians as being practically cowards. They never merited the charge. Cowards living in a country inhabited by hardy mountaineers and infested by wolves and tigers must surely find an early grave. Have you ever visited our fields? I assure you that our agriculturists sleep fearlessly on their farms even today; but the English and you and I would hesitate to sleep where they sleep. Strength lies in absence of fear, not in the quantity of flesh and muscle we may have on our bodies. Moreover, I must remind you who desire Home Rule that, after all, the Bhils, the Pindaris, and the Thugs are our own countrymen. To conquer them is your and my work. So long as we fear our own brethren, we are unfit to reach the goal.

Chapter 9

The Condition of India
(Continued): Railways

Reader: You have deprived me of the consolation I used to have regarding peace in India.

Editor: I have merely given you my opinion on the religious aspect, but when I give you my views as to the poverty of India, you will perhaps begin to dislike me because what you and I have hitherto considered beneficial for India no longer appears to me to be so.

Reader: What may that be?

Editor: Railways, lawyers and doctors have impoverished the country so much so that, if we do not wake up in time, we shall be ruined.

Reader: I do now, indeed, fear that we are not likely to agree at all. You are attacking the very institutions which we have hitherto considered to be good.

Editor: It is necessary to exercise patience. The true inwardness of the evils of civilization you will understand with difficulty.

Doctors assure us that a consumptive clings to life even when he is about to die. Consumption does not produce apparent hurt—it even produces a seductive colour about a patient's face so as to induce the belief that all is well. Civilization is such a disease and we have to be very wary.

Reader: Very well, then. I shall hear you on the railways.

Editor: It must be manifest to you that, but for the railways, the English could not have such a hold on India as they have. The railways, too, have spread the bubonic plague. Without them, the masses could not move from place to place. They are the carriers of plague germs. Formerly we had natural segregation. Railways have also increased the frequency of famines because, owing to facility of means of locomotion, people sell out their grain and it is sent to the dearest markets. People become careless and so the pressure of famine increases. Railways accentuate the evil nature of man. Bad men fulfil their evil designs with greater rapidity. The holy places of India have become unholy. Formerly, people went to these places with very great difficulty. Generally, therefore, only the real devotees visited such places. Nowadays rogues visit them in order to practise their roguery.

Reader: You have given a one-sided account. Good men can visit these places as well as bad men. Why do they not take the fullest advantage of the railways?

Editor: Good travels at a snail's pace—it can, therefore, have little to do with the railways. Those who want to do good are not selfish, they are not in a hurry, they know that to impregnate people with good requires a long time. But evil has wings. To build a house takes time. Its destruction takes none. So the railways can become a distributing agency for the evil one only.

It may be a debatable matter whether railways spread famines, but it is beyond dispute that they propagate evil.

Reader: Be that as it may, all the disadvantages of railways are more than counterbalanced by the fact that it is due to them that we see in India the new spirit of nationalism.

Editor: I hold this to be a mistake. The English have taught us that we were not one nation before and that it will require centuries before we become one nation. This is without foundation. We were one nation before they came to India. One thought inspired us. Our mode of life was the same. It was because we were one nation that they were able to establish one kingdom. Subsequently they divided us.

Reader: This requires an explanation.

Editor: I do not wish to suggest that because we were one nation we had no differences, but it is submitted that our leading men travelled throughout India either on foot or in bullock-carts. They learned one another's languages and there was no aloofness between them. What do you think could have been the intention of those farseeing ancestors of ours who established Setubandha (Rameshwar) in the South, Jagannath in the East and Hardwar in the North as places of pilgrimage? You will admit they were no fools. They knew that worship of God could have been performed just as well at home. They taught us that those whose hearts were aglow with righteousness had the Ganges in their own homes. But they saw that India was one undivided land so made by nature. They, therefore, argued that it must be one nation. Arguing thus, they established holy places in various parts of India, and fired the people with an idea of nationality in a manner unknown in other parts of the world.

And we Indians are one as no two Englishmen are. Only you and I and others who consider ourselves civilized and superior persons imagine that we are many nations. It was after the advent of railways that we began to believe in distinctions, and you are at liberty now to say that it is through the railways that we are beginning to abolish those distinctions. An opium-eater may argue the advantage of opium-eating from the fact that he began to understand the evil of the opium habit after having eaten it. I would ask you to consider well what I had said on the railways.

Reader: I will gladly do so, but one question occurs to me even now. You have described to me the India of the pre-Mahomedan period, but now we have Mahomedans, Parsis and Christians. How can they be one nation? Hindus and Mahomedans are old enemies. Our very proverbs prove it. Mahomedans turn to the West for worship, whilst Hindus turn to the East. The former look down on the Hindus as idolaters. The Hindus worship the cow, the Mahomedans kill her. The Hindus believe in the doctrine of non-killing, the Mahomedans do not. We thus meet with differences at every step. How can India be one nation?

Chapter 10

The Condition of India (Continued): The Hindus and the Mahomedans

Editor: Your last question is a serious one and yet, on careful consideration, it will be found to be easy of solution. The question arises because of the presence of the railways, of the lawyers and of the doctors. We shall presently examine the last two. We have already considered the railways. I should, however, like to add that man is so made by nature as to require him to restrict his movements as far as his hands and feet will take him. If we did not rush about from place to place by means of railways and such other maddening conveniences, much of the confusion that arises would be obviated. Our difficulties are of our own creation. God set a limit to a man's locomotive ambition in the construction of his body. Man immediately proceeded to discover means of overriding the limit. God gifted man with intellect that he might know his Maker. Man abused it so that he might forget his Maker. I am so constructed that I can only serve my immediate neighbours, but in my conceit I pretend to have discovered that I must with my body serve every individual in the Universe. In thus attempting the impossible, man comes in contact with different natures, different religions, and is utterly confounded. According to this reasoning, it must be apparent to you that railways are a most dangerous institution. Owing to them, man has gone further away from his Maker.

Reader: But I am impatient to hear your answer to my question. Has the introduction of Mahomedanism not unmade the nation?

Editor: India cannot cease to be one nation because people belonging to different religions live in it. The introduction of foreigners does not necessarily destroy the nation; they merge in it. A country is one nation only when such a condition obtains in it. That country must have a faculty for assimilation. India has ever been such a country. In reality there are as many religions as there are individuals; but those who are conscious of the spirit of nationality do not interfere with one another's religion. If they do, they are not fit to be considered a nation. If the Hindus believe that India should be peopled only by Hindus, they are living in dreamland. The Hindus, the Mahomedans, the Parsis and the Christians who have made India their country are fellow countrymen, and they will have to live in unity, if only for their own interest. In no part of the world are one nationality and one religion synonymous terms; nor has it ever been so in India.

Reader: But what about the inborn enmity between Hindus and Mahomedans?

Editor: That phrase has been invented by our mutual enemy. When the Hindus and Mahomedans fought against one another, they certainly spoke in that strain. They have long since ceased to fight. How, then, can there be any inborn enmity? Pray remember this too, that we did not cease to fight only after British occupation. The Hindus flourished under Moslem sovereigns and Moslems under the Hindu. Each party recognized that mutual fighting was suicidal, and that neither party would abandon its religion by force of arms. Both parties, therefore, decided to live in peace. With the English advent quarrels recommenced.

The proverbs you have quoted were coined when both were fighting; to quote them now is obviously harmful. Should we not remember that many Hindus and Mahomedans own the same ancestors and the same blood runs through their veins? Do people become enemies because they change their religion? Is the God of the Mahomedan different from the God of the Hindu? Religions are different roads converging to the same point. What does it matter that we take different roads so long as we reach the same goal? Wherein is the cause for quarrelling?

Moreover, there are deadly proverbs as between the followers of Shiva and those of Vishnu, yet nobody suggests that these two do not belong to the same nation. It is said that the Vedic religion is different from Jainism, but the followers of the respective faiths are not different nations. The fact is that we have become enslaved and, therefore, quarrel and like to have our quarrels decided by a third party. There are Hindu iconoclasts as there are Mahomedan. The more we advance in true knowledge, the better we shall understand that we need not be at war with those whose religion we may not follow.

Reader: Now I would like to know your views about cow-protection.

Editor: I myself respect the cow, that is, I look upon her with affectionate reverence. The cow is the protector of India because, being an agricultural country, she is dependent on the cow. The cow is a most useful animal in hundreds of ways. Our Mahomedan brethren will admit this.

But, just as I respect the cow, so do I respect my fellow-men. A man is just as useful as a cow no matter whether he be a Mahomedan or a Hindu. Am I, then, to fight with or kill a Mahomedan in order to save a cow? In doing so, I would become an enemy of the Mahomedan as well as of the cow. Therefore, the only method I know of protecting the cow is that I should approach my Mahomedan brother and urge him for the sake of the country to join me in protecting her. If he would not listen to me I should let the cow go for the simple reason that the matter is beyond my ability. If I were overfull of pity for the cow, I should sacrifice my life to save her but not take my brother's. This, I hold, is the law of our religion. When men become obstinate, it is a difficult thing. If I pull one way, my Moslem brother will pull another. If I put on superior airs, he will return the compliment. If I bow to him gently, he will do it much more so; and if he does not, I shall not be considered to have done wrong in having bowed. When the Hindus became insistent, the killing of cows increased. In my opinion, cow-protection societies may be considered cow-killing societies. It is a disgrace to us that we should need such societies. When we forgot how to protect cows, I suppose we needed such societies. What am I to do when a blood-brother is on the point of killing a cow? Am I to kill him, or to fall down at his feet and implore him? If you admit that I should adopt the latter course, I must do the same to my Moslem brother.

Who protects the cow from destruction by Hindus when they cruelly ill-treat her? Whoever reasons with the Hindus when they mercilessly belabour the progeny of the cow with their sticks? But this has not prevented us from remaining one nation.

Lastly, if it be true that the Hindus believe in the doctrine of non-killing and the Mahomedans do not, what, pray, is the duty of the former? It is not written that a follower of the religion of Ahimsa (non-killing) may kill a fellow-man. For him the way is straight. In order to save one being, he may not kill another. He can only plead—therein lies his sole duty.

But does every Hindu believe in Ahimsa? Going to the root of the matter, not one man really practises such a religion because we do destroy life. We are said to follow that religion because we want to obtain freedom from liability to kill any kind of life. Generally speaking, we may observe that many Hindus partake of meat and are not, therefore, followers of Ahimsa. It is, therefore, preposterous to suggest that the two cannot live together amicably because the Hindus believe in Ahimsa and the Mahomedans do not.

These thoughts are put into our minds by selfish and false religious teachers. The English put the finishing touch. They have habit of writing history; they pretend to study the manners and customs of all peoples. God has given us a limited mental capacity, but they usurp the function of the Godhead and indulge in novel experiments. They write about their own researches in most laudatory terms and hypnotize us into believing them. We in our ignorance then fall at their feet.

Those who do not wish to misunderstand things may read up the *Koran*, and they will find therein hundreds of passages acceptable to the Hindus; and the *Bhagavad-gita* contains passages to which not a Mahomedan can take exception. Am I to dislike a Mahomedan because there are passages in the *Koran* I do not understand or like? It takes two to make a quarrel. If I do not want to quarrel with a Mahomedan, the latter will be powerless to foist a quarrel on me; and, similarly, I should be powerless if a Mahomedan refuses his assistance to quarrel with me. An arm striking the air will become disjointed. If everyone will try to understand the core of his own religion and adhere to it, and will not allow false teachers to dictate to him, there will be no room left for quarrelling.

Reader: But will the English ever allow the two bodies to join hands?

Editor: This question arises out of your timidity. It betrays our shallowness. If two brothers want to live in peace, is it possible for a third party to separate them? If they were to listen to evil counsels we would consider them to be foolish. Similarly, we Hindus and Mahomedans would have to blame our folly rather than the English, if we allowed them to put us asunder. A clay pot would break through impact, if not with one stone, then with another. The way to save the pot is not to keep it away from the danger point but to bake it so that no stone would break it. We have then to make our hearts of perfectly baked clay. Then we shall be steeled against all danger. This can be easily done by the Hindus. They are superior in numbers; they pretend that they are more educated; they are, therefore, better able to shield themselves from attack on their amicable relations with the Mahomedans.

There is mutual distrust between the two communities. The Mahomedans, therefore, ask for certain concessions from Lord Morley. Why should the Hindus oppose this? If the Hindus desisted, the English would notice it, the Mahomedans would gradually begin to trust the Hindus, and brotherliness would be the outcome. We should be ashamed to take our quarrels to the English. Everyone can find out for himself that the Hindus can lose nothing by desisting. That man who has inspired confidence in another has never lost anything in this world.

I do not suggest that the Hindus and the Mahomedans will never fight. Two brothers living together often do so. We shall sometimes have our heads broken. Such a thing ought not to be necessary, but all men are not equitable. When people are in a rage, they do many foolish things. These we have to put up with. But when we do quarrel, we certainly do not want to engage counsel and resort to English or any law-courts. Two men fight; both have their heads broken, or one only. How shall a third party distribute justice amongst them? Those who fight may expect to be injured.

༺ ⁓ **Chapter 11** ⁓ ༻

The Condition of India
(Continued): Lawyers

Reader: You tell me that when two men quarrel they should not go to a law-court. This is astonishing.

Editor: Whether you call it astonishing or not, it is the truth. And your question introduces us to the lawyers and the doctors. My firm opinion is that the lawyers have enslaved India, have accentuated Hindu-Mahomedan dissensions and have confirmed English authority.

Reader: It is easy enough to bring these charges, but it will be difficult for you to prove them. But for the lawyers, who would have shown us the road to independence? Who would have protected the poor? Who would have secured justice? For instance, the late Manomohan Ghose defended many a poor man free of charge. The Congress, which you have praised so much, is dependent for its existence and activity upon the work of the lawyers. To denounce such an estimable class of men is to spell injustice, and you are abusing the liberty of the Press by decrying lawyers.

Editor: At one time I used to think exactly like you. I have no desire to convince you that they have never done a single good thing. I honour Mr. Ghose's memory. It is quite true that he helped the poor. That the Congress owes the lawyers something is believable. Lawyers are also men, and there is something good in every man. Whenever instances of lawyers having done good can be brought forward, it will be found that the good is due to them as men rather than as lawyers. All I am concerned with is to show you that the profession teaches immorality; it is exposed to temptation from which few are saved.

The Hindus and the Mahomedans have quarrelled. An ordinary man will ask them to forget all about it; he will tell them that both must be more or less at fault, and will advise them no longer to quarrel. But they go to lawyers. The latter's duty is to side with their clients and to find out ways and arguments in favour of the clients, to which they (the clients) are often strangers. If they do not do so, they will be considered to have degraded their profession. The lawyers, therefore, will, as a rule, advance quarrels instead of repressing them. Moreover, men take up that profession, not in order to help others out of their miseries, but to enrich themselves. It is one of the avenues of becoming wealthy and their interest exists in multiplying disputes. It is within my knowledge that they are glad when men have disputes. Petty pleaders actually manufacture them. Their touts, like so many leeches, suck the blood of the poor people. Lawyers are men who have little to do. Lazy people, in order to indulge in luxuries, take up such professions. This is a true statement. Any other argument is a mere pretension. It is the lawyers who have discovered that theirs is an honourable profession. They frame laws as they frame their own praises. They decide what fees they will charge and they put on so much side that poor people almost consider them to be heaven-born.

Why do they want more fees than common labourers? Why are their requirements greater? In what way are they more profitable to the country than the labourers? Are those who do good entitled to greater payment? And, if they have done anything for the country for the sake of money, how shall it be counted as good? Those who know anything of the Hindu-Mahomedan quarrels know that they have been often due to the intervention of lawyers. Some families have been ruined through them; they have made brothers enemies. Principalities, having come under the lawyers' power, have become loaded with debt. Many have been robbed of their all. Such instances can be multiplied. But the greatest injury they have done to the country is that they have tightened the English grip. Do you think that it would be possible for the English to carry on their Government without law-courts? It is wrong to consider that courts are established for the benefit of the people. Those who want to perpetuate their power do so through the courts. If people were to settle their own quarrels, a third party would not be able to exercise any authority over them. Truly, men were less unmanly when they settled their disputes either by fighting or by asking their relatives to decide for them. They became more unmanly and cowardly when they resorted to the courts of law. It was certainly a sign of savagery when they settled their disputes by fighting. Is it any the less so, if I ask a third party to decide between you and me? Surely, the decision of a third party is not always right. The parties alone know who is right. We, in our simplicity and ignorance, imagine that a stranger, by taking our money, gives us justice.

The chief thing, however, to be remembered is that without lawyers courts could not have been established or conducted and without the latter the English could not rule. Supposing that there were only English judges, English pleaders and English police, they could only rule over the English. The English could not do without Indian judges and Indian pleaders. How the pleaders were made in the first instance and how they were favoured you should understand well. Then you will have the same abhorrence for the profession that I have. If pleaders were to abandon their profession, and consider it just as degrading as prostitution, English rule would break up in a day. They have been instrumental in having the charge laid against us that we love quarrels and courts as fish love water. What I have said with reference to the pleaders necessarily applies to the judges; they are first cousins; and the one gives strength to the other.

❦ Chapter 12 ❦

The Condition of India (Continued): Doctors

Reader: I now understand the lawyers; the good they may have done is accidental. I feel that profession is certainly hateful. You, however, drag in the doctors also, how is that?

Editor: The views I submit to you are those I have adopted. They are not original. Western writers have used stronger terms regarding both lawyers and doctors. One writer has likened the whole modern system to the Upas tree. Its branches are represented by parasitical professions, including those of law and medicine, and over the trunk has been raised the axe of true religion. Immorality is the root of the tree. So you will see that the views do not come right out of my mind but represent the combined experiences of many. I was at one time a great lover of the medical profession. It was my intention to become a doctor for the sake of the country. I no longer hold that opinion, I now understand why the medicine men (the *vaids*) among us have not occupied a very honourable status.

The English have certainly effectively used the medical profession for holding us. English physicians are known to have used their profession with several Asiatic potentates for political gain.

Doctors have almost unhinged us. Sometimes I think that quacks are better than highly qualified doctors. Let us consider: the business of a doctor is to take care of the body, or, properly speaking, not even that. Their business is really to rid the body of diseases that may afflict it. How do these diseases arise? Surely by our negligence or indulgence. I overeat, I have indigestion, I go to a doctor, he gives me medicine, I am cured. I overeat again, I take his pills again. Had I not taken the pills in the first instance, I would have suffered the punishment deserved by me and I would not have overeaten again. The doctor intervened and helped me to indulge myself. My body thereby certainly felt more at ease; but my mind became weakened. A continuance of a course of medicine must, therefore, result in loss of control over the mind. I have indulged in vice, I contract a disease, a doctor cures me, the odds are that I shall repeat the vice.

Had the doctor not intervened, nature would have done its work, and I would have acquired mastery over myself, would have been freed from vice and would have become happy.

Hospitals are institutions for propagating sin. Men take less care of their bodies and immorality increases. European doctors are the worst of all. For the sake of a mistaken care of the human body, they kill annually thousands of animals. They practise vivisection. No religion sanctions this. All say that it is not necessary to take so many lives for the sake of our bodies.

These doctors violate our religious instinct. Most of their medical preparations contain either animal fat or spirituous liquors; both of these are tabooed by Hindus and Mahomedans. We may pretend to be civilized, call religious prohibitions a superstition and want only to indulge in what we like. The fact remains that the doctors induce us to indulge, and the result is that we have become deprived of self-control and have become effeminate. In these circumstances, we are unfit to serve the country. To study European medicine is to deepen our slavery.

It is worth considering why we take up the profession of medicine. It is certainly not taken up for the purpose of serving humanity. We become doctors so that we may obtain honours and riches. I have endeavoured to show that there is no real service of humanity in the profession, and that it is injurious to mankind. Doctors make a show of their knowledge, and charge exorbitant fees. Their preparations, which are intrinsically worth a few pence, cost shillings. The populace, in its credulity and in the hope of ridding itself of some disease, allows itself to be cheated. Are not quacks then, whom we know, better than the doctors who put on an air of humaneness?

Chapter 13

What Is True Civilization?

Reader: You have denounced railways, lawyers and doctors. I can see that you will discard all machinery. What, then, is civilization?

Editor: The answer to that question is not difficult. I believe that the civilization India has evolved is not to be beaten in the world. Nothing can equal the seeds sown by our ancestors. Rome went, Greece shared the same fate; the might of the Pharaohs was broken; Japan has become Westernised; of China nothing can be said; but India is still, somehow or other, sound at the foundation. The people of Europe learn their lessons from the writings of the men of Greece or Rome, which exist no longer in their former glory. In trying to learn from them, the Europeans imagine that they will avoid the mistakes of Greece and Rome. Such is their pitiable condition. In the midst of all this India remains immovable and that is her glory. It is a charge against India that her people are so uncivilized, ignorant and stolid, that it is not possible to induce them to adopt any changes. It is a charge really against our merit. What we have tested and found true on the anvil of experience, we dare not change. Many thrust their advice upon India, and she remains steady. This is her beauty: it is the sheet-anchor of our hope.

Civilization is that mode of conduct which points out to man the path of duty. Performance of duty and observance of morality are convertible terms. To observe morality is to attain mastery over our mind and our passions. So doing, we know ourselves. The Gujarati equivalent for civilization means "good conduct".

If this definition be correct, then India, as so many writers have shown, has nothing to learn from anybody else, and this is as it should be. We notice that the mind is a restless bird; the more it gets the more it wants, and still remains unsatisfied. The more we indulge our passions, the more unbridled they become. Our ancestors, therefore, set a limit to our indulgences. They saw that happiness was largely a mental condition. A man is not necessarily happy because he is rich, or unhappy because he is poor. The rich are often seen to be unhappy, the poor to be happy. Millions will always remain poor. Observing all this, our ancestors dissuaded us from luxuries and pleasures. We have managed with the same kind of plough as existed thousands of years ago. We have retained the same kind of cottages that we had in former times and our indigenous education remains the same as before. We have had no system of life-corroding competition. Each followed his own occupation or trade and charged a regulation wage. It was not that we did not know how to invent machinery, but our forefathers knew that if we set our hearts after such things, we would become slaves and lose our moral fibre. They, therefore, after due deliberation decided that we should only do what we could with our hands and feet. They saw that our real happiness and health consisted in a proper use of our hands and feet. They further reasoned that large cities were a snare and a useless encumbrance and that people would not be happy in them, that there would be gangs of thieves and robbers, prostitution and vice flourishing in them and that poor men would be robbed by rich men. They were, therefore, satisfied with small villages. They saw that kings and their swords were inferior to the sword of ethics, and they, therefore, held the sovereigns of the earth to be inferior to the Rishis and the Fakirs. A nation with a constitution like this is fitter to teach others than to learn from others. This nation had courts, lawyers and doctors, but they were all within bounds. Everybody knew that these professions were not particularly superior; moreover, these *vakils* and *vaids* did not rob people; they were considered people's dependants, not their masters. Justice was tolerably fair. The ordinary rule was to avoid courts. There were no touts to lure people into them. This evil, too, was noticeable only in and around capitals. The common people lived independently and followed their agricultural occupation. They enjoyed true Home Rule.

And where this cursed modern civilization has not reached, India remains as it was before. The inhabitants of that part of India will very properly laugh at your new-fangled notions. The English do not rule over them, nor will you ever rule over them. Those in whose name we speak we do not know, nor do they know us. I would certainly advise you and those like you who love the motherland to go into the interior that has yet been not polluted by the railways and to live there for six months; you might then be patriotic and speak of Home Rule.

Now you see what I consider to be real civilization. Those who want to change conditions such as I have described are enemies of the country and are sinners.

Reader: It would be all right if India were exactly as you have described it, but it is also India where there are hundreds of child widows, where two-year-old babies are married, where twelve-year-old girls are mothers and housewives, where women practise polyandry, where the practice of Niyoga obtains, where, in the name of religion, girls dedicate themselves to prostitution, and in the name of religion sheep and goats are killed. Do you consider these also symbols of the civilization that you have described?

Editor: You make a mistake. The defects that you have shown are defects. Nobody mistakes them for ancient civilization. They remain in spite of it. Attempts have always been made and will be made to remove them. We may utilize the new spirit that is born in us for purging ourselves of these evils. But what I have described to you as emblems of modern civilization are accepted as such by its votaries. The Indian civilization, as described by me, has been so described by its votaries. In no part of the world, and under no civilization, have all men attained perfection. The tendency of the Indian civilization is to elevate the moral being, that of the Western civilization is to propagate immorality. The latter is godless, the former is based on a belief in God. So understanding and so believing, it behoves every lover of India to cling to the old Indian civilization even as a child clings to the mother's breast.

⤜⟡⟿ **Chapter 14** ⬱⟡⤛

How Can India Become Free?

Reader: I appreciate your views about civilization. I will have to think over them. I cannot take them in all at once. What, then, holding the views you do, would you suggest for freeing India?

Editor: I do not expect my views to be accepted all of a sudden. My duty is to place them before readers like yourself. Time can be trusted to do the rest. We have already examined the conditions for freeing India, but we have done so indirectly; we will now do so directly. It is a world-known maxim that the removal of the cause of a disease results in the removal of the disease itself. Similarly if the cause of India's slavery be removed, India can become free.

Reader: If Indian civilization is, as you say, the best of all, how do you account for India's slavery?

Editor: This civilization is unquestionably the best, but it is to be observed that all civilizations have been on their trial. That civilization which is permanent outlives it. Because the sons of India were found wanting, its civilization has been placed in jeopardy. But its strength is to be seen in its ability to survive the shock. Moreover, the whole of India is not touched. Those alone who have been affected by Western civilization have become enslaved. We measure the universe by our own miserable foot-rule. When we are slaves, we think that the whole universe is enslaved. Because we are in an abject condition, we think that the whole of India is in that condition. As a matter of fact, it is not so, yet it is as well to impute our slavery to the whole of India. But if we bear in mind the above fact, we can see that if we become free, India is free. And in this thought you have a definition of Swaraj. It is Swaraj when we learn to rule ourselves. It is, therefore, in the palm of our hands. Do not consider this Swaraj to be like a dream. There is no idea of sitting still. The Swaraj that I wish to picture is such that, after we have once realized it, we shall endeavour to the end of our life- time to persuade others to do likewise. But such Swaraj has to be experienced, by each one for himself. One drowning man will never save another. Slaves ourselves, it would be a mere pretension to think of freeing others. Now you will have seen that it is not necessary for us to have as our goal the expulsion of the English. If the English become Indianised, we can accommodate them. If they wish to remain in India along with their civilization, there is no room for them. It lies with us to bring about such a state of things.

Reader: It is impossible that Englishmen should ever become Indianised.

Editor: To say that is equivalent to saying that the English have no humanity in them. And it is really beside the point whether they become so or not. If we keep our own house in order, only those who are fit to live in it will remain. Others will leave of their own accord. Such things occur within the experience of all of us.

Reader: But it has not occurred in history.

Editor: To believe that what has not occurred in history will not occur at all is to argue disbelief in the dignity of man. At any rate, it behoves us to try what appeals to our reason. All countries are not similarly conditioned. The condition of India is unique. Its strength is immeasurable. We need not, therefore, refer to the history of other countries. I have drawn attention to the fact that, when other civilizations have succumbed, the Indian has survived many a shock.

Reader: I cannot follow this. There seems little doubt that we shall have to expel the English by force of arms. So long as they are in the country we cannot rest. One of our poets say that slaves cannot even dream of happiness. We are day by day becoming weakened owing to the presence of the English. Our greatness is gone; our people look like terrified men. The English are in the country like a blight which we must remove by every means.

Editor: In your excitement, you have forgotten all we have been considering. We brought the English, and we keep them. Why do you forget that our adoption of their civilization makes their presence in India at all possible? Your hatred against them ought to be transferred to their civilization. But let us assume that we have to drive away the English by fighting, how is that to be done?

Reader: In the same way as Italy did it. What was possible for Mazzini and Garibaldi is possible for us. You cannot deny that they were very great men.

❮❯ Chapter 15 ❮❯

Italy and India

Editor: It is well that you have instanced Italy. Mazzini was a great and good man; Garibaldi was a great warrior. Both are adorable; from their lives we can learn much. But the condition of Italy was different from that of India. In the first instance, the difference between Mazzini and Garibaldi is worth noting. Mazzini's ambition was not and has not yet been realized regarding Italy. Mazzini has shown in his writings on the duty of man that every man must learn how to rule himself. This has not happened in Italy. Garibaldi did not hold this view of Mazzini's. Garibaldi gave and every Italian took arms. Italy and Austria had the same civilization; they were cousins in this respect. It was a matter of tit for tat. Garibaldi simply wanted Italy to be free from the Austrian yoke. The machinations of Minister Cavour disgrace that portion of the history of Italy. And what has been the result? If you believe that because Italians rule Italy the Italian nation is happy, you are groping in darkness. Mazzini has shown conclusively that Italy did not become free. Victor Emanuel gave one meaning to the expression; Mazzini gave another. According to Emanuel,

Cavour and even Garibaldi, Italy meant the King of Italy and his henchmen. According to Mazzini, it meant the whole of the Italian people, that is, its agriculturists. Emanuel was only its servant. The Italy of Mazzini still remains in a state of slavery. At the time of the so-called national war, it was a game of chess between two rival kings with the people of Italy as pawns. The working classes in that land are still unhappy. They, therefore, indulge in assassination, rise in revolt, and rebellion on their part is always expected. What substantial gain did Italy obtain after the withdrawal of the Austrian troops? The gain was only nominal. The reforms for the sake of which the war was supposed to have been undertaken have not yet been granted. The condition of the people in general still remains the same. I am sure you do not wish to reproduce such a condition in India. I believe that you want the millions of India to be happy, not that you want the reins of Government in your hands. If that be so, we have to consider only one thing: how can the millions obtain self-rule? You will admit that people under several Indian princes are being ground down. The latter mercilessly crush them. Their tyranny is greater than that of the English, and if you want such tyranny in India, then we shall never agree. My patriotism does not teach me that I am to allow people to be crushed under the heel of Indian princes if only the English retire. If I have the power, I should resist the tyranny of Indian princes just as much as that of the English. By patriotism I mean the welfare of the whole people, and if I could secure it at the hands of the English, I should bow down my head to them. If any Englishman dedicated his life in securing the freedom of India, resisting tyranny and serving the land, I should welcome that Englishman as an Indian.

Again, India can fight like Italy only when she has arms. You have not considered this problem at all. The English are splendidly armed; that does not frighten me, but it is clear that, to pit ourselves against them in arms, thousands of Indians must be armed. If such a thing be possible, how many years will it take? Moreover, to arm India on a large scale is to Europeanize it. Then her condition will be just as pitiable as that of Europe. This means, in short, that India must accept European civilization, and if that is what we want, the best thing is that we have among us those who are so well trained in that civilization. We will then fight for a few rights, will get what we can and so pass our days. But the fact is that the Indian nation will not adopt arms, and it is well that it does not.

Reader: You are over-stating the facts. All need not be armed. At first, we shall assassinate a few Englishmen and strike terror; then, a few men who will have been armed will fight openly. We may have to lose a quarter of a million men, more or less, but we shall regain our land. We shall undertake guerilla warfare, and defeat the English.

Editor: That is to say, you want to make the holy land of India unholy. Do you not tremble to think of freeing India by assassination? What we need to do is to sacrifice ourselves. It is a cowardly thought, that of killing others. Whom do you suppose to free by assassination? The millions of India do not desire it. Those who are intoxicated by the wretched modern civilization think these things.

Those who will rise to power by murder will certainly not make the nation happy. Those who believe that India has gained by Dhingra's act and other similar acts in India make a serious mistake. Dhingra was a patriot, but his love was blind. He gave his body in a wrong way; its ultimate result can only be mischievous.

Reader: But you will admit that the English have been frightened by these murders, and that Lord Morley's reforms are due to fear.

Editor: The English are both a timid and a brave nation. England is, I believe, easily influenced by the use of gunpowder. It is possible that Lord Morley has granted the reforms through fear, but what is granted under fear can be retained only so long as the fear lasts.

❧ Chapter 16 ❧

Brute Force

Reader: This is a new doctrine, that what is gained through fear is retained only while the fear lasts. Surely, what is given will not be withdrawn?

Editor: Not so. The Proclamation of 1857 was given at the end of a revolt, and for the purpose of preserving peace. When peace was secured and people became simple-minded, its full effect was toned down. If I cease stealing for fear of punishment, I would recommence the operation as soon as the fear is withdrawn from me. This is almost a universal experience. We have assumed that we can get men to do things by force and, therefore, we use force.

Reader: Will you not admit that you are arguing against yourself? You know that what the English obtained in their own country they obtained by using brute force. I know you have argued that what they have obtained is useless, but that does not affect my argument. They wanted useless things and they got them. My point is that their desire was fulfilled. What does it matter what means they adopted? Why should we not obtain our goal, which is good, by any means whatsoever, even by using violence? Shall I think of the means when I have to deal with a thief in the house? My duty is to drive him out anyhow. You seem to admit that we have received nothing, and that we shall receive nothing by petitioning. Why, then, may we not do so by using brute force? And, to retain what we may receive, we shall keep up the fear by using the same force to the extent that it may be necessary. You will not find fault with a continuance of force to prevent a child from thrusting its foot into fire. Somehow or other we have to gain our end.

Editor: Your reasoning is plausible. It has deluded many. I have used similar arguments before now. But I think I know better now, and I shall endeavour to undeceive you. Let us first take the argument that we are justified in gaining our end by using brute force because the English gained theirs by using similar means. It is perfectly true that they used brute force and that it is possible for us to do likewise, but by using similar means we can get only the same thing that they got. You will admit that we do not want that. Your belief that there is no connection between the means and the end is a great mistake. Through that mistake even men who have been considered religious have committed grievous crimes. Your reasoning is the same as saying that we can get a rose through planting a noxious weed. If I want to cross the ocean, I can do so only by means of a vessel; if I were to use a cart for that purpose, both the cart and I would soon find the bottom. "As is the God, so is the votary", is a maxim worth considering. Its meaning has been distorted and men have gone astray. The means may be likened to a seed, the end to a tree; and there is just the same inviolable connection between the means and the end as there is between the seed and the tree. I am not likely to obtain the result flowing from the worship of God by laying myself prostrate before Satan. If, therefore, anyone were to say: "I want to worship God; it does not matter that I do so by means of Satan," it would be set down as ignorant folly. We reap exactly as we sow. The English in 1833 obtained greater voting power by violence. Did they by using brute force better appreciate their duty? They wanted the right of voting, which they obtained by using physical force. But real rights are a result of performance of duty; these rights they have not obtained.

We, therefore, have before us in England the force of everybody wanting and insisting on his rights, nobody thinking of his duty. And, where everybody wants rights, who shall give them to whom? I do not wish to imply that they do no duties. They don't perform the duties corresponding to those rights; and as they do not perform that particular duty, namely, acquire fitness, their rights have proved a burden to them. In other words, what they have obtained is an exact result of the means they adopted. They used the means corresponding to the end. If I want to deprive you of your watch, I shall certainly have to fight for it; if I want to buy your watch, I shall have to pay you for it; and if I want a gift, I shall have to plead for it; and, according to the means I employ, the watch is stolen property, my own property, or a donation. Thus we see three different results from three different means. Will you still say that means do not matter?

Now we shall take the example given by you of the thief to be driven out. I do not agree with you that the thief may be driven out by any means. If it is my father who has come to steal I shall use one kind of means. If it is an acquaintance I shall use another; and in the case of a perfect stranger I shall use a third. If it is a white man, you will perhaps say you will use means different from those you will adopt with an Indian thief. If it is a weakling, the means will be different from those to be adopted for dealing with an equal in physical strength; and if the thief is armed from top to toe, I shall simply remain quiet. Thus we have a variety of means between the father and the armed man. Again, I fancy that I should pretend to be sleeping whether the thief was my father or that strong armed man. The reason for this is that my father would also be armed and I should succumb to the strength possessed by either and allow my things to be stolen. The strength of my father would make me weep with pity; the strength of the armed man would rouse in me anger and we should become enemies. Such is the curious situation. From these examples we may not be able to agree as to the means to be adopted in each ease. I myself seem clearly to see what should be done in all these cases, but the remedy may frighten you. I therefore hesitate to place it before you. For the time being I will leave you to guess it, and if you cannot, it is clear you will have to adopt different means in each case. You will also have seen that any means will not avail to drive away the thief. You will have to adopt means to fit each case. Hence it follows that your duty is *not* to drive away the thief by any means you like.

Let us proceed a little further. That well-armed man has stolen your property; you have harboured the thought of his act; you are filled with anger; you argue that you want to punish that rogue, not for your own sake, but for the good of your neighbours; you have collected a number of armed men, you want to take his house by assault; he is duly informed of it, he runs away; he too is incensed. He collects his brother-robbers, and sends you a defiant message that he will commit robbery in broad daylight. You are strong, you do not fear him, you are prepared to receive him. Meanwhile, the robber pesters your neighbours. They complain before you. You reply that you are doing all for their sake; you do not mind that your own goods have been stolen. Your neighbours reply that the robber never pestered them before, and that he commenced his depredations only after you declared hostilities against him. You are between Scylla and Charybdis. You are full of pity for the poor men. What they say is true. What are you to do? You will be disgraced if you now leave the robber alone. You, therefore, tell the poor men: "Never mind. Come, my wealth is yours, I will give you arms, I will teach you how to use them; you should belabour the rogue; don't you leave him alone." And so the battle grows; the robbers increase in numbers; your neighbours have deliberately put themselves to inconvenience. Thus the result of wanting to take revenge upon the robber is that you have disturbed your own peace; you are in perpetual fear of being robbed and assaulted; your courage has given place to cowardice. If you will patiently examine the argument, you will see that I have not overdrawn the picture. This is one of the means. Now let us examine the other. You set this armed robber down as an ignorant brother; you intend to reason with him at a suitable opportunity; you argue that he is, after all, a fellow-man; you do not know what prompted him to steal. You, therefore, decide that, when you can, you will destroy the man's motive for stealing. Whilst you are thus reasoning with yourself, the man comes again to steal. Instead of being angry with him, you take pity on him. You think that this stealing habit must be a disease with him. Henceforth, you, therefore, keep your doors and windows open, you change your sleeping-place, and you keep your things in a manner most accessible to him. The robber comes again and is confused as all this is new to him; nevertheless, he takes away your things. But his mind is agitated. He inquires about you in the village, he comes to learn about your broad and loving heart, he repents, he begs your pardon, returns you your things, and leaves off the stealing habit. He becomes your servant, and you find for him honourable employment. This is the second method. Thus, you see, different means have brought about totally different results. I do not wish to deduce from this that robbers will act in the above manner or that all will have the same pity and love like you, but I only wish to show that fair means alone can produce fair results, and that, at least in the majority of cases, if not indeed in all, the force of love and pity is infinitely greater than the force of arms. There is harm in the exercise of brute force, never in that of pity.

Now we will take the question of petitioning. It is a fact beyond dispute that a petition, without the backing of force, is useless. However, the late Justice Ranade used to say that petitions served a useful purpose because they were a means of educating people. They give the latter an idea of their condition and warn the rulers. From this point of view, they are not altogether useless. A petition of an equal is a sign of courtesy; a petition from a slave is a symbol of his slavery. A petition backed by force is a petition from an equal and, when he transmits his demand in the form of a petition, it testifies to his nobility. Two kinds of force can back petitions. "We shall hurt you if you do not give this," is one kind of force; it is the force of arms, whose evil results we have already examined. The second kind of force can thus be stated: "If you do not concede our demand, we shall be no longer your petitioners. You can govern us only so long as we remain the governed; we shall no longer have any dealings with you." The force implied in this may be described as love-force, soul-force or, more popularly but less accurately, passive resistance. This force is indestructible. He who uses it perfectly understands his position. We have an ancient proverb which literally means:

"One negative cures thirty-six diseases." The force of arms is powerless when matched against the force of love or the soul.

Now we shall take your last illustration, that of the child thrusting its foot into fire. It will not avail you. What do you really do to the child? Supposing that it can exert so much physical force that it renders you powerless and rushes into fire, then you cannot prevent it. There are only two remedies open to you—either you must kill it in order to prevent it from perishing in the flames, or you must give your own life because you do not wish to see it perish before your very eyes.

You will not kill it. If your heart is not quite full of pity, it is possible that you will not surrender yourself by preceding the child and going into the fire yourself. You, therefore, helplessly allow it to go into the flames. Thus, at any rate, you are not using physical force. I hope you will not consider that it is still physical force, though of a low order, when you would forcibly prevent the child from rushing towards the fire if you could.

That force is of a different order and we have to understand what it is.

Remember that, in thus preventing the child, you are minding entirely its own interest; you are exercising authority for its sole benefit. Your example does not apply to the English. In using brute force against the English you consult entirely your own, that is the national interest. There is no question here either of pity or of love. If you say that the actions of the English, being evil, represent fire, and that they proceed to their actions through ignorance, and that therefore they occupy the position of a child and that you want to protect such a child, then you will have to overtake every evil action of that kind by whomsoever committed and, as in the case of the evil child, you will have to sacrifice yourself. If you are capable of such immeasurable pity, I wish you well in its exercise.

Chapter 17

Passive Resistance

Reader: Is there any historical evidence as to the success of what you have called soul-force or truth-force? No instance seems to have happened of any nation having risen through soul-force. I still think that the evil-doers will not cease doing evil without physical punishment.

Editor: The poet Tulsidas has said: "Of religion, pity, or love, is the root, as egotism of the body. Therefore, we should not abandon pity so long as we are alive." This appears to me to be a scientific truth. I believe in it as much as I believe in two and two being four. The force of love is the same as the force of the soul or truth. We have evidence of its working at every step. The universe would disappear without the existence of that force. But you ask for historical evidence. It is, therefore, necessary to know what history means. The Gujarati equivalent means: "It so happened." If that is the meaning of history, it is possible to give copious evidence. But, if it means the doings of kings and emperors, there can be no evidence of soul-force or passive resistance in such history, You cannot expect silver ore in a tin mine. History, as we know it, is a record of the wars of the world, and so there is a proverb among Englishmen that a nation which has no history, that is, no wars, is a happy nation. How kings played, how they became enemies of one another, how they murdered one another, is found accurately recorded in history, and if this were all that had happened in the world, it would have been ended long ago. If the story of the universe had commenced with wars, not a man would have been found alive today. Those people who have been warred against have disappeared as, for instance, the natives of Australia of whom hardly a man was left alive by the intruders. Mark, please, that these natives did not use soul-force in self-defence, and it does not require much foresight to know that the Australians will share the same fate as their victims. "Those that take the sword shall perish by the sword." With us the proverb is that professional swimmers will find a watery grave.

The fact that there are so many men still alive in the world shows that it is based not on the force of arms but on the force of truth or love. Therefore, the greatest and most unimpeachable evidence of the success of this force is to be found in the fact that, in spite of the wars of the world, it still lives on.

Thousands, indeed tens of thousands, depend for their existence on a very active working of this force. Little quarrels of millions of families in their daily lives disappear before the exercise of this force. Hundreds of nations live in peace. History does not and cannot take note of this fact. History is really a record of every interruption of the even working of the force of love or of the soul. Two brothers quarrel; one of them repents and re-awakens the love that was lying dormant in him; the two again begin to live in peace; nobody takes note of this. But if the two brothers, through the intervention of solicitors or some other reason take up arms or go to law—which is another form of the exhibition of brute force—their doings would be immediately noticed in the Press, they would be the talk of their neighbours and would probably go down to history. And what is true of families and communities is true of nations. There is no reason to believe that there is one law for families and another for nations. History, then, is a record of an interruption of the course of nature. Soul-force, being natural, is not noted in history.

Reader: According to what you say, it is plain that instances of this kind of passive resistance are not to be found in history. It is necessary to understand passive resistance more fully. It will be better, therefore, if you enlarge upon it.

Editor: Passive resistance is a method of securing rights by personal suffering; it is the reverse of resistance by arms. When I refuse to do a thing that is repugnant to my conscience, I use soul-force. For instance, the Government of the day has passed a law which is applicable to me. I do not like it. If by using violence I force the Government to repeal the law, I am employing what may be termed body-force. If I do not obey the law and accept the penalty for its breach, I use soul-force. It involves sacrifice of self.

Everybody admits that sacrifice of self is infinitely superior to sacrifice of others. Moreover, if this kind of force is used in a cause that is unjust, only the person using it suffers. He does not make others suffer for his mistakes. Men have before now done many things which were subsequently found to have been wrong. No man can claim that he is absolutely in the right or that a particular thing is wrong because he thinks so, but it is wrong for him so long as that is his deliberate judgment. It is therefore meet that he should not do that which he knows to be wrong, and suffer the consequence whatever it may be. This is the key to the use of soul-force.

Reader: You would then disregard laws—this is rank disloyalty. We have always been considered a law-abiding nation. You seem to be going even beyond the extremists. They say that we must obey the laws that have been passed, but that if the laws be bad, we must drive out the law-givers even by force.

Editor: Whether I go beyond them or whether I do not is a matter of no consequence to either of us. We simply want to find out what is right and to act accordingly. The real meaning of the statement that we are a law-abiding nation is that we are passive resisters. When we do not like certain laws, we do not break the heads of law-givers but we suffer and do not submit to the laws. That we should obey laws whether good or bad is a new-fangled notion. There was no such thing in former days. The people disregarded those laws that they did not like and suffered the penalties for their breach. It is contrary to our manhood if we obey laws repugnant to our conscience. Such teaching is opposed to religion and means slavery. If the Government were to ask us to go about without any clothing, should we do so? If I were a passive resister, I would say to them that I would have nothing to do with their law. But we have so forgotten ourselves and become so compliant that we do not mind any degrading law. A man who has realized his manhood, who fears only God, will fear no one else. Man-made laws are not necessarily binding on him. Even the Government does not expect any such thing from us. They do not say: "You must do such and such a thing," but they say: "If you do not do it, we will punish you." We are sunk so low that we fancy that it is our duty and our religion to do what the law lays down. If man will only realize that it is unmanly to obey laws that are unjust, no man's tyranny will enslave him. This is the key to Self-Rule or Home-Rule.

It is a superstition and ungodly thing to believe that an act of a majority binds a minority. Many examples can be given in which acts of majorities will be found to have been wrong and those of minorities to have been right. All reforms owe their origin to the initiation of minorities in opposition to majorities. If among a band of robbers a knowledge of robbing is obligatory, is a pious man to accept the obligation? So long as the superstition that men should obey unjust laws exists, so long will their slavery exist. And a passive resister alone can remove such a superstition.

To use brute-force, to use gunpowder, is contrary to passive resistance, for it means that we want our opponent to do by force that which we desire but he does not. And if such a use of force is justifiable, surely he is entitled to do likewise by us. And so we should never come to an agreement. We may simply fancy, like the blind horse moving in a circle round a mill, that we are making progress. Those who believe that they are not bound to obey laws which are repugnant to their conscience have only the remedy of passive resistance open to them. Any other must lead to disaster.

Reader: From what you say I deduce that passive resistance is a splendid weapon of the weak, but that when they are strong they may take up arms.

Editor: This is gross ignorance. Passive resistance, that is, soul-force, is matchless. It is superior to the force of arms. How, then, can it be considered only a weapon of the weak? Physical-force men are strangers to the courage that is requisite in a passive resister. Do you believe that a coward can ever disobey a law that he dislikes? Extremists are considered to be advocates of brute force. Why do they, then, talk about obeying laws? I do not blame them. They can say nothing else. When they succeed in driving out the English and they themselves become governors, they will want you and me to obey their laws. And that is a fitting thing for their constitution. But a passive resister will say he will not obey a law that is against his conscience, even though he may be blown to pieces at the mouth of cannon.

What do you think? Wherein is courage required in blowing others to pieces from behind a cannon, or with a smiling face to approach a cannon and be blown to pieces? Who is the true warrior—he who keeps death always as a bosom-friend, or he who controls the death of others? Believe me that a man devoid of courage and manhood can never be a passive resister.

This however, I will admit: that even a man weak in body is capable of offering this resistance. One man can offer it just as well as millions. Both men and women can indulge in it. It does not require the training of an army; it needs no jiu-jitsu. Control over the mind is alone necessary, and when that is attained, man is free like the king of the forest and his very glance withers the enemy.

Passive resistance is an all-sided sword, it can be used anyhow; it blesses him who uses it and him against whom it is used. Without drawing a drop of blood it produces far-reaching results. It never rusts and cannot be stolen. Competition between passive resisters does not exhaust. The sword of passive resistance does not require a scabbard. It is strange indeed that you should consider such a weapon to be a weapon merely of the weak.

Reader: You have said that passive resistance is a speciality of India. Have cannons never been used in India?

Editor: Evidently, in your opinion, India means its few princes. To me it means its teeming millions on whom depends the existence of its princes and our own. Kings will always use their kingly weapons. To use force is bred in them. They want to command, but those who have to obey commands do not want guns: and these are in a majority throughout the world. They have to learn either body-force or soul-force. Where they learn the former, both the rulers and the ruled become like so many madmen; but where they learn soul force, the commands of the rulers do not go beyond the point of their swords, for true men disregard unjust commands. Peasants have never been subdued by the sword, and never will be. They do not know the use of the sword, and they are not frightened by the use of it by others. That nation is great which rests its head upon death as its pillow. Those who defy death are free from all fear. For those who are labouring under the delusive charms of brute-force, this picture is not overdrawn. The fact is that, in India, the nation at large has generally used passive resistance in all departments of life. We cease to co-operate with our rulers when they displease us. This is passive resistance.

I remember an instance when, in a small principality, the villagers were offended by some command issued by the prince. The former immediately began vacating the village. The prince became nervous, apologized to his subjects and withdrew his command. Many such instances can be found in India. Real Home Rule is possible only where passive resistance is the guiding force of the people. Any other rule is foreign rule.

Reader: Then you will say that it is not at all necessary for us to train the body?

Editor: I will certainly not say any such thing. It is difficult to become a passive resister unless the body is trained. As a rule, the mind, residing in a body that has become weakened by pampering, is also weak, and where there is no strength of mind there can be no strength of soul. We shall have to improve our physique by getting rid of infant marriages and luxurious living. If I were to ask a man with a shattered body to face a cannon's mouth I should make a laughing-stock of myself

Reader: From what you say, then, it would appear that it is not a small thing to become a passive resister, and, if that is so, I should like you to explain how a man may become one.

Editor: To become a passive resister is easy enough but it is also equally difficult. I have known a lad of fourteen years become a passive resister; I have known also sick people do likewise; and I have also known physically strong and otherwise happy people unable to take up passive resistance. After a great deal of experience it seems to me that those who want to become passive resisters for the service of the country have to observe perfect chastity, adopt poverty, follow truth, and cultivate fearlessness.

Chastity is one of the greatest disciplines without which the mind cannot attain requisite firmness. A man who is unchaste loses stamina, becomes emasculated and cowardly. He whose mind is given over to animal passions is not capable of any great effort. This can be proved by innumerable instances. What, then, is a married person to do is the question that arises naturally; and yet it need not. When a husband and wife gratify the passions, it is no less an animal indulgence on that account. Such an indulgence, except for perpetuating the race, is strictly prohibited. But a passive resister has to avoid even that very limited indulgence because he can have no desire for progeny. A married man, therefore, can observe perfect chastity. This subject is not capable of being treated at greater length. Several questions arise: How is one to carry one's wife with one, what are her rights, and other similar questions. Yet those who wish to take part in a great work are bound to solve these puzzles.

Just as there is necessity for chastity, so is there for poverty. Pecuniary ambition and passive resistance cannot well go together. Those who have money are not expected to throw it away, but they are expected to be indifferent about it. They must be prepared to lose every penny rather than give up passive resistance.

Passive resistance has been described in the course of our discussion as truth-force. Truth, therefore, has necessarily to be followed and that at any cost. In this connection, academic questions such as whether a man may not lie in order to save a life, etc., arise, but these questions occur only to those who wish to justify lying. Those who want to follow truth every time are not placed in such a quandary; and if they are, they are still saved from a false position.

Passive resistance cannot proceed a step without fearlessness. Those alone can follow the path of passive resistance who are free from fear, whether as to their possessions, false honour, their relatives, the government, bodily injuries or death. These observances are not to be abandoned in the belief that they are difficult. Nature has implanted in the human breast ability to cope with any difficulty or suffering that may come to man unprovoked. These qualities are worth having, even for those who do not wish to serve the country. Let there be no mistake, as those who want to train themselves in the use of arms are also obliged to have these qualities more or less. Everybody does not become a warrior for the wish. A would-be warrior will have to observe chastity and to be satisfied with poverty as his lot. A warrior without fearlessness cannot be conceived of. It may be thought that he would not need to be exactly truthful, but that quality follow real fearlessness. When a man abandons truth, he does so owing to fear in some shape or form. The above four attributes, then, need not frighten anyone. It may be as well here to note that a physical-force man has to have many other useless qualities which a passive resister never needs. And you will find that whatever extra effort a swordsman needs is due to lack of fearlessness. If he is an embodiment of the latter, the sword will drop from his hand that very moment. He does not need its support. One who is free from hatred requires no sword. A man with a stick suddenly came face to face with a lion and instinctively raised his weapon in self-defence. The man saw that he had only prated about fearlessness when there was none in him. That moment he dropped the stick and found himself free from all fear.

Education

Reader: In the whole of our discussion, you have not demonstrated the necessity for education; we always complain of its absence among us. We notice a movement for compulsory education in our country. The Maharaja Gaekwar has introduced it in his territories. Every eye is directed towards them. We bless the Maharaja for it. Is all this effort then of no use?

Editor: If we consider our civilization to be the highest, I have regretfully to say that much of the effort you have described is of no use. The motive of the Maharaja and other great leaders who have been working in this direction is perfectly pure. They, therefore, undoubtedly deserve great praise. But we cannot conceal from ourselves the result that is likely to flow from their effort.

What is the meaning of education? It simply means a knowledge of letters. It is merely an instrument, and an instrument may be well used or abused. The same instrument that may be used to cure a patient may be used to take his life, and so may a knowledge of letters. We daily observe that many men abuse it and very few make good use of it; and if this is a correct statement, we have proved that more harm has been done by it than good.

The ordinary meaning of education is a knowledge of letters. To teach boys reading, writing and arithmetic is called primary education. A peasant earns his bread honestly. He has ordinary knowledge of the world. He knows fairly well how he should behave towards his parents, his wife, his children and his fellow-villagers. He understands and observes the rules of morality. But he cannot write his own name. What do you propose to do by giving him a knowledge of letters? Will you add an inch to his happiness? Do you wish to make him discontented with his cottage or his lot? And even if you want to do that, he will not need such an education. Carried away by the flood of Western thought we came to the conclusion, without weighing pros and cons, that we should give this kind of education to the people. Now let us take higher education. I have learned Geography, Astronomy, Algebra, Geometry, etc. What of that? In what way have I benefited myself or those around me? Why have I learned these things? Professor Huxley has thus defined education: "That man I think has had a liberal education who has been so trained in youth that his body is the ready servant of his will and does with ease and pleasure all the work that as a mechanism it is capable of; whose intellect is a clear, cold, logic engine with all its parts of equal strength and in smooth working order ... whose mind is stored with a knowledge of the fundamental truths of nature ... whose passions are trained to come to heel by a vigorous will, the servant of a tender conscience ... who has learnt to hate all vileness and to respect others as himself. Such a one and no other, I conceive, has had a liberal education, for he is in harmony with nature. He will make the best of her and she of him."

If this is true education, I must emphatically say that the sciences I have enumerated above I have never been able to use for controlling my senses. Therefore, whether you take elementary education or higher education, it is not required for the main thing. It does not make men of us. It does not enable us to do our duty.

Reader: If that is so, I shall have to ask you another question. What enables you to tell all these things to me? If you had not received higher education, how would you have been able to explain to me the things that you have?

Editor: You have spoken well. But my answer is simple: I do not for one moment believe that my life would have been wasted, had I not received higher or lower education. Nor do I consider that I necessarily serve because I speak. But I do desire to serve and in endeavouring to fulfill that desire, I make use of the education I have received. And, if I am making good use of it, even then it is not for the millions, but I can use it only for such as you, and this supports my contention. Both you and I have come under the bane of what is mainly false education. I claim to have become free from its ill effect, and I am trying to give you the benefit of my experience and in doing so, I am demonstrating the rottenness of this education.

Moreover, I have not run down a knowledge of letters in all circumstances. All I have now shown is that we must not make of it a fetish. It is not our *Kamadhuk* [Mythical cow, yielding whatever is wished for]. In its place it can be of use and it has its place when we have brought our senses under subjection and put our ethics on a firm foundation. And then, if we feel inclined to receive that education, we may make good use of it. As an ornament it is likely to sit well on us. It now follows that it is not necessary to make this education compulsory.

Our ancient school system is enough. Character-building has the first place in it and that is primary education. A building erected on that foundation will last.

Reader: Do I then understand that you do not consider English education necessary for obtaining Home Rule?

Editor: My answer is yes and no. To give millions a knowledge of English is to enslave them. The foundation that Macaulay laid of education has enslaved us. I do not suggest that he had any such intention, but that has been the result. Is it not a sad commentary that we should have to speak of Home Rule in a foreign tongue?

And it is worthy of note that the systems which the Europeans have discarded are the systems in vogue among us. Their learned men continually make changes. We ignorantly adhere to their cast-off systems. They are trying each division to improve its own status. Wales is a small portion of England. Great efforts are being made to revive a knowledge of Welsh among Welshmen. The English Chancellor, Mr. Llyod George, is taking a leading part in the movement to make Welsh children speak Welsh. And what is our condition? We write to each other in faulty English, and from this even our M.A.s are not free; our best thoughts are expressed in English; the proceedings of our Congress are conducted in English; our best newspapers are printed in English. If this state of things continues for a long time, posterity will—it is my firm opinion—condemn and curse us.

It is worth noting that, by receiving English education, we have enslaved the nation. Hypocrisy, tyranny, etc., have increased; English-knowing Indians have not hesitated to cheat and strike terror into the people. Now, if we are doing anything for the people at all, we are paying only a portion of the debt due to them.

Is it not a painful thing that, if I want to go to a court of justice, I must employ the English language as a medium, that when I become a barrister, I may not speak my mother-tongue and that someone else should have to translate to me from my own language? Is not this absolutely absurd? Is it not a sign of slavery? Am I to blame the English for it or myself? It is we, the English-knowing Indians that have enslaved India. The curse of the nation will rest not upon the English but upon us.

I have told you that my answer to your last question is both yes and no. I have explained to you why it is yes. I shall now explain why it is no.

We are so much beset by the disease of civilization that we cannot altogether do without English education. Those who have already received it may make good use of it wherever necessary. In our dealings with the English people, in our dealings with our own people, when we can only correspond with them through that language, and for the purpose of knowing how disgusted they (the English) have themselves become with their civilization, we may use or learn English, as the case may be. Those who have studied English will have to teach morality to their progeny through their mother-tongue and to teach them another Indian language; but when they have grown up, they may learn English, the ultimate aim being that we should not need it. The object of making money thereby should be eschewed. Even in learning English to such a limited extent we shall have to consider what we should learn through it and what we should not. It will be necessary to know what sciences we should learn. A little thought should show you that immediately we cease to care for English degrees, the rulers will prick up their ears.

Reader: Then what education shall we give?

Editor: This has been somewhat considered above, but we will consider it a little more. I think that we have to improve all our languages. What subjects we should learn through them need not be elaborated here. Those English books which are valuable, we should translate into the various Indian languages. We should abandon the pretension of learning many sciences. Religious, that is ethical, education will occupy the first place. Every cultured Indian will know in addition to his own provincial language, if a Hindu, Sanskrit; if a Mahomedan, Arabic; if a Parsee, Persian; and all, Hindi. Some Hindus should know Arabic and Persian; some Mahomedans and Parsees, Sanskrit. Several Northerners and Westerners should learn Tamil. A universal language for India should be Hindi, with the option of writing it in Persian or Nagari characters. In order that the Hindus and the Mahomedans may have closer relations, it is necessary to know both the characters. And, if we can do this, we can drive the English language out of the field in a short time. All this is necessary for us, slaves. Through our slavery the nation has been enslaved, and it will be free with our freedom.

Reader: The question of religious education is very difficult.

Editor: Yet we cannot do without it. India will never be godless. Rank atheism cannot flourish in this land. The task is indeed difficult. My head begins to turn as I think of religious education. Our religious teachers are hypocritical and selfish; they will have to be approached. The Mullas, the Dasturs and the Brahmins hold the key in their hands, but if they will not have the good sense, the energy that we have derived from English education will have to be devoted to religious education. This is not very difficult. Only the fringe of the ocean has been polluted and it is those who are within the fringe who alone need cleansing. We who come under this category can even cleanse ourselves because my remarks do not apply to the millions. In order to restore India to its pristine condition, we have to return to it. In our own civilization there will naturally be progress, retrogression, reforms, and reactions; but one effort is required, and that is to drive out Western civilization. All else will follow.

❦ Chapter 19 ❦

Machinery

Reader: When you speak of driving out Western civilization, I suppose you will also say that we want no machinery.

Editor: By raising this question, you have opened the wound I have received. When I read Mr. Dutt's *Economic History of India*, I wept; and as I think of it again my heart sickens. It is machinery that has impoverished India. It is difficult to measure the harm that Manchester has done to us. It is due to Manchester that Indian handicraft has all but disappeared.

But I make a mistake. How can Manchester be blamed? We wore Manchester cloth and this is why Manchester wove it. I was delighted when I read about the bravery of Bengal. There were no cloth-mills in that presidency. They were, therefore, able to restore the original hand-weaving occupation. It is true Bengal encourages the mill-industry of Bombay. If Bengal had proclaimed a boycott of *all* machine-made goods, it would have been much better.

Machinery has begun to desolate Europe. Ruination is now knocking at the English gates. Machinery is the chief symbol of modern civilization; it represents a great sin.

The workers in the mills of Bombay have become slaves. The condition of the women working in the mills is shocking. When there were no mills, these women were not starving. If the machinery craze grows in our country, it will become an unhappy land. It may be considered a heresy, but I am bound to say that it were better for us to send money to Manchester and to use flimsy Manchester cloth than to multiply mills in India. By using Manchester cloth we only waste our money; but by reproducing Manchester in India, we shall keep our money at the price of our blood, because our very moral being will be sapped, and I call in support of my statement the very mill-hands as witnesses. And those who have amassed wealth out of factories are not likely to be better than other rich men. It would be folly to assume that an Indian Rockefeller would be better than the American Rockefeller. Impoverished India can become free, but it will be hard for any India made rich through immorality to regain its freedom. I fear we shall have to admit that moneyed men support British rule; their interest is bound up with its stability. Money renders a man helpless. The other thing which is equally harmful is sexual vice. Both are poison. A snake-bite is a lesser poison than these two, because the former merely destroys the body but the latter destroy body, mind and soul. We need not, therefore, be pleased with the prospect of the growth of the mill-industry.

Reader: Are the mills, then, to be closed down?

Editor: That is difficult. It is no easy task to do away with a thing that is established. We, therefore, say that the non-beginning of a thing is supreme wisdom. We cannot condemn mill-owners; we can but pity them. It would be too much to expect them to give up their mills, but we may implore them not to increase them. If they would be good they would gradually contract their business. They can establish in thousands of households the ancient and sacred handlooms and they can buy out the cloth that may be thus woven. Whether the mill-owners do this or not, people can cease to use machine-made goods.

Reader: You have so far spoken about machine-made cloth, but there are innumerable machine-made things. We have either to import them or to introduce machinery into our country.

Editor: Indeed, our gods even are made in Germany. What need, then, to speak of matches, pins and glassware? My answer can be only one. What did India do before these articles were introduced? Precisely the same should be done today. As long as we cannot make pins without machinery, so long will we do without them. The tinsel splendour of glassware we will have nothing to do with, and we will make wicks, as of old, with home-grown cotton and use hand-made earthen saucers for lamps. So doing, we shall save our eyes and money and support Swadeshi and so shall we attain Home Rule. It is not to be conceived that all men will do all these things at one time or that some men will give up all machine-made things at once. But, if the thought is sound, we shall always find out what we can give up and gradually cease to use it. What a few may do, others will copy; and the movement will grow like the coconut of the mathematical problem. What the leaders do, the populace will gladly do in turn. The matter is neither complicated nor difficult. You and I need not wait until we can carry others with us. Those will be the losers who will not do it, and those who will not do it, although they appreciate the truth, will deserve to be called cowards.

Reader: What, then, of the tram-cars and electricity?

Editor: This question is now too late. It signifies nothing. If we are to do without the railways we shall have to do without the tram-cars. Machinery is like a snake-hole which may contain from one to a hundred snakes. Where there is machinery there are large cities; and where there are large cities, there are tram-cars and railways; and there only does one see electric light. English villages do not boast of any of these things. Honest physicians will tell you that where means of artificial locomotion have increased, the health of the people has suffered. I remember that when in a European town there was a scarcity of money, the receipts of the tramway company, of the lawyers and of the doctors went down and people were less unhealthy. I cannot recall a single good point in connection with machinery. Books can be written to demonstrate its evils.

Reader: Is it a good point or a bad one that all you are saying will be printed through machinery?

Editor: This is one of those instances which demonstrate that sometimes poison is used to kill poison. This, then, will not be a good point regarding machinery. As it expires, the machinery, as it were, says to us: "Beware and avoid me. You will derive no benefits from me and the benefit that may accrue from printing will avail only those who are infected with the machinery-craze."

Do not, therefore, forget the main thing. It is necessary to realize that machinery is bad. We shall then be able gradually to do away with it. Nature has not provided any way whereby we may reach a desired goal all of a sudden. If, instead of welcoming machinery as a boon, we should look upon it as an evil, it would ultimately go.

❦ Chapter 20 ❦

Conclusion

Reader: From your views I gather that you would form a third party. You are neither an extremist nor a moderate.

Editor: That is a mistake. I do not think of a third party at all. We do not all think alike. We cannot say that all the moderates hold identical views. And how can those who want only to serve have a party? I would serve both the moderates and the extremists. Where I differ from them, I would respectfully place my position before them and continue my service.

Reader: What, then, would you say to both the parties?

Editor: I would say to the extremists: "I know that you want Home Rule for India; it is not to be had for your asking. Everyone will have to take it for himself. What others get for me is not Home Rule but foreign rule; therefore, it would not he proper for you to say that you have obtained Home Rule if you have merely expelled the English. I have already described the true nature of Home Rule. This you would never obtain by force or arms. Brute force is not natural to Indian soil. You will have, therefore, to rely wholly on soul-force. You must not consider that violence is necessary at any stage for reaching our goal."

I would say to the moderates: "Mere petitioning is derogatory; we thereby confess inferiority. To say that British rule is indispensable, is almost a denial of the Godhead. We cannot say that anybody or anything is indispensable except God. Moreover, common sense should tell us that to state that, for the time being, the presence of the English in India is a necessity, is to make them conceited.

"If the English vacated India, bag and baggage, it must not be supposed that she would be widowed. It is possible that those who are forced to observe peace under their pressure would fight after their withdrawal. There can be no advantage in suppressing an eruption; it must have its vent. If, therefore, before we can remain at peace, we must fight amongst ourselves, it is better that we do so. There is no occasion for a third party to protect the weak. It is this so-called protection which has unnerved us. Such protection can only make the weak weaker. Unless we realize this, we cannot have Home Rule. I would paraphrase the thought of an English divine and say that anarchy under Home Rule was better than orderly foreign rule. Only, the meaning that the learned divine attached to Home Rule is different from Indian Home Rule according to my conception. We have to learn, and to teach others, that we do not want the tyranny of either English rule or Indian rule."

If this idea were carried out, both the extremists and the moderates could join hands. There is no occasion to fear or distrust one another.

Reader: What, then, would you say to the English?

Editor: To them I would respectfully say: "I admit you are my rulers. It is not necessary to debate the question whether you hold India by the sword or by my consent. I have no objection to your remaining in my country, but although you are the rulers, you will have to remain as servants of the people. It is not we who have to do as you wish, but it is you who have to do as we wish. You may keep the riches that you have drained away from this land, but you may not drain riches henceforth. Your function will be, if you so wish, to police India; you must abandon the idea of deriving any commercial benefit from us. We hold the civilization that you support to be the reverse of civilization. We consider our civilization to be far superior to yours. If you realize this truth, it will be to your advantage and, if you do not, according to your own proverb, you should only live in our country in the same manner as we do. You must not do anything that is contrary to our religions. It is your duty as rulers that for the sake of the Hindus you should eschew beef, and for the sake of Mahomedans you should avoid bacon and ham. We have hitherto said nothing because we have been cowed down, but you need not consider that you have not hurt our feelings by your conduct. We are not expressing our sentiments either through base selfishness or fear, but because it is our duty now to speak out boldly. We consider your schools and law courts to be useless. We want our own ancient schools and courts to be restored.

"The common language of India is not English but Hindi. You should, therefore, learn it. We can hold communication with you only in our national language.

"We cannot tolerate the idea of your spending money on railways and the military. We see no occasion for either. You may fear Russia; we do not. When she comes we shall look after her. If you are with us, we may then receive her jointly. We do not need any European cloth. We shall manage with articles produced and manufactured at home. You may not keep one eye on Manchester and the other on India. We can work together only if our interests are identical.

"This has not been said to you in arrogance. You have great military resources. Your naval power is matchless. If we wanted to fight with you on your own ground, we should be unable to do so, but if the above submissions be not acceptable to you, we cease to play the part of the ruled. You may, if you like, cut us to pieces. You may shatter us at the cannon's mouth. If you act contrary to our will, we shall not help you; and without our help, we know that you cannot move one step forward.

"It is likely that you will laugh at all this in the intoxication of your power. We may not be able to disillusion you at once; but if there be any manliness in us, you will see shortly that your intoxication is suicidal and that your laugh at our expense is an aberration of intellect. We believe that at heart you belong to a religious nation. We are living in a land which is the source of religions. How we came together need not be considered, but we can make mutual good use of our relations.

"You, English, who have come to India are not good specimens of the English nation, nor can we, almost half-Anglicized Indians, be considered good specimens of the real Indian nation. If the English nation were to know all you have done, it would oppose many of your actions. The mass of the Indians have had few dealings with you. If you will abandon your so-called civilization and search into your own scriptures, you will find that our demands are just. Only on condition of our demands being fully satisfied may you remain in India; and if you remain under those conditions, we shall learn several things from you and you will learn many from us. So doing we shall benefit each other and the world. But that will happen only when the root of our relationship is sunk in a religions soil."

Reader: What will you say to the nation?

Editor: Who is the nation?

Reader: For our purposes it is the nation that you and I have been thinking of, that is, those of us who are affected by European civilization, and who are eager to have Home Rule.

Editor: To these I would say, "It is only those Indians who are imbued with real love who will be able to speak to the English in the above strain without being frightened, and only those can be said to be so imbued who conscientiously believe that Indian civilization is the best and that the European is a nine days' wonder. Such ephemeral civilizations have often come and gone and will continue to do so. Those only can be considered to be so imbued who, having experienced the force of the soul within themselves, will not cower before brute-force, and will not, on any account, desire to use brute-force. Those only can be considered to have been so imbued who are intensely dissatisfied with the present pitiable condition, having already drunk the cup of poison.

"If there be only one such Indian, he will speak as above to the English and the English will have to listen to him.

"These are not demands, but they show our mental state. We shall get nothing by asking; we shall have to take what we want, and we need the requisite strength for the effort and that strength will be available to him only who will act thus:

1. He will only on rare occasions make use of the English language.
2. If a lawyer, he will give up his profession, and take up a hand-loom.

3. If a lawyer, he will devote his knowledge to enlightening both his people and the English.

4. If a lawyer, he will not meddle with the quarrels between parties but will give up the courts, and from his experience induce the people to do likewise.

5. If a lawyer, he will refuse to be a judge, as he will give up his profession.

6. If a doctor, he will give up medicine, and understand that rather than mending bodies, he should mend souls.

7. If a doctor, he will understand that no matter to what religion he belongs, it is better that bodies remain diseased rather than that they are cured through the instrumentality of the diabolical vivisection that is practised in European schools of medicine.

8. Although a doctor, he will take up a hand-loom, and if any patients come to him, will tell them the cause of their diseases, and will advise them to remove the cause rather than pamper them by giving useless drugs; he will understand that if by not taking drugs, perchance the patient dies, the world will not come to grief and that he will have been really merciful to him.

9. Although a wealthy man, yet regardless of his wealth, he will speak out his mind and fear no one.

10. If a wealthy man, he will devote his money to establishing hand-looms, and encourage others to use hand-made goods by wearing them himself.

11. Like every other Indian, he will know that this is a time for repentance, expiation and mourning.

12. Like every other Indian, he will know that to blame the English is useless, that they came because of us, and remain also for the same reason, and that they will either go or change their nature only when we reform ourselves.

13. Like others, he will understand that at a time of mourning, there can be no indulgence, and that, whilst we are in a fallen state, to be in gaol or in banishment is much the best.

14. Like others, he will know that it is superstition to imagine it necessary that we should guard against being imprisoned in order that we may deal with the people.

15. Like others, he will know that action is much better than speech; that it is our duty to say exactly what we think and face the consequences and that it will be only then that we shall be able to impress anybody with our speech.

16. Like others, he will understand that we shall become free only through suffering.

17. Like others, he will understand that deportation for life to the Andamans is not enough expiation for the sin of encouraging European civilization.

18. Like others, he will know that no nation has risen without suffering; that, even in physical warfare, the true test is suffering and not the killing of others, much more so in the warfare of passive resistance.

19. Like others, he will know that it is an idle excuse to say that we shall do a thing when the others also do it; that we should do what we know to be right, and that others will do it when they see the way; that when I fancy a particular delicacy, I do not wait till others taste it; that to make a national effort and to suffer are in the nature of delicacies; and that to suffer under pressure is no suffering."

Reader: This is a large order. When will all carry it out?

Editor: You make a mistake. You and I have nothing to do with the others. Let each do his duty. If I do my duty, that is, serve myself, I shall be able to serve others. Before I leave you, I will take the liberty of repeating:

1. Real home-rule is self-rule or self-control.
2. The way to it is passive resistance: that is soul-force or love-force.
3. In order to exert this force, Swadeshi in every sense is necessary.
4. What we want to do should be done, not because we object to the English or because we want to retaliate but because it is our duty to do so. Thus, supposing that the English remove the salt-tax, restore our money, give the highest posts to Indians, withdraw the English troops, we shall certainly nor use their machine-made goods, nor use the English language, nor many of their industries. It is worth noting that these things are, in their nature, harmful; hence we do not want them. I bear no enmity towards the English but I do towards their civilization.

In my opinion, we have used the term "Swaraj" without understanding its real significance. I have endeavoured to explain it as I understand it, and my conscience testifies that my life henceforth is dedicated to its attainment.